(38) *Basic*

Speech

Experiences

FIFTH REVISED EDITION

by
CLARK S. CARLILE
Idaho State University

CLARK PUBLISHING CO.
P. O. Box 205
POCATELLO, IDAHO 83201

TO

The Idaho State University Speech and Drama Department Staff
who work and play as a team—who labor untiringly to teach and
advise hundreds of students each year who complete two credits
of speech as a graduation requirement . . . . .

LITHOGRAPHED BY JOHN S. SWIFT CO., INC., ST. LOUIS • CHICAGO • NEW YORK • CINCINNATI • CLEVELAND
(PRINTED IN U. S. A.)

The foreword to a previous edition (see below) still represents my philosophy of a speech text. In this fifth revised edition I have updated all bibliographies and included many new sample speeches. In fifteen instances new speeches of Idaho State University students and faculty have been used and the authors named. The other sample speeches are my own. Minor changes appear elsewhere in this new edition, but otherwise it remains very close to the previous edition except "Communication, A Few Ideas About It" has been added. I urge all students to prepare their speeches carefully and to strive for the finest work they are capable of doing.

CLARK S. CARLILE

FOREWORD

THIS BOOK WAS WRITTEN FOR STUDENTS AND TEACHERS who want to teach and learn speech by the simple process of giving speeches.

To those teachers who are plagued by the everlasting question of "What shall I assign my students for their next speeches?" this text provides thirty-eight completely worked-out projects. These speech projects are of the kind a student will be asked to continue in real life situations when he no longer is enrolled in a speech course. They are practical because they meet the needs of students who will be tomorrow's business and social leaders. The teacher may assign any one of the speaking experiences and know that the student will have all the information he needs in the assignment in order to prepare and present a dedication speech, a eulogy, a sales talk, an after dinner speech, a panel, a debate, a speech to inform, or any one of dozens of others.

The text is adaptable and flexible. Any sequence of assignments a teacher desires may be scheduled. Any specific assignment may be modified as an instructor wishes. Any basic speech text may be used as a supplement, since each speech assignment carries references to leading speech texts.

The student's job is made easy because he knows from each assignment what he must do to fulfill adequately the purpose of a specific speech. He knows because the assignment specifies clearly what he must do. The requirements, such as time limits, outlining, organizing, and reading source materials, are not easy. They are not intended to be easy. They are basic to all good speech making, and while some students may complain that it takes too much effort to time a speech properly, to make a complete sentence outline, to read two or more sources, and to rehearse aloud, yet these same students will quickly discover that as a result of such preparation they can present excellent speeches. They will see their grades go up; they will experience new thrills of self-confidence, and they will speak capably, largely because they will have learned that good speaking is carefully prepared speaking.

A speech course, well taught, and earnestly applied by the student, does more than train a person for public speaking. With this training comes the feeling of self-adequacy so necessary to mature personality. Also developed is greater ease in expressing one's thoughts and feelings effectively and understandably, which permits a relationship with people that can erase much confusion in ordinary business and social communication. An awareness of the need for honest and reliable talk should be one of the goals every thoughtful speech student strives to achieve, for without it democracies fall and demagogues flourish.

No person can afford to be satisfied with mediocrity in speech - or anything else.

CLARK S. CARLILE

TABLE OF CONTENTS

SUGGESTIONS FOR THE SPEECH TEACHER

1. Most speech assignments in this text may be altered and thus repeated numerous times without creating a sense of monotony in students' minds. No teacher should accept a student's complaint that he has just done a certain speech and therefore should not do another speech like it. Great speakers do not reach this state of mind. Students seldom rise above mediocrity unless they are willing to continually strive for improvement by repeated practice and experience. Stress this point to them.

2. Variety in assignments may be achieved as follows:
   (a) Require the use of visual aids, i.e., charts, graphs, pictures, or similar illustrations which are prepared on cardboard sheets or easels. (b) Require blackboard use in assignments. (c) Have the speaker use a student assistant during a speech. (d) The use of quotations, one or more, may be stipulated. (e) Use one or more anecdotes within a speech. (f) Use two or more jokes, socially acceptable for mixed groups, that apply to points within the speech. (g) Hold a three-to-five-minute question period following the speech. (h) Permit questions from the listeners at any time throughout the speech. Appoint a student chairman to moderate as needed, permitting questions only, not heckling. (i) Designate certain speeches that require suits and ties for the boys and heels and hose for the girls, to be worn by all participants. (j) Designate combinations of the above suggestions that must be used within a given speech.

3. To teach sentence outlining and organization, prepare dittoed copies of scrambled outlines which students are assigned to unscramble. Symbols may be scrambled, sentences may be scrambled, or both may be. It's fun. Correct them in class. Students may wish to prepare scrambled outlines which they trade with each other to be unscrambled.

4. Assign different students to evaluate each speech that is presented. Immediately following a speech the student evaluator will go to the front of the room and, using notes, make a three-minute critique of the speech just completed. Grade the evaluator. This may, for variety, be a written evaluation due the next day. The speech appraisal in the back of this text may be used as a guide.

5. Appoint a different student chairman one day in advance of each class period whose duties are to collect speech outlines, arrange them according to the order of speakers, make a list of speakers and topics from the outlines, and hand the outlines in proper arrangement to the instructor to be graded during student speeches. The chairman then introduces each speaker and his topic. Following the last speech he comments briefly about the day's assignment and speeches, after which he turns the class back to the instructor. The chairman should sit on the front row, step before the class to make each introduction, be orderly, businesslike, and clever. The instructor may grade his work as chairman.

6. Appoint a timekeeper whose duty is to raise his hand briefly to signal the minimum time and to raise his hand again at the maximum time limit, keeping it up until the speaker concludes. Or require each speaker to be his own timekeeper.

7. Members of the class may be graded on their listening behavior. Communication is a two-way proposition - it must have an audience and a speaker. The audience should observe closely and thus not repeat errors they note in other speakers. The more attention a listener gives, the more he will get from a speaker.

8. Occasionally the class may select, by secret ballot, the person presenting the outstanding speech and designate him "Speaker of the Day."

9. For special training and interest, assign students to interview local officials to learn how a court case is conducted. Or have the class visit a court and observe it. Require students to know exactly what procedures are followed then set up a mock crime situation within the class. Hold a jury trial. This might require several weeks to complete.

10. Using the sales talk as a basis, conduct a sales contest in which the student actually sells an article to the class. Local businessmen will often provide sales articles. The public may be invited to an evening sales contest in which local businessmen will act as judges.

11. Books on speech teaching are listed for teachers' reference:

Balcer, Charles Lewis, and Seabury, H. F., Teaching Speech in Today's Secondary Schools, Holt, Rinehart and Winston, 1965.

Lewis, George, and Others, Teaching Speech, Charles E. Merrill Pub. Co., 1969.

Mulgrave, Dorothy Irene, Speech For the Classroom Teacher, Prentice-Hall, Inc., 3d ed., 1955.

Nelson, Oliver W., and LaRusso, D. A., Oral Communication in the Secondary School Classroom, Prentice-Hall, Inc., 1970.

Ogilvie, Mardel, Teaching Speech in the High School, Appleton-Century-Crofts, Inc., 1961.

Robinson, Karl F., and Kerikas, E. J., Teaching Speech, Methods and Materials, David McKay Company, Inc., 1963.

Streeter, Donald C., A Speech Handbook for Teachers, Prentice-Hall, Inc., 1964.

12. Books on speech correction which may be of help to teachers are as follows:

Anderson, Virgil, Improving the Child's Speech, Oxford University Press, 1953.

Battin, Rosabell Ray, and Haug, C.O., Speech and Language Delay, C. C. Thomas Publishers, 2d ed., 1968.

Berry, Mildred Freburg, Language Disorders of Children, Appleton-Century-Crofts, Inc., 1969.

Berry, Mildred F. and Eisenson, Jon, Speech Disorders: Principles and Practices of Therapy, Appleton-Century-Crofts, Inc., 2d ed., 1964.

Carrell, James Aubrey, Disorders of Articulation, Prentice-Hall, Inc., 1968.

Davis, Hallowell, and Silverman, S. Richard, Hearing and Deafness, Holt, Rinehart, and Winston, 3d ed., 1970.

Eisenson, Jon, and Ogilvie, Mardel, Speech Correction in the Schools, The Macmillan Company, 2d ed., 1963.

Johnson, Wendell, and Others, Speech Handicapped School Children, Harper and Row Publishers, 3d ed., 1967.

Johnson, Wendell, Stuttering and What You Can Do About It, The Interstate, 1961.

Jones, Merritt, and Pettas, Mary, Speech Improvement, Wadsworth Pub. Co., Inc., 1969.

Mayer, Lyle V., Fundamentals of Voice and Diction, W. C. Brown Co., 1968.

Palmer, Charles E., Speech and Hearing Problems: A Guide for Teachers and Parents, C. C. Thomas, 1961.

Rochmis, Lyda N., and Doob, Dorothy, Speech Therapy, John Day Co., Inc., 1970.

Sheehan, Joseph Green, and Others, Stuttering, Harper and Row, Publishers, 1970.

Sloane, Howard N., and MacAulay, B. D., eds., Operant Procedures in Remedial Speech and Language Training, Houghton Mifflin Co., 1967.

Spriestersbach, D. C., and Sherman, D. H., eds., Cleft Palate and Communication, Academic Press, 1968.

Van Hattum, Rolland James, ed., Clinical Speech in the Schools, C. C. Thomas Publishers, 1969.

Van Riper, Charles and Irwin, John V., Voice and Articulation, Prentice-Hall, Inc., 1958.

West, Robert William, and Ansberry, Merle, The Rehabilitation of Speech, Harper and Row, Publishers, 4th ed., 1968.

Zemlin, Willard R., Speech and Hearing Science, Prentice-Hall, Inc., 1968.

SUGGESTED ORDER OF ASSIGNMENTS

1. Chapter 1   Your First Speech
2. Chapter 2   Recording a Speech
3. Page x   Where to go to Find Sources and Materials
4. Page xi   Making an Outline of Your Speech
5. Page xiii   How to Prepare a Good Speech
6. Page xvi   How to Begin a Speech
7. Page xviii   How to End a Speech
8. Chapter 3   Speech of Personal Experience
9. Chapter 4   The Pet Peeve or Opinion Speech
10. Chapter 6   The Pantomime
11. Chapter 5   The Speech to Develop Bodily Action and Gesture
12. Chapter 7   Speech of Self Explanation and Fear Confession
13. Chapter 8   The Speech to Inform
14. Chapters 25-26 The Nominating Speech and Accepting a Nomination or Office
                    (One student should nominate, another accept the nomination.)
15. Chapter 16   The Introduction Speech
16. Chapters 19-20 Presenting a Gift or Award and Accepting a Gift or Award
                    (One student should present, another should accept.)
17. Chapter 9   The Speech to Stimulate or Arouse
18. Chapter 29   Making an Announcement

Note: From this point on the instructor should assign from the remaining chapters or repeat Chapters 8 and 9 using special requirements as suggested under point "2" in "Suggestions For The Speech Teacher."

HINTS ON OUTLINING, ASSIGNING, GRADING, AND CRITICISM

Using the above "Suggested Order of Assignments" as a guide you will note that students begin the course by presenting their first speech, Chapter I, on the second or third day class meets, thus quickly becoming acquainted with the speaking act and their reactions to it. It is followed by Chapter 2, "Recording A Speech". This gives them activity first which they want, and secondly gives the teacher an idea of his students' abilities and needs. These two experiences provide a common ground for the entire class and show them they can profit by further study and practice.

Outlining should be taught early, perhaps shortly after the second performance, Chapter 2, "Recording A Speech". Students should study pp. xi - xii, then do scrambled outlines as noted under Suggestions For The Speech Teacher, point 3-page vii. Whether they like it or not, students must learn to determine their purpose then to organize their ideas by outlining them in complete sentences which demand complete thoughts. This forces students to formulate definite ideas (not vague ones) and to arrange them in logical sequence. Admittedly it is not easy but to be understood by an audience it is necessary. Otherwise a rambling, disconnected, meaningless speech usually results.

It is advisable to give students a speaking assignment in writing one week in advance and to set specific dates when the speech is due. Consider it as an oral examination. Students failing to meet the assignment on time (except for extreme emergency or illness) should forfeit their opportunity to speak and receive an "F" grade. If this policy is not established overdue speeches will become the daily routine, lesson plans will be useless, and chaos will follow because a few lazy and uncaring students will seek favoritism. This alone can cause any course, speech or otherwise, to lose interest and value.

Grading speeches may be based on the outline (including neatness and spelling), and on the presentation including choice of topic and depth of ideas. Glibness, careless last minute preparation, habitual easy-personal-experience-type topics, and inadequate language use should be penalized since they contribute little or nothing to the class or the speaker. This policy should be clarified early in the course so students will know what is required.

Both oral and written evaluations may be offered by the instructor and students. By first mentioning "what you liked about the speech" followed by "suggestions for improvement", the evaluations do not tend to destroy confidence. Favorable comments may be offered on the initial speeches to build feelings of acceptance within speakers; however, ideas relative to improvement may be introduced on general bases to the entire class, say at the end of the hour following the first speech. Once the class has established a feeling of unity and purpose, after one or two speeches, comments concerning individual improvement are in order. When students have presented four or five speeches they may be assigned to prepare evaluation charts which they will suggest to the class in oral presentations, using the blackboard to illustrate.

A speech class should be enjoyable for students and teacher but not a place to play or party. Learning is fun and satisfying for all when a feeling of accomplishment is involved. A well taught speech class provides such a feeling of accomplishment besides a mastery of ideas and knowledge.

WHERE TO GO TO FIND SOURCES AND MATERIALS

One of the biggest problems confronting students in speech courses is that of finding materials on subjects which interest them. Actually this problem is easy to solve if the student is willing to "look around a bit" to find sources of information and to read what he finds. In preparing a speech, no student should say he cannot find enough material unless he has actually checked all of the possible sources.

The question which occurs most often concerning source materials is: "Where do I go to find these materials?" Aside from one's personal experience and interviews with business men, teachers, parents, and friends, there is one great source, the greatest and most valuable of all; namely, the Library. Here a person can find just about anything he wants, provided he is willing to look for it. It may well be admitted that whatever a person is hunting for will not be "growing on trees." It will be in books, magazines, newspapers, and pamphlets - often filed away on unfrequented shelves in the library but it will be there. To find these forgotten sources or others, there is one sure method - ask the librarian to help locate materials for a speech on (subject). In most cases, a librarian will provide more materials in ten minutes than the student can digest in several hours.

Besides going to the librarian for assistance, there are many sources which an individual can check for himself. A person should learn what these sources are and how to use them if he wishes to learn how to find speech materials quickly. A representative group of these research tools is listed below:

1. The card catalogue: check here for title and/or author of materials kept in the library.

2. Encyclopedias:
   A. General:
      (1) Encyclopedia Britannica: general information.
      (2) Encyclopedia Americana: general information.
      (3) New International Encyclopedia: general information.
   B. Special:
      (1) Encyclopedia of the Social Sciences: relates to social sciences.
      (2) McLaughlin. Cyclopedia of American Government.
      (3) Monroe. Cyclopedia of Education: concerns the history and philosophy of education.
      (4) Hastings. Encyclopedia of Religion and Ethics: contains articles concerning all the religions of the world.
      (5) Mythology of All Races: just what the title implies.

3. Yearbooks:
   A. Americana Annual: a source of current events.
   B. Britannica Book of the Year: a record of events from 1937 to date.
   C. New International Yearbook: a condensation of the world's progress from the year 1907- .
   D. World Almanac and Book of Facts, from 1868- : crammed full of information, largely statistical on hundreds of subjects.
   E. Stateman's Yearbook: statistical and historical information of the states of the world.
   F. The American Yearbook: a compilation of events and progress of the U. S.

4. Handbooks:
   A. Ploetz's Manual of Universal History: a history of the world in chronological outline.
   B. Political Handbook of the World: concerns party programs, world leaders, and the press.

5. Indexes:
   A. Poole's Index to Periodical Literature: covers years up to 1906; useful for finding old material on hundreds of topics.
   B. Reader's Guide to Periodical Literature: covers years since 1900; lists sources of information in practically every field.
   C. New York Times Index: lists information which is to be found in copies of the New York Times.
   D. Industrial Arts Index: an index to articles on engineering, business and commerce.
   E. Agricultural Index: index to articles in periodicals and bulletins pertaining to agriculture.
   F. Education Index: index to articles in periodicals and bulletins pertaining to education.

6. Biographical Dictionaries:
   A. Dictionary of National Biography: an encyclopedia of English biography of deceased persons. Kept up to date with supplements. Alphabetically arranged.
   B. Dictionary of American Biography: an encyclopedia of American biography of deceased persons. Kept up to date with supplements. Alphabetically arranged.
   C. Who's Who: principally English biographies and a few internationally famous names.
   D. Who's Who in America (biennial): brief biographies of notable living persons of the United States.
   E. National Cyclopedia of American Biography: the most complete list of American living and dead famous persons available in any one source.
   F. Webster's Biographical Dictionary: contains brief biographies of ancient and modern persons of international fame.
   G. Current Biography: short biographies of living people who are in the news today.

7. Special Dictionaries:
   A. Weseen. Dictionary of American Slang.
   B. Mawson. Dictionary of Foreign Terms.
   C. Keller's Dictionary of Dates: a record of early history by countries.

8. Quotations from Literature:
   A. Stevenson. The Home Book of Quotations: approx. 50,000; arranged alphabetically by subject.
   B. Hoyt. New Cyclopedia of Practical Quotations: taken from the speech and writings of all nations. (Includes Concordance.)
   C. Bartlett's Familiar Quotations: traces quotations to their sources in ancient and modern literature.

9. Government Publications: these materials cover almost unlimited fields. Ask the librarian about them.

10. There are many other sources available on the above subjects and subjects not included here. Ask the librarian for assistance in locating them.

MAKING AN OUTLINE OF YOUR SPEECH

Below is a sample complete sentence outline. If you will study it carefully, you will note that every statement is a complete sentence. There are no incomplete sentences. There are no compound sentences. The outline is logically organized and divided into three parts - the introduction, body, and conclusion.

There are numerous ways to develop an outline and numerous sections into which it can be divided. The method followed by any one person is a matter of choice. If your instructor prefers a particular method of outlining, he will tell you what it is. The important point to remember when constructing an outline (which is the skeleton of a speech) is that it must make sense - logical sense, which is easily followed.

It takes time and effort to construct a complete sentence outline; yet the time and energy one spends in building a good outline will pay big dividends in improved speaking. The student must do his best.

Type of speech: _____Informative_____   Name: _____Your name_____

Number of words in outline: _____124_____   Date: _____October 25, 1975_____

Purpose of this speech: (What do you want your audience to learn, to think, to believe, to feel, or do because of this speech?)

I want my audience to have a better understanding of stagefright.
_____

Title: STAGEFRIGHT - LET'S UNDERSTAND IT

Introduction:
- I. You may have been asked to make a speech.
  - A. Your heart may have skipped a beat.
  - B. Perspiration may have broken out.
  - C. Anxiety may have swept over you.
    - 1. I want to discuss this anxiety called stagefright.

Body:
- I. All normal persons are subject to stagefright.
  - A. It is natural reaction to the unknown.
    - 1. Speakers are not sure of what will happen.
      - a. They may forget.
      - b. They may have language difficulties.
      - c. The audience may disapprove many ways.
- II. Causes of stagefright are varied.
  - A. It may relate to unpleasant experiences or limited background.
  - B. It may spring from "old wives" tales.
- III. Stagefright can be controlled.
  - A. Thoroughly preparing and presenting many speeches is advisable.
  - B. Understanding stagefright is essential.

Conclusion:
- I. Fearful speakers can become outstanding.
  - A. History gives many examples.
    - 1. You can master stagefright if you try.

Sources of Information:
Buehler, E. Christian, and Linkugel, W. A., Speech Communication, Harper & Row, Publishers, 1969, pp. 74-81.
Oliver, Robert T., and Cortright, R. L., Effective Speech, Holt, Rinehart and Winston, Inc., 5th ed., 1970, pp. 51-58.
Verderber, Rudolph F., The Challenge of Effective Speaking, Wadsworth Publishing Company, Inc., 1970, pp. 55-56.

SAMPLE COPY OF SPEAKER'S NOTES

Below is a sample copy of notes a speaker might use in presenting a five to six minute speech on stagefright. Observe that each word stands for an idea, that each word is large enough to be easily seen at a glance, and that the size of the paper on which the notes are written is about equal to that of a postal card. Speaking notes should serve only as a guide, not as a crutch. The actual speech should be in the mind of the speaker, not in a mass of notes.

Hold your card of notes by the lower right hand corner between your thumb and forefinger.

STAGEFRIGHT

1. SYMPTOMS

2. NATURAL FEARS

3. CAUSES

4. CONTROLS

5. BECOME OUTSTANDING

HOW TO PREPARE A GOOD SPEECH

The first law of good speaking is adequate preparation.

Preparing a good speech is like preparing to run a four-forty yard dash in a track meet. Each requires many trial runs before the event actually starts. To attempt a speech without preparation is just as foolhardy as to attempt a quarter-mile run without practice. The well-trained and conditioned racer makes it look easy, just as does the well-prepared speaker. To an uninformed person, both the speaker and the racer may appear to be performing effortlessly and impromptu, yet in most cases nothing could be farther from the truth. Only many hours of intense preparation make it possible for the good speaker and the good athlete to display great ability. If there is any doubt about this point in the mind of any reader he should ask the man who makes speeches or who runs races.

There are several initial requisites which should be considered at this time in order to explain adequate speech preparation. Here they are:

I. YOUR SUBJECT - Consider it.

    A. You should be sure you can find sufficient material on your subject, otherwise your speech may be too short, devoid of quantity as well as quality.

    B. You should be sure the subject you plan to discuss is appropriate to you, your audience and the occasion. Any subject not adjusted to these three factors simply is inadequate. If you are in doubt, consult your instructor.

    C. You should be certain that your subject can be adequately discussed in the time allotted for your speech. Preliminary investigation, narrowing the subject, and a few "trial runs" will clear up doubts about this phase of preparation.

    D. Since it takes time for ideas to grow and develop, you should weigh carefully the time you allow yourself for preparation, otherwise your speech may not be past the infant stage when you present it, and frankly an audience dislikes seeing a baby when it comes to see a full-grown man.

    E. The importance of selecting a suitable subject need not be stressed since it is so obvious, however, you should decide whether your topic is too technical, trivial, trite or broad. If it falls in any one of these categories then it must be altered accordingly or a new topic be chosen.

    F. The title of your speech should be provocative, brief, relative to your subject, and interesting. It is one of the first things your audience will read about in the papers or hear before you speak. A good title can add immeasurably to the initial interest in your speech.

II. THINK OF YOUR AUDIENCE

    A. To best adapt your material to your audience, you must understand the people in it. It is your obligation to find out what kind of people will likely come to hear you. How old will they be? What will their occupations be? What is their social standing? Their education? Their religion? Their prejudices and beliefs? Their wealth? What do they want from you? So long as you are taking the time of ten or fifteen persons, perhaps several hundred, you will be wise to give them a speech which is worth their time. You can be much surer you will do this if you analyze your audience. This isn't something to be done on a moment's notice. Rather it will require a definite investigation from you, but it will be well worth your efforts, provided you adapt your remarks to what you find out.

III. THE MECHANICS OF SPEECH PREPARATION

Now that you have considered your subject and analyzed your audience, you are ready to begin the mechanical preparation of your speech. Here are the steps to follow:

    A. Decide on the purpose of your speech, that is, what do you want to accomplish with your speech? What reaction do you want from the people who hear you? Do you want them to understand an idea better? To appreciate something more? To be thankful? To feel honored? To change their minds? To become stirred up and aroused about something? To perform an act, such as to vote for or against a candidate or contribute to a fund or join an organization? In your own mind it is absolutely essential that you know definitely what you want your speech to do to your listeners. If you don't have this point settled, then you really don't know why you are giving your speech or why you organized it the way you did or why you are telling your audience "thus and so." In reality you don't know what you want and nobody else does. You cannot expect your audience to get anything from your speech if you yourself don't know what you want them to get. One of the most pronounced causes of poor speaking lies in the elementary fact that the speaker has nothing in mind that he wants to accomplish with his speech. This need not happen to you if you decide on a purpose and direct all your efforts towards achieving it.

B. Your next step is to gather material for your speech. Consult the chapter in this text entitled "Where To Go To Find Sources and Materials." Having located various materials, you should take comprehensive notes on what you decide to use. Be sure to indicate your sources exactly and completely. This includes the specific names of the magazines or books the material was taken from, titles of articles, authors' full names, dates of publication, and chapters or pages where the material was found. If a source is a person, identify him completely by title, position, occupation, etc. These data, telling exactly where you got your material, will prove most beneficial when someone later asks you where you found your material. The validity of your remarks will be no greater than the sources you use.

C. Your third step is to organize the material in an orderly and logical sequence. This means that all examples, analogies, facts, quotations, and other evidence which you use to support main ideas must be in their proper place where they will do the most good. The best way to achieve organization that is progressive and unified is to prepare a complete sentence outline of your speech. For a fuller understanding of a complete sentence outline, study the example elsewhere in this text under the chapter heading "Making An Outline of Your Speech." A complete sentence outline will assist you in formulating and crystallizing complete thoughts prior to presenting the speech. Without this procedure you will discover it is exceedingly difficult to prepare and present a quality speech.

D. Step number four is wording your speech. Here you must decide what words you will use when you expand your complete sentence outline into a full speech. To get in mind the words you want to use, you should employ the method best suited to you, however, two recommended methods follow. (Complete word-for-word memorization is not recommended.) One method for wording your speech is to write it out in full, then read your manuscript aloud several times to master the general ideas and the necessary details. After doing this, you should construct a set of very brief notes containing only the main ideas of your speech and rehearse aloud from them until you master the general wording and the order of the main points. Do not rehearse by mumbling in a monotone or by "thinking about" your wording. It is permissible and usually advisable to memorize the introduction and conclusion, but not the body of your speech.

A second method for wording your speech is to rehearse aloud from your complete sentence outline or other outline until you have attained a definite mastery of the words you plan to use. Here again it will be wise to memorize the introduction and conclusion although you should not memorize the rest of your speech word for word. You should, of course, memorize the sequence of your main points irrespective of how you practice. The number of times needed for oral rehearsal will depend solely on you, but probably it will be at least four to six times and quite possibly even more, regardless of what method you use. In any case, if you plan to use notes while speaking, be sure to use the final copy of your speaking notes during your last few rehearsals.

One of the best ways to rehearse a speech is to stand before a mirror so that you may observe your posture, bodily actions and gestures. Some students object to using a mirror saying that it bothers them to observe themselves. This is a flimsy excuse since those same students know they must speak before their classmates who will be forced, through courtesy, to observe them while they stumble through actions, gestures and various postures which they themselves couldn't bear to see reflected in a mirror. A few "trial runs" before a mirror will vastly improve most speeches and speakers. Of course, it will be helpful to rehearse by using a wire or tape recorder in order to check your speech by listening to play-backs. A video tape (with audio) is unexcelled.

E. Step number five involves the development of a mental attitude of the speaker towards himself and the entire speaking situation. He will be wise to expect nervousness and stage fright during his first few speeches. He should realize quite clearly that although his stage fright will largely disappear after a reasonably short while, his nervousness just before speaking probably will not. He should look upon it as a form of energy that will keep his speaking on a more vigorous plane than would otherwise be possible were he entirely devoid of nervous feelings. His attitude should tell him he will gain self-confidence and poise as he makes more speeches, but not to expect a miracle. The mental attitude should be one in which the student recognizes his own weaknesses, but is not morbidly disturbed because he isn't a great success on his first attempts. He should be willing to seek advice from his instructor, to make honest efforts toward a more adequate preparation of his speeches since this is the greatest guarantee for good speaking, and gradually as he progresses he should take pride in his own personal improvement and feelings of self-confidence. Every beginning speaker should look forward to a feeling of adequacy and personal satisfaction, for if he does, and if he possesses a healthy mental attitude, he is sure to attain these goals - and good speech.

BIBLIOGRAPHY FOR HOW TO PREPARE A GOOD SPEECH

Buehler, E. Christian, and Linkugel, W. A., Speech Communication, Harper & Row, Publishers, 1969, pp. 96-102.

Gilman, Wilbur E., and Others, An Introduction to Speaking, The Macmillan Company, 2d ed., 1968, pp. 6-24.

Hance, Kenneth G., and Others, Principles of Speaking, Wadsworth Publishing Company, Inc., 2d ed., 1969, Chapter 2.

Jensen, J. Vernon, Perspectives on Oral Communication, Holbrook Press, Inc., 1970, Chapter 2.

McAuley, Jack G., Speech, The Essential Elements, Burgess Publishing Company, 1968, Chapters 2-11.

Monroe, Alan H., and Ehninger, Douglas, Principles of Speech Communication, 6th brief ed., 1969, Chapter 1.

Nadeau, Ray E., A Basic Rhetoric of Speech Communication, Addison-Wesley Publishing Company, 1969, Part 2.

Oliver, Robert T., and Cortright, R. L., Effective Speech, Holt, Rinehart and Winston, Inc., 5th ed., 1970, Part 3.

Oliver, Robert T., and Others, Communicative Speaking and Listening, Holt, Rinehart and Winston, Inc., 4th ed., 1968, Chapter 3.

Ross, Raymond S., Speech Communication, Prentice-Hall, Inc., 2d ed., 1970, Chapter 7.

Tacey, William S., Business and Professional Speaking, Wm. C. Brown Company, Publishers, 1970, Chapter 6.

Verderber, Rudolph F., The Challenge of Effective Speaking, Wadsworth Publishing Company, Inc., 1970, Part 2.

Williams, Barbara, Purposeful Communication, Kendall/Hunt Publishing Company, 1970, Chapter 3.

HOW TO BEGIN A SPEECH

Note: Students may be assigned to prepare and present sample introductions.

The Introduction

An introduction to a speech is what a man's trousers are to full dress when he goes out to dinner, they are a necessity. Without them he is undressed and he shocks many people. A speech without an introduction is undressed, it shocks many people. It can be said that with few exceptions every speech demands a pair of trousers, i.e., an introduction. It has also been said that every speaker has the audience's attention when he rises to speak and that if he loses the attention, it is after he begins to speak, hence the importance of the introduction becomes apparent.

There are several purposes a speaker normally wishes to achieve by means of his introductory remarks in order to be most effective. These purposes may be listed as follows:

I. One purpose of the introduction may be to gain attention, arouse the interest and excite the curiosity of listeners. This may be effected in numerous ways.

   A. The speaker may refer to the occasion and purpose of the meeting with a few brief remarks explaining and commenting on why the audience have gathered on this occasion. He may refer to special interests of the audience and show how his subject is connected with these interests. In no way should he apologize for his speech.

   B. The speaker may pay the audience a genuine compliment relative to their hospitality, their interest in the subject to be discussed, their concern over bettering their community, their progressive educational program, the outstanding leadership of the group sponsoring the speech. The sincerity of the speaker should be genuine since the audience's judgment of his speech will be strongly influenced by his opening phrases.

   C. The speaker may open by telling a story (human interest, humorous, exciting, etc.) that catches interest and arouses curiosity. He should of course link the story to his subject. If the story is not related to the subject, it should not be told.

   D. The speaker may refer to a recent incident that the audience is acquainted with. Example: "Three persons were burned to death a week ago because of a school house which had improper fire escape exits." This paves the way for his discourse, the need for a new school house.

   E. The speaker may use a quotation to open his remarks and set the stage for the introduction of his ideas. The quotation should be relevant to what he plans to say and be tied to his thoughts with a few brief explanations. He should not prolong this type of introduction too much.

   F. The speaker may use a novel idea or a striking statement to arouse curiosity and interest or to gain attention. This should not be overdone. If it is sensationalism it will lose its punch because the remainder of the speech cannot be so shocking.

   Example of an introduction to a speech on atomic power is:
   "It is hard to imagine fifty thousand persons destroyed in a few seconds - it is hard to imagine a ship driven around the world on a glass of water, or a rocket shot to the moon on a pound of metal, yet the day may not be far off when atomic power will make these possibilities either horrible or helpful realities."

   G. The speaker may refer to a preceding speaker and his thoughts in order to secure interest and attention, however, too much elaboration should not occur.

   Example:
   "Ladies and Gentlemen: The preceding speaker, Mr. McIntosh, has given you a peculiarly striking and graphic picture of what we may expect within the next ten years in the development of atomic power. I would like to expand his ideas further by telling you how this power may be harnessed so that it will wash your dishes and heat your houses."

   H. The speaker may put pertinent and challenging questions to the audience to arouse their curiosity. "Did you know that . . . ? Do you want such to happen to you?" etc. These questions should have a bearing on the material which is to follow, otherwise they will be just so much noise.

I.   Various combinations of the above suggestions may provide an effective introduction. The combinations which should be used will depend on the audience, occasion, speaker, speech and environment.

II.   A second purpose of the introduction may be to prepare and open the minds of the hearers for the thoughts which are to come. This is particularly necessary if the audience is hostile. It may be accomplished by giving background and historical information so that the audience can and will understand the subject. This purpose may be further achieved if the speaker establishes his right to speak by recounting the research he has done on his subject, by naming prominent persons associated with him in his endeavor, and by modestly telling of certain honors, offices and awards he has received as a result of his accomplishments in fields closely related to his topic.

III.   A speaker's third objective of an introduction may be to indicate the direction and purpose of his speech and the end it will reach. This may be achieved by stating generally his subject and by announcing and explaining the thesis of his talk. To give only a naked statement of the topic is not enough. It is uninteresting and in most cases dull. An appropriate and interesting exposition of any general statement of the subject should be made in reference to the topic. In other words, to announce only the title of a speech and to consider this an adequate introduction is a grave mistake.

> Example:
> "Ladies and Gentlemen: I have chosen to speak with you today on the subject of crime, which is costing our nation untold billions of dollars annually. It is my desire to explain to you the causes of crime as well as the preventions. It is only when crime is understood that people are enabled to combat it and decrease its scope."

There are a few points to remember when preparing and delivering an introduction. Dullness and triteness, undue length of opening remarks, false leads that are not followed up, stories which are suggestive or risque used only to fill time, or a mere announcement of the topic should all be avoided. Any apologies or remarks which might be construed to be apologies for the speech should definitely be omitted. There is nothing so invigorating, so appreciated, so likely to secure good will as an introduction which provides an original, fresh and sparkling meeting between the audience and the speaker and his subject. Work for it.

Generally speaking, an introduction is prepared last. This is practical because a speaker needs to have the body of his talk outlined and his ideas developed and ripe before he can best determine how they should be introduced. The length of an introduction may vary considerably; however, it should not comprise more than one-fourth of the entire speech. It may comprise much less.

One more important aspect of the beginning of a speech is the speaker's behavior before he takes the platform and after he gets there. If he is sitting on stage in full view of his audience he should remain comfortably and calmly alert, yet politely seated. People are carefully appraising him while he waits. Feminine speakers while seated should be careful not to cross their knees. Crossing the ankles is permissible, although it is safer to keep both feet on the floor with the knees together. When the speaker is introduced, he should rise easily without delay or noise and move to his place on the platform. After arriving there, a few seconds should elapse while he deliberately surveys the scene before him. Then after addressing the chairman, if he has not already done so, he is ready to begin his introductory remarks.

BIBLIOGRAPHY FOR THE INTRODUCTION OF A SPEECH

Buehler, E. Christian, and Linkugel, W. A., Speech Communication, Harper & Row, Publishers, 1969, pp. 138-146.
McAuley, Jack G., Speech, The Essential Elements, Burgess Publishing Company, 1968, Chapter 6.
Monroe, Alan H., and Ehninger, Douglas, Principles of Speech Communication, Scott, Foresman and Company, 6th brief ed., 1969, Chapter 9.
Oliver, Robert T., and Cortright, R. L., Effective Speech, Holt, Rinehart and Winston, Inc., 5th ed., 1970, Chapter 11.
Ross, Raymond S., Speech Communication, Prentice-Hall, Inc., 2d ed., 1970, Chapter 7.
Tacey, William S., Business and Professional Speaking, Wm. C. Brown Company, Publishers, 1970, Chapter 6.
Verderber, Rudolph F., The Challenge of Effective Speaking, Wadsworth Publishing Company, Inc., 1970, Chapter 4.
Williams, Barbara, Purposeful Communication, Kendall/Hunt Publishing Company, 1970, Chapter 3.

HOW TO END A SPEECH

Note: Students may be assigned to prepare and present sample conclusions.

The Conclusion

A day is never ended without a sunset of some kind. If the sunset is captivating the entire day is often long remembered because of its impressive ending. A speech is much the same. It must have an ending and to be most successful the ending should be impressive.

The conclusion brings together all the thoughts, emotions, discussions, arguments, and feelings which the speaker has tried to communicate to his audience. The closing words should make a powerful emotional impression on the listeners, since in most cases logic alone is insufficient to move an audience to act or believe as the speaker suggests. Not only this but the conclusion is the last opportunity to emphasize the point of the speech. It should be a natural culmination of all that has been spoken. It should not be weak, insipid remarks which are begun or ended just as the speaker starts a hesitating but very obvious journey towards his chair.

The conclusion should be, <u>without exception</u>, one of the most carefully prepared parts of a speech. Just when it should be prepared is largely a matter of opinion. Some authorities advise preparing it first because such a practice enables a speaker to point his talk toward a predetermined end. Other speakers suggest preparing the conclusion last because this procedure allows a person to draw his final words from the full draft of his speech. Regardless of when a conclusion is prepared, there is one point on which all authorities agree and it is that the conclusion must be carefully worded, carefully organized, carefully rehearsed and in most cases committed to memory or nearly so. The conclusion should be brief, generally not more than one-eighth to one-tenth of the entire speech, perhaps less, depending on the speech, the speaker, the audience, the occasion and the environment in which the speech is delivered. A conclusion should never bring in new material, since such an action requires a discussion of the new material which in turn unnecessarily prolongs the speech. Also the introduction of new material brings about an undesirable anticlimax and frequently irritates an audience because a speaker runs past a perfect place to stop.

When a speaker moves into his conclusion, it should be obvious that he is closing his remarks. His intentions should be so clear that he should not have to tell the audience what he is doing by saying, "In conclusion . . . "

The importance of the delivery of a conclusion cannot be overemphasized. The total organism, mind, body and soul, must be harmoniously at work. The eye contact should be direct, the gestures and actions appropriate, the posture alert, and the voice sincere, distinct and well articulated. The speaker's effort in delivering the conclusion may be likened to a foot racer who culminates an entire race in one great, last surge of power as he lunges toward the tape - and victory.

Now that you have been told what should be contained within a conclusion, there remains one major question which is, "How do you actually go about attaining these ends, i.e., what methods should be used?"

There are numerous ways to develop a conclusion. Some of the better known are listed as follows:

1. <u>Summary</u> is a method often utilized in closing a speech. It is sometimes expressed by restatement of the speech title, of the purpose, of some specific phrase that has been used several times in the speech, by an apt quotation, either prose or poetry, which adroitly says what the speaker wishes to be said, or by any other means which tends to bring the main point of the speech into final focus for the audience. An example of a very brief summary is contained in the following words which were once used by a speaker to summarize a speech against Hitler's aggression in Czechoslovakia:

   Example:
   "Czechoslovakia will live again! The hordes of Hitler, the Huns of Europe, the intrigue of Berlin shall not swallow up this mighty and prideful people. They shall rise up and fight their horrible aggressor. Yes, Czechoslovakia will live again!"

2. <u>Recapitulation</u> may be used in longer formal speeches when it is necessary to restate points in a <u>one, two, three order</u>. The danger of this method is that it may become monotonous and uninteresting. Short speeches do not require this type of conclusion, since the points are easily

remembered. A short speech may close with the last main point if it is a <u>strong</u> point. Usually, however, more is needed to close a speech, even a short one.

Example of recapitulation in a speech favoring world federation:
"To be sure that we all understand my reasons for believing as I do let me restate my main points. First, world federation is the only type of government which will save the world from destroying itself. Second, world federation is the only type of government which is acceptable to the several nations, and third, world federation is the most democratic type of world government yet conceived by man. It is for these reasons that I favor the establishment of a world government."

3. A striking <u>anecdote</u>, an <u>analogy</u>, or a <u>simile</u> may be employed as closing remarks, or any one of them or a suitable combination of them may be interwoven with the summary or recapitulation type of conclusion. One conclusion which utilizes the analogy for a speech concerning old cars is:

Example:
"These old cars of ours are like the wonderful one horse shay. Let us hope that they, too, do not suddenly fall apart, scattering nuts and bolts across our neighbor's lawn."

4. An <u>emotionalized or idealized statement of the thesis</u> may serve as a useful conclusion. If the thesis were "American Honesty," one conclusion of the above type could be:

Example:
"Honesty is and always has been the moral fibre of our country. Honesty is the heritage of over two hundred million Americans. To this criterion of national manliness the world pays respect and offers admiration. It reveres American honesty as a true indication of Christian living. Let us not blot out this bright star which outshines all the myriads of lesser lights. Let us continue to deserve the right to be known as the world's most honest nation."

5. There may be a <u>powerful restatement of the thesis</u>. If the subject were "America's Might," the final words could be:

Example:
"America will live forever, strong, defiant to aggression, relentless in attack, mighty in defense, humble before God."

6. A <u>vivid illustration of the central idea</u> may fittingly conclude a speech. If it were on the Navy's might, the following words could be used:

Example:
"The famous words of John Paul Jones, who said he had not yet begun to fight, are emblazoned again across the world's horizon, for tonight the American Navy launched ten new battle ships!"

7. A <u>call for action from the audience</u> may clinch a speech. It must of course pertain to the ideas of the speaker. This is an excellent type of conclusion, particularly when the purpose has been to stimulate or to get action from the audience. If a speech were on "Building Good Government," a conclusion could be:

Example:
"Let us no longer sit here doing nothing while the crooked politicians corrupt our government and steal our money. Let's go out one by one, by two's and three's or by the hundreds and vote for clean government and honest officials. Let's do it tomorrow - it's election day and our only hope!"

One final word of warning is this: When the speech is done the speaker should hold the floor for a second or two (this cannot be stressed enough), then return to his chair, seat himself politely and remain seated until the chairman adjourns the audience. Display or frivolity of any kind on the part of the speaker <u>after the speech</u> may sharply alter many good impressions which he has made while on the platform. A person should not let his actions portray how well or how poorly he thinks he has done on his speech. The audience will decide this point.

BIBLIOGRAPHY FOR THE CONCLUSION OF A SPEECH

Buehler, E. Christian, and Linkugel, W. A., Speech Communication, Harper & Row, Publishers, 1969, pp. 157-161.

McAuley, Jack G., Speech, The Essential Elements, Burgess Publishing Company, 1968, Chapter 6.

Monroe, Alan H., and Ehninger, Douglas, Principles of Speech Communication, Scott, Foresman and Company, 6th brief ed., 1969, Chapter 9.

Nadeau, Ray E., A Basic Rhetoric of Speech Communication, Addison-Wesley Publishing Company, 1969, pp. 80-81.

Oliver, Robert T., and Cortright, R. L., Effective Speech, Holt, Rinehart and Winston, Inc., 5th ed., 1970, Chapter 11.

Ross, Raymond S., Speech Communication, Prentice-Hall, Inc., 2d ed., 1970, Chapter 7.

Samovar, Larry, and Mills, Jack, Oral Communication, Message and Response, Wm. C. Brown Company, Publishers, 1968, Chapter 6.

Strother, Edward S., and Huckleberry, A. W., The Effective Speaker, Houghton Mifflin Company, 1968, pp. 175-183.

Tacey, William S., Business and Professional Speaking, Wm. C. Brown Company, Publishers, 1970, Chapter 6.

Verderber, Rudolph F., The Challenge of Effective Speaking, Wadsworth Publishing Company, Inc., 1970, Chapter 4.

Williams, Barbara, Purposeful Communication, Kendall/Hunt Publishing Company, 1970, Chapter 3.

COMMUNICATION -- A FEW IDEAS ABOUT IT

Communication may not be what you think so let's first agree on what it is. Basically whenever you do anything (intentionally or not) that causes people to see, smell, hear, taste or feel you, they receive messages from you. Most people think communication occurs only when someone speaks, yet you know how people gesture with their hands, nod their heads, move their legs or shoulders, smile or frown, raise eye brows or wiggle their noses all the while they talk. These physical movements which you see tell more sometimes than what is said with the speaker's words. Actually what a person does is express his feelings and ideas two ways simultaneously, one way with words and another with bodily movements. It is almost impossible to talk without accompanying physical movements, thus a person often sends out messages he does not intend to send because of these movements. An example would'be an individual who tells you he is unafraid with words but you know he is scared to death by observing his movements. An embarrassed or frightened person often communicates how he feels by his actions.

The point is, communication occurs anytime someone else sees and/or hears you, and what you communicate may be what you intended or it may not be. However, words are one of your most powerful communication devices.

As a small child learning to talk, every word you learned had a special meaning to you because of your association with it. The word "puppy" meant only your puppy because to you there was no other. And so it was with all your words, each had your own special meaning and everytime you spoke, your words referred to the meaning you gave them. This remained true as you grew from childhood and will remain true all your life. Your words now carry broader meanings because you have learned there are many kinds of puppies but you still attach your meaning to your words. The trouble in trying to convey (symbolize) your ideas to someone else is that for every word you speak the listener interprets it with his special meaning which is different from yours. When this happens he does not fully understand you. It means that you communicated something but not exactly what you intended.

The process of putting words together in phrases and sentences to represent your feelings and ideas is called encoding. A listener has to interpret your words by sorting out ideas they create in his mind, which is called decoding, somewhat like figuring out a message sent in secret code.

Still another way you communicate when talking is how loud, how fast, how high or low your voice is -- all reflect meanings about things for which you have no specific words. People hearing you usually can tell by your vocal variety whether you are happy, sad, tired or angry. A good example would be the way a friend greets you when he says, "Good morning." You know instantly something is bothering him because he communicated this feeling by his voice quality, perhaps he muttered his words, possibly by a frown on his face or the way he walked, but he communicated this feeling whether he intended to or not. Because people don't have words to completely express all their thoughts and feelings they use vocal variety and thousands of muscular movements in addition to their words.

Since words have different meanings to the speaker and listener the question rises, "How does one talk so he can be understood more precisely?" Perhaps the best way is to use accurate and specific words. For example do not say, "It was bright colored." Instead say, "It was red and orange." Instead of, "He was a big man," say, "He was six feet three inches tall and weighed 225 pounds." Omit words such as pretty, nice, beautiful, bad, good, great, very, most, much, fast, slow and similar terms with generalized meanings. In other words say specifically what you mean, use correct grammar, articulate clearly, and pronounce distinctly. And finally, say it in as few words as possible. Don't make a listener decode fifty words to get your message when you can say the same thing using twenty five.

You also tell people all about yourself by your appearance. Neatly pressed clean clothes, carefully groomed hair, no offensive odors, clean hands, face, and body, all communicate by sight and smell what you are. The person who ignores these fundamental facts about his appearance communicates as plainly as if he carried a large sign reading, "I'M DIRTY AND SMELL BAD. STAY AWAY FROM ME." And people will. (He won't get a job either.)

Everyone also communicates by taste and touch. Kiss a tiny baby and it actually tastes; it feels so delicate and fragile you instinctively protect it. The baby has communicated. Shaking hands with friends in greeting, holding hands with the opposite sex and kissing, all communicate by taste, touch, smell, sight, and sound. Think about these ideas a minute and I believe you will agree.

Now in a broader sense you hear much about business, social, political, economic, and educational communication. It's popular to say, "He didn't communicate," to explain misunderstandings, however, it would be more appropriate to say, "He wasn't specific," or "He wasn't definite," or "He wasn't accurate," or "He used technical language," or "He wasn't complete." You could say in many instances, "He didn't speak plainly," or "He wrote sloppily and misspelled words." or "He did not signal (communicate) his message when he was supposed to." (Too early or too late).

On the other side it can be said that some people don't listen to understand but instead to argue and talk about their own thoughts. They don't read carefully, or they hear and read only a part of what is said and pretend they heard and read everything. Thus they only partially decode messages they receive and foolishly wonder why they don't understand.

We can summarize these remarks when we say communication can be improved by being definite, specific, accurate and complete in speaking and writing. When receiving messages we must listen, observe, and read carefully and completely. It's that simple. Add to these communication principles, attentiveness, appropriate bodily movements and gestures, a clean and neat personal appearance and an earnest desire to understand or to be understood.

Here's an interesting device. Next time you argue with someone try to restate his point of view so he will say, "That's exactly what I mean." Have him restate your views likewise. Do this on every point of disagreement then each will know what the other is talking about. Continue your discussion only if you both can do this.

Chapter 1

YOUR FIRST SPEECH

This speech is due:
Time limits: None.
Speaking notes: Tear off those at the end of this chapter.

PURPOSE OF YOUR FIRST SPEECH

This speech is your first to be presented in this course. Your first speech gives you a chance to stand before your classmates and to tell them something about yourself. You are not expected to give a long biographical account of your life; that is not what is wanted. By answering the questions at the end of this assignment, you introduce yourself to your audience (classmates) and you make your first speech. You will get the feel of standing on your feet and talking before a group of persons. Since you must start somewhere, this experience will provide a good beginning.

HOW TO PREPARE FOR YOUR FIRST TALK

One reason for making your first talk is to tell your audience enough concerning yourself that they will know something about you. In other words, they will get acquainted. Another purpose of this experience is to give you an opportunity to learn what it is like to see many persons sitting before you waiting to hear what you have to say. Some students get a thrill from it; others get a scare. Actually the scare is only a feeling that comes to a speaker because certain glands in his body are functioning more than they usually do in a speech situation. Because people dislike the feeling caused by their glandular functions, they say they are scared. Instead of being scared of speaking, they are scared of a normal physical action taking place within themselves. They associate this feeling with speechmaking and, tying the two together, say, "speaking scares them."

To be scared is normal. To be nervous is normal. To be tense is normal. You must experience these feelings; otherwise you would be as lifeless as an old shirt. These feelings are present in football players before and during a game. Great actors have them. Great speakers have them. Nervousness is the high octane gas which provides these persons the drive to give life to their performances. They want a normal amount of it because they use it. You see, they control their nervousness (energy) and that is all you need to do. Do not try to rid yourself of nervousness entirely; you will gain control of this power. As you give more speeches throughout this course, you will discover your control growing stronger - and that is what you want.

Study the questions at the end of this assignment. Decide generally how you will answer them. It will help you to practice aloud several times by standing in front of a mirror while you speak. Do not memorize your answers word for word, since this would make your remarks sound like a recitation.

HOW TO PRESENT YOUR FIRST SPEECH

Tear the questions along the perforated line so that you may take them with you to be used as notes. Do this before your instructor asks you to speak.

When your name is called walk quietly to the front of the room. Avoid "stomping" your feet, clicking your heels on the floor, or calling unnecessary attention to yourself. When you get there, stand politely on both feet. Do not place one foot forward, throw out a hip and rest your weight on your rear foot, assuming a bashful boy slouch. Keep your weight on both feet or on your slightly forward foot. An attitude of a soldier at attention or any similar stance is undesirable. Be alert and polite, and you may be sure that you look all right.

Let your hands hang loosely at your sides unless you care to bring the one holding your notes up in front of you. It is certainly permissible to place a hand in your pocket, on a table top, or a chair back, if you do not call attention to the act. Grasp your notes lightly between the thumb and index finger. Do not palm them, roll, crumple, twist or disfigure them in any way by continuous handling. When you refer to your notes, raise them high enough that you do not need to lower your head to glance at them.

If you feel like moving around a few paces, do so naturally, without shuffling or scraping your feet. When you are not changing positions, stand still and keep your feet quiet.

When you begin your speech, talk with your normal voice just as you would if you were telling about yourself to a group of good friends. Good speaking is good conversation. Make an introductory statement for a beginning. Show some interest in your remarks. Be sure that everyone can hear you. Look your audience directly in the eyes; however, avoid a shifty, flitting type of gaze that never really stops anywhere. You may look at certain persons in different parts of the group, since you cannot very well look at everybody during the short time you are speaking.

When you are ready to close your remarks, conclude with a brief summarizing statement. Pause at least two seconds after your final words; then go easily and politely to your chair. Do not rush or hurry or crumple your notes into a wad and shove them in your pocket. Upon reaching your chair, avoid slouching down in it, sprawling out, heaving a big sigh and in general going through a pantomime which says in effect, "Boy, I'm glad that's over!" You may feel that way; however, this is one time that advertising does not pay. Sit comfortably in your chair and remember that you are still giving impressions of yourself. If you have done your best, no one will complain.

IMPROVE YOUR VOCABULARY

Gambol - (gam'bol) n. or v. - Play, rollick, frolic, romp, frisk, to leap and skip about. Example: The neighbor's child would <u>gambol</u> about like a young colt.

<u>Look</u> - Do you use this word too much? If so, you can improve your vocabulary and conversation by giving <u>look</u> a rest. Synonyms are: gage, inspect, observe, regard, survey, scan, discern, contemplate, glance, etc.

BIBLIOGRAPHY FOR YOUR FIRST SPEECH

Buehler, E. Christian, and Linkugel, W. A., <u>Speech Communication</u>, Harper & Row, Publishers, 1969, pp. 96-103.

Culp, Ralph Borden, <u>Basic Types of Speech</u>, Wm. C. Brown Company, Publishers, 1968, Chapter 1.

Hance, Kenneth G., and Others, <u>Principles of Speaking</u>, Wadsworth Publishing Company, 2d ed., 1969, Part 3.

Monroe, Alan H., and Ehninger, Douglas, <u>Principles of Speech Communication</u>, Scott, Foresman and Company, 6th brief ed., 1969, Chapter 1.

Oliver, Robert T., and Cortright, R. L., <u>Effective Speech</u>, Holt, Rinehart and Winston, Inc., 5th ed., 1970, Parts 3 & 4.

Ross, Raymond S., <u>Speech Communication</u>, Prentice-Hall, Inc., 2d ed., 1970, Chapter 7.

Verderber, Rudolph F., <u>The Challenge of Effective Speaking</u>, Wadsworth Publishing Company, Inc., 1970, Part 2.

Williams, Barbara, <u>Purposeful Communication</u>, Kendall/Hunt Publishing Company, 1970, Chapter 4.

- -

(Copy the notes below). Use them while giving the information they request.)

1. My name is (what shall we call you?)
2. Where and how did you spend your childhood? Explain.
3. Tell about your home town.
4. What is your hobby? Explain.
5. Who are your favorite movie actor and actress? Why?
6. What is your favorite sport? Why?
7. Conclude with a summarizing statement about your school plans.

RECORDING A SPEECH

This speech is due:
Time limits: See your instructor for the exact time.
Speaking notes: Ten or fifteen words should be enough.

PURPOSE OF RECORDING A SPEECH

This assignment is proposed in order that you may hear and judge your own speaking. It calls for a speech that you will record and keep for yourself as a record of how you talked when this course started. At a later date near the end of the course, you may wish to make another recording to compare with your first recording, thus noting your progress.

EXPLANATION OF A RECORDED SPEECH

A recorded speech may be any kind for any occasion. It simply is a speech which is recorded and played back at will. In other words, it becomes a record in voice rather than a record in writing. These are its chief purposes: rebroadcasting from a radio station, private use, or classroom study. Its special feature is the time limit placed on the speaker. Its time has to be observed within a matter of seconds. Any person who is not willing to adhere to the time limit pays for disc space he does not use because his speech is short. If he has too much speech and runs out of time, he either makes an awkward conclusion or is cut off in the middle of a sentence or summary.

Occasions for recording a speech occur any time a speech needs to be preserved for later use. Occasions may arise in the home, school, church, club, business, politics, government, theatre, radio station, and the like.

SUGGESTED TOPICS FOR RECORDING

If you are recording a speech during the first part of the school year with the thought in mind that you will make a later recording for purposes of comparison, it might be wise to use the first speech experience suggested in this book, the one in which you introduced yourself to the class. If you do not care to do this, check through the many possibilities listed under "Suggested Topics" in each of the other speech experiences. Be sure your selection meets the time limit which you will be required to observe. Consult your instructor for further information.

If this is your first recording or you are inexperienced, do not try to be profound in your remarks. Rather, select a topic which will best represent you at your present stage of development as a speaker. On the other hand, if you merely wish to make a recording of a speech, your topic will have little to do with it.

HOW TO PREPARE A SPEECH FOR RECORDING

For this particular speech your purpose is to secure a record of your speaking ability. Decide according to the first assignment notes what you are going to say; then practice aloud until you have your thoughts well in mind, but not memorized. Know the general outline of your ideas.

If you choose to speak on some other topic, simply prepare it as you would any speech by observing good speech preparation practices. In all cases observe your time limits within ten seconds if possible.

Should you choose to read your speech (with your instructor's consent), organize it as you would any speech. Keep it right on the nose as to time.

HOW TO PRESENT A SPEECH FOR RECORDING

You should begin your speech by saying, "This is (George Jones) speaking on (date) . . . " After your first sentence, go ahead with your talk. Speak in your natural voice as you normally would. Be careful not to vary the distance from the microphone by moving your head a great deal or your recording may be loud at first and then weak. Also avoid coughing, clearing your throat, sneezing, or shouting into the "mike." Ask your instructor how close to stand to the microphone; however, ten inches is considered a good distance.

While speaking, watch your progress so that you may be sure to finish before your time runs out.

If you use notes, avoid rustling them near the microphone. Any sound they make will be picked up and exaggerated. When one piece of paper is finished, let it quietly drop from your hands to the floor.

SPECIAL NOTES

If discs are used for recordings, the following may apply. When a group of recordings is concluded, the instructor may play them back to the class; then members of the class may discuss the individual speakers. Points to listen for are the whistled "s," nasality, harshness, resonance, pitch, force, articulation, pronunciation . . . .

The instructor, at his discretion, may keep the records on file until the end of the course when a final recording may be made for comparative purposes. The student may then receive the record with a speech on each side for his own use and analysis.

Blank discs may be procured from a local music store or if the instructor wishes, he may write to various record-making companies for them. He should ask for educational discounts, regardless of where he gets them. Each student should be prepared to pay for the disc used in making his recording unless the school provides for this expense.

If a wire or tape recorder is used, there will be no expense attached unless the spool is retained for future reference. Should this be done, another spool will be needed to replace it. Even in this case, the used spool may be filed until near the end of the term at which time it can be reused without cost.

IMPROVE YOUR VOCABULARY

On the nose - This is a term used in radio to designate that the speaker or actor concluded his performance exactly on time. Learn to use it when talking about radio. Example: He finished his speech on the nose.

Hot - Use synonyms for this word. It is overworked. Examples are: burning, scorching, boiling, heated, excited, strong, raging, fiery, etc.

Chapter 3

SPEECH OF PERSONAL EXPERIENCE

This speech is due:
Time limits: 3-4 minutes.
Speaking notes: 10-word maximum limit.
Source of information: Use your own personal experience.
Outline of speech: Prepare a 50-100 word complete sentence outline to be handed to your instructor when you rise to speak. He may wish to write criticisms on it regarding your speech. Write the number of words in upper left hand corner of the paper. Use the form at the end of this chapter.

PURPOSE OF A SPEECH OF PERSONAL EXPERIENCE

You take a step forward in your speaking experience when you present a speech of personal experience. While this speech is essentially about yourself, it still requires a definite preparation and interesting presentation. You should learn the importance of these two requirements early in your speech training. Aside from becoming acquainted with these aspects of speechmaking, you should feel increased confidence and poise as a result of this speech experience. Your ease before the group will improve noticeably. By giving your best to this speech you will achieve a creditable improvement and desirable personal satisfaction.

EXPLANATION OF A SPEECH OF PERSONAL EXPERIENCE

A speech of personal experience may be one of any four basic types: that is, the speech may be given to (1) inform, (2) to stimulate or arouse, (3) to convince, or (4) to entertain. The specific purpose of your remarks will determine which of these types you plan to present. If you want to tell of funny or amusing personal experiences, you will plan to entertain your listeners. If you wish to tell how you trap muskrats, your purpose will be to inform your listeners. It is advisable to confine your efforts to one of these two kinds of speeches. To attempt either of the others this early would be too hazardous to recommend now. You should study the chapter elsewhere in this book that deals with the type of speech you plan to present.

All this speech requires from you is a good thorough preparation. You must know the order in which you plan to tell of your experiences. You also need to know how you will tell them, that is, the words you will use. This does not mean you are to memorize your speech. Do not memorize your speech either now or later. This point will be discussed in subsequent paragraphs under the headings: "How To Prepare a Speech of Personal Experience" and "How To Present a Speech of Personal Experience."

Unlimited occasions for a speech of personal experience occur at all kinds of meetings - such as before school assemblies, clubs, business meetings, religious gatherings, and other groups. You have probably heard such a speech from a war veteran, a war correspondent, from a missionary, a newspaper reporter, a great athlete, or from a person like yourself who tells what has happened to him.

SUGGESTED TOPICS FOR A SPEECH OF PERSONAL EXPERIENCE

1. Wrecks
2. Conflagrations
3. Falling through ice
4. Swimming
5. Hunting
6. Camping
7. Hiking
8. Climbing
9. Racing - any kind
10. Sports contests
11. Rodeos
*12. A trip
13. Flying
14. An experiment
15. Sickness
16. Wrestling
17. At a carnival
18. Embarrassment
19. A funny incident
20. Building something
21. Speaker's choice

* Do not choose this topic unless you have more to tell than items, such as; the time you started, where you ate your meals, the hotels you stayed in, the cities you passed through, and when you returned. A speech of this kind should carry some element of special interest which makes it different from any ordinary trip.

HOW TO CHOOSE A TOPIC FOR A SPEECH OF PERSONAL EXPERIENCE

Read the foregoing list of topics carefully. They are intended to suggest ideas to you. If you have had an exciting experience similar to one of them, select it for your speech. Whatever you decide to talk about should be vivid in your memory and quite clear. As you think about it you may feel prickly chills race up your spine, you may laugh, you may feel sad. But whatever it is, the experience should be personal.

Do not begin stalling before making a choice of topic because you do not know anything interesting to talk about. This is an old, worn-out excuse which explorers used before Columbus; they could not make up their minds about what to discover. In all likelihood they did not try. The topic that you choose will not be interesting in itself. It is your responsibility to plan to tell the personal experience in an interesting way. You can do this with a little effort. Choose a topic without delay, and then read the rest of this assignment to find out how to prepare and present a speech on the topic you have chosen.

HOW TO PREPARE A SPEECH OF PERSONAL EXPERIENCE

First, decide on your purpose for giving this speech. Do you want to inform your listeners? Do you want to entertain them? It will be wise to work toward one of these ends for this speech. Having decided this point, your next step is to find out how you go about informing or entertaining. You may do this by reading the chapter in this text dealing with these types of talks.

Now let us assume that you know generally what is expected of you when you give your speech. Let us assume, too, that you have your purpose constantly before you (to entertain or to inform). Now develop your speech in the following order:

I. Outline your speech in considerable detail. This means that you must set up the order of events you want to talk about.
   A. Be sure your outline places these events in their most effective order throughout your talk. A little thought about arrangement will tell you how to place your ideas.
      1. In arranging what you will talk about, include your own personal feelings and reactions, the activities of other persons or animals, and objects that made your experience thrilling, exciting, funny, . . . This will add interest.

II. Practice your speech aloud before friends and in front of a mirror. Do this until you have memorized the sequence of events, not the words. You will quite naturally tend to memorize certain words and phrases and this is all right. But do not under any circumstances memorize the whole speech word for word. Every time you rehearse you will tell the same things, but never with exactly the same words. Each rehearsal will set the pattern of your speech more firmly in mind until after several practices (the number depends on the individual) you will be able to present your speech with full confidence and the knowledge that you know what you are going to say; that is, you know the events and feelings you are going to talk about and describe.

III. Make a final evaluation of your speech before marking it "ready for presentation." Ask yourself the following questions and be sure that your speech answers each question adequately.
   A. Does your speech merely list a series of persons, places, things, and time without telling what happened to these persons and things? (You should vitalize these persons and things by describing what happened and by pointing out unusual or exciting incidents, such as; dangers, or humorous occurrences.) Avoid unnecessary details.
   B. Is your speech about you only? If so, you can improve it by talking about the influences that were operating in your presence. For example, if you rescued a drowning person, do not be satisfied to say, "I jumped in and pulled him out." Tell what he was doing, describe his struggles, tell how deep the water was, how far he was from shore, recount your fears and other feelings as you pulled him toward shore, tell how the current almost took you under, demonstrate the way you held him by the hair, . . . Emphasize such items as your fatigue and near exhaustion as you fought to stay afloat. Here is an example of a "thriller": "We were in swimming. I guess we'd been in about an hour. John got the cramps and yelled

for help. I swam over and pulled him out. He almost took me under once, but I got him out and gave him artificial respiration. I learned that when I was a kid. Boy, I sure was scared."
(Author's note: Was this an interesting story of an experience? It could have been, had it been told with vividness and description.)
C. Do you have a curiosity-arousing introduction, one that catches the attention? Check this point carefully.
D. Do you have a conclusion? A speech is never finished without one.

HOW TO PRESENT A SPEECH OF PERSONAL EXPERIENCE

Your attitude regarding yourself and your audience will exert a singular influence upon you and your listeners. You should have a sincere desire to entertain or inform. If it is information that you earnestly desire to give, then you must try to make your audience understand what you are telling. If it is entertainment you want to provide, then you must strive to give enjoyment by amusing and causing smiles and perhaps some laughter. You should not feel that what you have to say is simply not interesting and never was, which is the attitude of some students. Consider for a moment the child who runs to you eagerly, grasps your hand, and excitedly tells you about a big dog two doors down the street. His story no doubt captivates your interest; yet there is nothing inherently interesting about a big dog you have seen many times. Why then are you interested? The answer lies largely in the extreme desire of the child to tell you something. He wants you to understand him, and therein lies the basic secret of giving information to which people will listen attentively. You must have a desire to make your audience understand you or enjoy what you are saying.

As for your bodily actions and gestures, demonstrate those points which you can. Let your arms and hands gesture whenever you feel an impulse to do so; otherwise, your hands may hang comfortably at your sides, rest easily on a table top or chair back, or be placed conveniently in a pocket. Be calm about putting your hands anywhere. Change your stage position by moving laterally a few feet. This will cause attention to be drawn to your presentation.

Use your voice normally and conversationally. Talk earnestly and loudly enough to be heard by everyone present. If you are truly interested in your audience's understanding you, your voice modulation and force will take care of themselves very well.

If you use speaking notes, observe the ten-word maximum limit. Have these written in large handwriting so that they may be easily read. Use a paper at least three by five inches in size, preferably larger. Do not fiddle with the paper or roll it into a tube. Hold the notes calmly between your thumb and forefinger in either hand. When referring to your notes, raise them to a level that permits you to glance at them without bowing your head. Do not try to hide them, nor act ashamed of using them. They are your map. Treat them as casually as you would a road map were you taking a trip.

IMPROVE YOUR VOCABULARY

Avid - (ăv'ĭd) a. To desire very much. Greedy, rapacious, eager, keen, anxious, athirst, etc.
    Example: He was an avid wrestling fan. Use this word three or four times daily until it is yours. It will give you a new and expressive term.

Get - Omit this word. Use a synonym to give variety to your speech. Here are examples: achieve, earn, gain, procure, secure, obtain, acquire, attain, receive, win, etc.

BIBLIOGRAPHY FOR SPEECH OF PERSONAL EXPERIENCE

Monroe, Alan H., and Ehninger, Douglas, Principles of Speech Communication, Scott, Foresman and Company, 6th brief ed., 1969, Chapter 1.
Williams, Barbara, Purposeful Communication, Kendall/Hunt Publishing Company, 1970, pp. 105-106.

PERSONAL EXPERIENCE SPEECH

By Gail Anderson

THE EARTH TREMBLED

"And Jesus uttered a loud cry, and breathed his last. And the curtain of the temple was torn in two, from top to bottom." Mark 15: 37-38. Good Friday holds a point in destiny unequaled since the dawning of all mankind. March 27, 1964, Good Friday alike, holds an eminent position in the stream of my life as the day of the Alaska earthquake.

I was thirteen at the time, living in Anchorage, Alaska. The fact was that a "Good Friday supper-time" sort of atmosphere was beginning to creep into the minds of each of the members of my family. We might even have been bored had it not been for the anticipation of the evening meal that was near completion.

The day was calm. My father was typically absorbed in the newspaper. "Kitchen-puttering" occupied my mother. My brother was both engaged and absorbed in some nonsensical whiling away of time. Snow was falling in a soft and gentle manner, combatting boredom with me. The subtle and peaceful cloaking it lent the earth, could only be viewed as ironic now, in the face of what was to come.

The snow was still falling when the hanging light fixtures began to swing and the rattle of furniture could be heard on the tile floor. At first, our reaction could only have been termed amusement. But our amusement soon became terror. As we stumbled down stairs and through doors, trying to avoid tumbling objects, we heard and felt the rumble of our earth mount. As the front door forcibly flung us into the mounds of snow in the front yard, the earth continued to roll and groan. And then sprawled on the sidewalk, the ground ceased to tease us with its laughing rumbles. Now it was cracking. Around me the snow was forming rifts as great expanses of the frozen earth were separating.

The noises somehow were strangely deafening. Hysterical cries of neighbors blended with the laughing of the earth and the creaking of the houses to produce a wicked sound system matched only by the horror of its backdrop.

Our station wagon bounced as if it were a rubber ball. The picture windows of the house were distorted to the point of being diamond-shaped. Trees on high-crumbling mountains in the distance were waving like a wheatfield in a breeze.

Finally the earth became dormant once again. Now it was still. And as the curtain of night shrouded our stricken Alaska, we were left to our contemplations. The hesitancy of the only partially existent radio gave our own woes a universality. Only then did we realize the encompassing scope of this earthquake. Sitting in my rocking chair (attempting to camouflage any further shaking), I heard of this demon which had left me alive and glad with my saved family, and spared home, but had taken the lives and homes of so many others.

In Anchorage the next day we saw the effects of disaster. Homes, schools, and businesses lay in ruin, paradoxically powdered with snow. But the people were together, helping one another. The homes left standing were crowded, but a unity of cause made these conditions endurable.

Immediately work began to rebuild, to restore. Radio announcers neglected their families to keep the people informed, as televisions and newspapers were not to be lines of communication for some time. People were living without heat, water, mail service, and many other things. Essentials were the essence of a united survival.

I wish that I could have understood the agonizing pleas for survival, for salvation. But only now, as my mind becomes a victim of time, do I have any understanding of the emotional or intellectual influence a natural disaster exercises on life and the perception of it.

And so, as on the original Good Friday, man was to be a recipient of one of the most vividly educational experiences in a lifetime. As the tragedy of the crucifixion and resurrection of Jesus Christ, the tragedy of the earthquake was to bring man closer to God, more desirous of salvation, and more understanding of both his God and himself.

SPEECH OUTLINE

Construct a neat, complete sentence outline on this sheet, tear it out, and hand it to your instructor when you rise to speak. He may wish to write criticisms of the outline and speech in the margins.

Type of speech:_____   Name:_____

Number of words in outline:_____   Date:_____

Purpose of this speech: (What do you want your audience to learn, to think, to believe, to feel, or do
                          because of this speech?)_____

_____

TITLE:

INTRODUCTION:

BODY:

CONCLUSION:

Instructor's comments may concern choice of topic, development of ideas, organization, language use, personal appearance, posture, physical activity, sources, and improvement.

(Write sources of information on back of sheet)

SOURCES FROM LITERATURE

(Fill out source requirements completely. Write "none listed" if an author's name or copyright date is not listed.)

1. Author's name _____

   Title of book or magazine used _____

   Title of article in above book or magazine _____

   Chapter and/or pages read _____

   Date of above publication _____

2. Author's name _____

   Title of book or magazine used _____

   Title of article in above book or magazine _____

   Chapter and/or pages read _____

   Date of above publication _____

3. Author's name _____

   Title of book or magazine used _____

   Title of article in above book or magazine _____

   Chapter and/or pages read _____

   Date of above publication _____

INTERVIEW SOURCES

1. Person interviewed _____ Date of interview _____

   His position, occupation, and location _____

   Why is he a reliable source? Be specific _____

   _____

2. Person interviewed _____ Date of interview _____

   His position, occupation, and location _____

   Why is he a reliable source? Be specific _____

   _____

PERSONAL EXPERIENCE OF SPEAKER

1. Tell (1) when, (2) where, and (3) conditions under which you became an authority on subject matter in

   your speech _____

   _____

   _____

   _____

Chapter 4

THE PET PEEVE OR OPINION SPEECH

This speech is due:
Time limits: None.
Speaking notes: Do as you like - you will probably be more effective without them.
Source of information: Yourself.
Outline of speech: None is required.
To the instructor: This speech usually works well after students have had two or three previous assignments.

PURPOSE OF THE PET PEEVE OR OPINION SPEECH

Thus far in your speeches you have probably felt varying degrees of nervousness and tension. As a result you may have taken stage fearfully, spoken in hushed and weak tones, used little or no bodily action, and scarcely any gestures. Perhaps you have not looked your audience in the eye (called eye contact) or you may have lacked sufficient enthusiasm. Such behavior on your part is probably caused by thinking of yourself and how you are doing.

One way to overcome tensions and nervousness is by talking of something about which you are intensely aroused. This speech is designed to give you the feeling of real, live speaking in which you cast aside all inhibitions, fears, and thoughts of yourself. See what you can do with it.

EXPLANATION OF THE PET PEEVE OR OPINION SPEECH

Your talk should be about your pet peeve. It should concern your innermost personal feelings on that peeve which causes you greater disturbance and anger or stronger feeling than anything else. It should make your blood boil just to think of it. It may be about something of recent occurrence or it may concern an event that happened some time ago. It must, however, be about an incident that is vivid in your memory. Probably it should be of recent date; otherwise, you may have cooled off too much to make a strong speech about it.

SUGGESTED TOPIC

My pet peeve - or anything else that stirs you up.

HOW TO PREPARE A SPEECH ABOUT A PET PEEVE

No particular preparation is required. All that you need do is to decide what your most annoying and irritating pet peeve is. Once you make your choice of peeve, mull over the irritating idea and make up your mind that you are going to "blow off a lot of steam" to your audience. If you wish to rehearse before presentation, so much the better. However, for this specific assignment you are not asked to practice. All that you are asked to do is to make sure that you are "red hot" about a particular subject. If you are, your preparation is sufficient for this speech.

HOW TO PRESENT YOUR SPEECH

There is just one way to deliver a speech about a pet peeve. Put your whole body and soul into it. Mean every word. Use plenty of force framed in dynamic and colorful language. Let a slow fire that has been smoldering within you suddenly explode. Pour hot verbal oil on the blaze and let it roar and burn! In other words, let yourself go as never before. Quit pussy footing around and acting like a meek little lamb that has lost its way. Be a man and do not be afraid to let the world know it. If your arms feel like waving, let them wave. If you feel like scowling in disgust - scowl. If you feel like shouting - shout. Whatever you do, just be sure you go all out. No doubt you will be surprised at your own ability - when you really "unload your pet peeve."

After your speech, the instructor and class will comment orally on your effectiveness. They should be able to tell you whether or not you really meant what you said. It will be helpful to you to find out how they reacted.

IMPROVE YOUR VOCABULARY

Banal - (băn'ăl, bā'năl) a. commonplace, hackeyed, trite. Example: Avoid banal language.

Give - Use a synonym for this very common verb. Here are a few examples; Bestow, cede, deliver, confer, communicate, donate, grant, impart, supply, present, etc.

BIBLIOGRAPHY FOR THE PET PEEVE OR OPINION SPEECH

These references will suggest helpful hints for improvement of your speech:

Buehler, E. Christian, and Linkugel, W. A., Speech Communication, Harper & Row, Publishers, 1969.
Hance, Kenneth G., and Others, Principles of Speaking, Wadsworth Publishing Company, 2d ed., 1969.
Williams, Barbara, Purposeful Communication, Kendall/Hunt Publishing Company, 1970, pp. 67-69.

PET PEEVE SPEECH

By William A. Baxter

LET'S NOT BECOME A NATION OF FOOLS

Many young people today are allowing themselves to be made to look like fools. In their idealism they are being duped into believing that utopia is possible. Were constructive efforts being attempted to achieve their goal, perhaps this great hoax could be rationalized. But no! Destruction is their key, and lawlessness their weapon. Let's take a closer look.

Many groups are being organized today. Members of these organizations paint a beautiful picture for our young people. They say they want to change America. They want complete equality, freedom, love, and respect for all men. Granted these are laudable aims; ideals for which our fathers fought and died, and which today men are defending with their lives. But let us now examine these groups formed for the sake of brotherly love.

One such group is a notorious black organization. They began in an effort to help colored people fight for civil rights. But check the newspapers and magazines reporting their activities. Destruction of property, terrorism, and murder appear to be their main methods. Do we have to believe that the only way to better ourselves in America is to kill everyone who does not believe as we do?

Other groups calling themselves "students for this" or "defenders for that," all formed for honorable or idealistic goals, have recently been arming themselves. Does the only way to brotherly love, freedom and equality lie in the destruction of our government and the abolition of the capitalistic system which have made America the powerful nation she is today? To me, this idea is revolting. Why can't we young people see that the way to accomplish reform is through the knowledgeable use of our democratic system? So our elected officials have made mistakes -- so have we all. This should not make us forget that we have a tool in our system which is much more powerful than all the guns held by militants and subversives. That tool is the pen. Used correctly, it will support those who work to achieve the will of the people; it will conquer those who have not the good of the country at heart; it will give powerful aid to those who are in a position to help us achieve the ideals for which we all hope.

Many young people today are fools. They use evil to fight evil. They haven't yet discovered there is a better way!

Chapter 5

THE SPEECH TO DEVELOP BODILY ACTION AND GESTURE

This speech is due:
Time limits: 4-5 minutes.
Speaking notes: 10-word maximum limit.
Sources of information: Two are required, preferably three. For each source give the specific magazine
    or book it was taken from, title of the article, author's full name, date of publication, and the chap-
    ter or pages telling where the material was found. If a source is a person, identify him complete-
    ly by title, position, occupation, etc. List these on the outline form.
Outline your speech: Prepare a 75-150 word complete sentence outline. Designate the exact number of
    words in your outline. Use the form at the end of this chapter.

PURPOSE OF THE SPEECH TO DEVELOP BODILY ACTION AND GESTURE

Speaking is a total bodily activity. To be really effective a person has to talk all over. He has to use his feet and legs, his hands and arms, his trunk, his head, his eyebrows - every part of him. Many beginning speakers do not realize this, despite the fact that they themselves use total bodily expression all the time in their normal conversation. One sees such speakers standing before a class very stiff and rigid making their speeches. They move only their vocal cords, their tongue and jaws. Actually, they are half speaking (communicating) because they are using only half of their communicating tools. If they would put all of their speaking power into action, they would include bodily action and gestures. A speech assign-ment of this kind is made because it will provide an experience which will demand that the speaker use bodily actions and gestures, and thus improve his speech.

EXPLANATION OF BODILY ACTION AND GESTURES IN SPEECH

A speech to illustrate bodily activity may be any kind, since bodily actions and gestures should be used in every speech with varying degrees. The purpose of your speech need not be influenced because bodily actions and gestures are required. These activities will be aids in assisting you to communicate in a manner which fulfills your purpose, regardless of what it is.

Bodily actions may be defined as the movements of the body as it changes places. Gestures may be defined as movements of individual parts of the body, such as: raising an eyebrow, shrugging the shoulders, pointing . . . .

This speech in which you will deliberately use bodily actions and gestures should be considered as an experience in which you plan to utilize your entire organism and then do it. By carrying through you will understand how much more effective you really are and thus set a pattern of speaking to be used in your future speeches.

As far as this writer knows, it is impossible to speak without some bodily action and gestures. Just because you may not be aware of all that goes on while you speak, in no sense means that you are not using some actions. Your very nervousness and stage fright elicit certain gestures which tell your aud-ience you are nervous. Now, if you substitute meaningful activity, you at once improve your communica-tion and release many nervous tensions which accompany speaking. The point to bear in mind is that all speech communication should be accompanied by appropriate and meaningful bodily actions and gestures, which should not be interpreted to mean that you must employ constant bodily movements and incessant gestures. Such monotony of motion would be nerve wracking to an audience. Someone once said that mod-eration is good to practice in all things. This is true of total bodily expression. Keep this in mind.

SUGGESTED TOPICS FOR SPEECHES TO DEVELOP BODILY ACTION AND GESTURES

1. How to saddle, bridle, and mount a horse.
2. How to take a picture.
3. How to use a golf club.
4. How to hold and pitch a baseball to make it curve.
5. How to catch and throw a football.
6. How to dribble and "shoot" a basketball.
7. How to box.
8. How to wrestle.

9. How to type properly.
10. How to write well.
11. How to revive a drowning person.
12. How to play a musical instrument.
13. How to cast with a fishing rod.
14. How to shoot a gun (pistol, rifle, shotgun).
15. How to fly an airplane.
16. How to milk a cow.
17. How to use a lasso.
18. How to give a referee's signals for any sport.
19. How to dance (different steps should be demonstrated and explained. Also different types of dancing such as square, tap, ballet . . .)
20. How to apply facial make-up correctly.
21. How to use bodily actions and gestures while speaking.
22. How to ice skate or roller skate.
23. How to construct something.
24. How to do card tricks (this must be a demonstration which uses bodily action and gesture - not a mere performance of a few tricks.)
25. How to ski, toboggan . . .
26. Speaker's choice.

HOW TO CHOOSE A TOPIC FOR A SPEECH TO DEVELOP BODILY ACTION AND GESTURE

Since the purpose of presenting this speech is to improve your use of bodily action and gesture, you should select a subject which you can demonstrate while talking about it. On the other hand, the purpose of the speech itself will be to inform your listeners. It will be wise then for you to choose a topic in which you are interested and about which you can find source materials. You must also adapt your material (your speech) to your audience; hence it must be suitable to them as well as to you.

Study the above list carefully; then make your decision. After your choice is made, stick to it even though you discover it more difficult to prepare than you had anticipated. Do not change topics just because you misjudged the amount of effort it would take for preparation.

It is important that you make your selection of a topic without delay, for this speech will require considerable planning. There is no reason to put off a decision regarding a topic. Make up your mind now; then pursue your materials until you have what you want.

HOW TO PREPARE A SPEECH TO DEVELOP BODILY ACTION AND GESTURE

In the speech to develop bodily action and gesture, your communicative purpose will be to inform your listeners in such a way that they understand what you are talking about. You will find out all about this type of speech by reading the chapter in this text, "The Speech to Inform." You develop your speech in the manner suggested for the informative speech.

In rehearsing this talk, you will need to practice bodily actions and gestures, as these will constitute a great part of this speech. These actions should not be memorized in detail, which would result in a mechanical performance on your part. Instead, you should stand before a mirror while you practice. If possible, use a large mirror that reflects your whole body rather than just the upper half of it. However, if only a small mirror is available, do the best you can with it. A friend who will watch you and give helpful criticisms will provide an excellent means for improvement.

While you rehearse, your efforts should be exerted to create a well-organized set of spontaneous actions. As stated above, you must not memorize these actions. They must be motivated by the earnestness of your desire to make your hearers understand you. You must feel impelled to use your body and hands in expressing yourself. These actions of your body and hands need not be like those of anybody else - they are your own, the same as your walk and style of dancing are your own. All that you need to do is to observe yourself in practice in order to eliminate awkwardness, undesirable posture and foot positions, and distracting mannerisms.

The thought is that if you are willing to try and to undergo a little self-inflicted criticism, you can develop your own style of gesture and bodily action. In doing this, it is advisable that you read several references on bodily action and gesture. However, for your assistance you may find it helpful to know of the following general types of hand and arm gestures:

1. Pointing - use the index finger. Have some vigor in this gesture. Do not use a half-crooked finger.
2. Palm up (one or both hands) - this is seen most when giving or receiving, whether it be an idea or an object.
3. Palm down (one or both hands) - this is used in rejecting, pushing things away from you. Imagine that a pup jumped on you, putting his front paws against your body. Push him away - palms down! The same goes for ideas while speaking.
4. Palm oblique, about shoulder high - this is used in cautioning. Imagine yourself patting a friend on the shoulder while you say, "Take it easy, John, there's danger ahead."
5. The clenched fist (it must be vigorously clenched so that the muscles stand out on the forearm and shoulder) - both fists may be used if the gesture is appropriate. Usually one fist clenches sympathetically with the other if the gesture is really meant. Use this gesture for emphasis. Do not pound the table. Just almost touch it on the down stroke, that is, if a table is around.

Your posture should be one of alertness in which you stand tall. Keep your weight on the balls of your feet and on the forward foot.

Bodily action should be free, relaxed, easy. It should have tonicity, vigor and coordination, without the appearance of extreme nervous tension, which is characterized by shuffling feet and restless tiger-like pacing. In moving to the left, lead with the left foot; to the right, with the right foot. Avoid crossing your legs in order to get started. Move quietly without "clomping" heels and scraping soles. Be sure that the movement is motivated and acts as a transition between ideas, as an emphasis, as a device for releasing bodily tension and holding attention. Use bodily action deliberately until you habitually make it a desirable part of your speech, a part that communicates meanings and ideas.

Before you consider this speech completely prepared, construct the outline indicated at the beginning of this chapter.

HOW TO PRESENT A SPEECH TO DEVELOP ACTION AND GESTURE
When you present this speech, approach the speaker's stand with the attitude of a person determined to win. Have no fear or shame that your gestures and actions will be wrong or inappropriate. Take pride in the fact that you are going to use your entire organism in speaking. With this attitude you cannot lose.

When you actually present your speech, concentrate on one point which will make the audience understand what you are informing them about. They have to understand you, or you will not be getting your ideas across (communicating). Now, while you are earnestly presenting your ideas, try to make them clearer by demonstrating what you have to say. Do this by acting out certain parts as you talk. If you tell the audience that it is best to mount a horse a certain way, show them how to do it. If you say a baseball should be thrown a certain way, demonstrate it with all the force and energy you would use were you actually pitching. If your demonstration is so vigorous that it makes you short of breath, so much the better; you will have been truly trying to show, as well as tell what you have to say. You may exhibit pictures, charts, diagrams, write on the blackboard . . . If you do, be sure that your equipment is ready for exhibition before you begin.

Do not be afraid to try; do your best, and you will do a good job. Plan to continue using bodily actions and gestures in your future speeches.

IMPROVE YOUR VOCABULARY

Furtive - (fûr'tĭv) a. done stealthily - sly, secret, covert, underhand, clandestine. Example: The cat cast a furtive glance toward the approaching dog. Use this word three times daily for three days. Make it a working part of your vocabulary.

Quiet - Omit this word for a week. Use a synonym to give your speech variety and to add new words to your vocabulary. Here are a few examples: calm, motionless, serene, placid, taciturn, reticent, hushed, inactive, uncommunicative, etc.

BIBLIOGRAPHY FOR THE SPEECH TO DEVELOP BODILY ACTION AND GESTURE

Buehler, E. Christian, and Linkugel, W. A., Speech Communication, Harper & Row, Publishers, 1969, pp. 89-93.

Ecroyd, Donald H., Speech in the Classroom, Prentice-Hall, Inc., 2d ed., 1969, Chapter 5.

Hance, Kenneth G., and Others, Principles of Speaking, Wadsworth Publishing Company, 2d ed., 1969, pp. 256-262.

McAuley, Jack G., Speech, The Essential Elements, Burgess Publishing Company, 1968, pp. 117-124.

Monroe, Alan H., and Ehninger, Douglas, Principles of Speech Communication, Scott, Foresman and Company, 6th brief ed., 1969, Chapter 4.

Oliver, Robert T., and Cortright, R. L., Effective Speech, Holt, Rinehart and Winston, Inc., 5th ed., 1970, Chapter 13.

Ross, Raymond S., Speech Communication, Prentice-Hall, Inc., 2d ed., 1970, Chapter 5.

SPEECH TO DEVELOP BODILY ACTION AND GESTURE
By Joann Bopp
START CANOEING AND ENJOY YOUR WEEKENDS

Props needed for this speech are canoe paddles, an armless chair, and a small rug. You should wear light weight sports clothes. Before you are asked to deliver your speech see that the chair is in front of the class. When you are called to speak carry the small rug and the paddles with you. Lay the paddles across the seat of the chair and spread the rug on the floor near the chair. You can now stand in front of the class or at the podium and begin your speech.

Wouldn't you like to get more fun and relaxation out of your leisure time? Those two-day weekends could be spent away from the busy, hurried city life that most of us lead. Just put a canoe on top of your car and head for water. A canoe can float on as little as four inches of water. A quiet lake or stream or pond may hold more fascination than you ever imagined. It is a delight to quietly skim over calm waters and see the natural beauty of the shoreline or catch a glimpse of wildlife going about their unhurried activities. A canoe could also bring the thrills of shooting rapids of a swift running river, but this is for the experienced boatman, or you can find much pleasure with little effort in canoeing secluded little bodies of water.

I would like to give you a few rules and demonstrations to show you how to canoe in a very short time. Number one rule is getting in and out of a craft correctly. Canoeing is often thought of as being very dangerous but the danger usually occurs when getting in or out of the canoe. To get in, you step first to the center, lengthwise, and place the other foot behind (demonstrate on rug). Then lower yourself to a kneeling position which is the correct canoeing position (demonstrate by kneeling on rug). There are braces across the canoe to lean against. Once you have established this low center of gravity the canoe has great stability. Getting out is just reverse. Keep your weight to the center as much as possible (demonstrate by getting off the rug).

These are the paddles (show paddles), they are made of fir, a soft wood which holds up well in water and is light weight. To select the paddle measure it to your height. It should come to about your chin (demonstrate). (Sit in the chair to demonstrate paddling strokes). To hold the paddle grip the end with one hand and with the other hand grasp it a little above the blade (demonstrate). Holding in this manner you are ready to start paddling.

The basic stroke is called the "cruising stroke," or the "bow stroke." Extend the paddle in front of you (demonstrations follow), close to the canoe, and dip into the water, bringing it straight back to the hip by pushing with the top hand and pulling with the lower hand. Now bring the paddle back and repeat. The paddling is usually done by a two man team called tandem paddling. In tandem paddling the person in front is the sternman who steers the boat. The person in the rear is the bowman and he provides the power. The bowman uses the bow stroke most of the time (demonstrations follow). The sternman uses the bow stroke also, but often makes a hook outward on the end of the stroke to keep the canoe on course. This version of the bow stroke is called the "J-stroke." The sternman also uses the "sweep stroke" for turning. It is a wide, sweeping, arc-like stroke made close to the water surface (demonstrate). To stop or go backwards the "backwater stroke" is used. Simply place the paddle into the water at right angles to the canoe and hold it firmly to stop (demonstrate). To go backwards reverse the "bow stroke" (demonstrate).

(Rise to a standing position with paddles in hand.)

This is by no means all there is to know about canoeing, but if you can accomplish these things you will be able to have fun. So to enjoy the outdoors and take a break from a humdrum routine I hope you will try canoeing. (Pick up rug, and with paddles and rug, resume your seat).

SPEECH OUTLINE

Construct a neat, complete sentence outline on this sheet, tear it out, and hand it to your instructor when you rise to speak. He may wish to write criticisms of the outline and speech in the margins.

Type of speech:_____   Name: _____

Number of words in outline:_____   Date: _____

Purpose of this speech: (What do you want your audience to learn, to think, to believe, to feel, or do because of this speech?)_____

_____

TITLE:

INTRODUCTION:

BODY:

CONCLUSION:

<u>Instructor's comments</u> may concern choice of topic, development of ideas, organization, language use, personal appearance, posture, physical activity, sources, and improvement.

(Write sources of information on back of sheet)

SOURCES FROM LITERATURE

(Fill out source requirements completely. Write "none listed" if an author's name or copyright date is not listed.)

1. Author's name _____

   Title of book or magazine used _____

   Title of article in above book or magazine _____

   Chapter and/or pages read _____

   Date of above publication _____

2. Author's name _____

   Title of book or magazine used _____

   Title of article in above book or magazine _____

   Chapter and/or pages read _____

   Date of above publication _____

3. Author's name _____

   Title of book or magazine used _____

   Title of article in above book or magazine _____

   Chapter and/or pages read _____

   Date of above publication _____

INTERVIEW SOURCES

1. Person interviewed _____ Date of interview _____

   His position, occupation, and location _____

   Why is he a reliable source?   Be specific _____

   _____

2. Person interviewed _____ Date of interview _____

   His position, occupation, and location _____

   Why is he a reliable source?   Be specific _____

   _____

PERSONAL EXPERIENCE OF SPEAKER

1. Tell (1) when, (2) where, and (3) conditions under which you became an authority on subject matter in

   your speech _____

   _____

   _____

THE PANTOMIME

This pantomime is due:
Time limits: 2-3 minutes.
Source of information: Yourself.
Outline of pantomime: Prepare a 50-100 word complete sentence outline of the pantomime you intend to
present. Write the number of words used in the upper right hand corner of the page. Hand it to
your instructor when you rise to take stage. Use the form at the end of this chapter.

PURPOSE OF THE PANTOMIME

This experience, a pantomime, should assist you in acquiring a new freedom of bodily actions and
gestures. As you perhaps have discovered by now, unhampered bodily action is highly important to effective speech. By producing a good pantomime you will emphasize all of the elements of speech except the
spoken word itself. In so doing, you will bring into play the silent but yet extremely important factors that
often speak what words cannot. Once you master these silent helpers you should find your speech improved. This pantomime is intended to help you to learn to use your bodily actions and gestures more
freely with the result that in your next speech you will talk all over instead of using only your voice.

EXPLANATION OF THE PANTOMIME

Pantomime is utilized as a part of drama, as an individual performance, and as a part of communicating. As you know, it involves only bodily action and gesture. It requires that you express ideas and
thoughts, emotions and feelings by actions instead of sound (voice). The purpose of pantomime is to tell
your audience with your actions what you normally would say with voice and action. If you have seen people
give a stage performance called pantomime, you have seen it as one generally thinks of it. However, every
time you observe someone telling someone else something without using his voice or the written word, you
see pantomime. We might say that pantomime accompanies the spoken word, if we think of pantomime as
actions. From this point of view, watch how your friends do pantomime while they talk. They beckon and
wave and show by a thousand different motions what they are trying to tell another person. Sometimes
they shrug their shoulders, kick their feet, frown, scowl, grin, smile, blink their eyes, wrinkle their fore-
heads, shake their heads from side to side or up and down. They use all these motions and many, many
more.

Some people actually carry on conversation and never utter a sound. They are the deaf-mutes who
talk with a highly organized sign language. As for yourself, you probably have talked to many of your
friends without speaking a word. Think of the times you have sent a sly wink across a room, have placed
a finger to your lips as you pursed them to indicate silence, or have crooked your finger toward yourself
and moved it rapidly to say in effect, "Come here." When you used these actions alone, they were pantomime. When you used them while you were speaking, they were a part of communication.

SUGGESTIONS FOR PANTOMIME

1. A robbery.	13. Studying.
2. Building something.	14. Escorting a date.
3. Flying an airplane.	15. Fishing.
4. Driving a car.	16. Giving.
5. Baking something.	17. Hunting for something.
6. Dressing.	18. Hunting wild game.
7. At a party.	19. Changing a tire.
8. Arguing.	20. Bowling.
9. Buying.	21. Pitching baseball.
10. Selling.	22. Boxing.
11. Singing.	23. Skating.
12. Hitch hiking.	24. Speaker's choice.

HOW TO CHOOSE AN ACT TO PANTOMIME

Look over the suggestions. Find one you know enough about that you can act it out in full detail.
Be sure you have an interest in the subject you plan to pantomime. Do not put off making a choice until
just before class time. If you do you will not have time to prepare an outline or practice, the lack of which
will definitely weaken your performance.

HOW TO PREPARE A PANTOMIME

Follow the methods you would normally use in preparing a speech regarding topic, audience, occasion, and rehearsal. Your purpose for this pantomime will be to work out a series of meaningful actions that tell something. It will help you to list (outline) the scenes you intend to present; then break them down into smaller and more detailed scenes until you have a complete series of well-planned actions. Your next step is rehearsal. Practice as many times as necessary to completely master your act. Ask a friend to observe you and offer helpful suggestions.

It is well to note here that you will have no reason for not utilizing the proper time limits. To prolong your act or to cut it short will be an indication of insufficient preparation. It is a rare case, indeed, in which the student has not sufficient time to prepare adequately.

HOW TO PRESENT A PANTOMIME

Before beginning your performance, make a thorough check to make certain that all the chairs or other properties you intend to use are in place. Any unusual use made of properties should be briefly explained to your audience. You may then announce your act or you may begin the performance at once and permit your audience to discover the act as it unfolds.

In presenting your pantomime, stay in character. Be watchful that you express fully what you desire to tell your audience. In most instances it is safe to "let yourself go" and not to worry about overacting. Your bodily actions, facial expressions and other gestures, if freely employed, should insure a successful portrayal. You should keep in mind that no one expects you to do a professional pantomime. The act is, in its final analysis, an experience that will help you to improve your speaking through better bodily action and gesture.

After concluding your performance, it will be helpful to you to remain on stage while your classmates comment on your act. They will tell you whether or not you communicated your ideas effectively. They will give you suggestions for improvement.

Helpful hints:
1. Complete any activity you start. For example, if you are dressing for a party, do not forget to put your shoes on.
2. Observe the timing of your movements so that they are natural.
3. At the conclusion of your act break character only after the last detail has been finished. Walk politely to the front of the stage and bow slightly to indicate that you have ended your pantomime.

IMPROVE YOUR VOCABULARY

Facile - (făs'ĭl) a. Easily done, easily surmounted or mastered, approachable, easily persuaded, yielding, pliant, "giving in" to an idea. Example: As a person he was facile, as a speaker he was firm. Use this word four times daily for a few days and it will be yours.

Entertain - Use a synonym for this word. One of the best ways to improve your vocabulary is to use synonyms. Here are some for entertain: amuse, beguile, cheer, disport, divert, enliven, gratify, recreate, please, etc.

BIBLIOGRAPHY FOR THE PANTOMIME

Goodman, Edward, Make Believe, the Art of Acting, Charles Scribner's Sons, 1956, pp. 22-26.
Howard, Vernon Linwood, Pantomimes, Charades and Skits, Sterling Publishing Company, Inc., 1959, entire book.
Hunt, Douglas and Hunt, Kari, Pantomime, the Silent Theatre, Atheneum Publishers, 1964, entire book.
Tanner, Fran Averett, Basic Drama Projects, Clark Publishing Company, 2d ed., 1972, Chapters 1 and 2.

SPEECH OUTLINE

Construct a neat, complete sentence outline on this sheet, tear it out, and hand it to your instructor when you rise to speak. He may wish to write criticisms of the outline and speech in the margins.

Type of speech:_____ Name:_____

Number of words in outline:_____ Date:_____

Purpose of this speech: (What do you want your audience to learn, to think, to believe, to feel, or do because of this speech?)_____

_____

TITLE:

INTRODUCTION:

BODY:

CONCLUSION:

<u>Instructor's comments</u> may concern choice of topic, development of ideas, organization, language use, personal appearance, posture, physical activity, sources, and improvement.

(Write sources of information on back of sheet)

SOURCES FROM LITERATURE

(Fill out source requirements completely. Write "none listed" if an author's name or copyright date is not listed.)

1. Author's name _____

    Title of book or magazine used _____

    Title of article in above book or magazine _____

    Chapter and/or pages read _____

    Date of above publication _____

2. Author's name _____

    Title of book or magazine used _____

    Title of article in above book or magazine _____

    Chapter and/or pages read _____

    Date of above publication _____

3. Author's name _____

    Title of book or magazine used _____

    Title of article in above book or magazine _____

    Chapter and/or pages read _____

    Date of above publication _____

INTERVIEW SOURCES

1. Person interviewed _____ Date of interview_____

    His position, occupation, and location _____

    Why is he a reliable source? Be specific _____

    _____

2. Person interviewed _____ Date of interview_____

    His position, occupation, and location _____

    Why is he a reliable source? Be specific _____

    _____

PERSONAL EXPERIENCE OF SPEAKER

1. Tell (1) when, (2) where, and (3) conditions under which you became an authority on subject matter in

    your speech _____

    _____

    _____

    _____

Chapter 7

SPEECH OF SELF-EXPLANATION AND FEAR CONFESSION

This speech is due:
Time limits: None.
Speaking notes: Make a list of your "speech fears" if you wish.
Outline of speech: Prepare a list of your fears on the form at the end of this assignment. Hand the list to
    your instructor when you rise to tell about yourself.

PURPOSE OF THE SPEECH OF SELF-EXPLANATION AND FEAR CONFESSION
    The speech of self-explanation and fear confession is unique. It is also important because it does a great deal for the student. By carrying it through, a person sometimes achieves a mastery over himself which before he had thought impossible. The student sees that practically all inexperienced speakers suffer similar fears and physical reactions, including apathy, speechlessness, short breath, dry mouth, weak knees, pain in the stomach, and nervous trembling. Because improvement so often is an immediate result of this speech experience, it is offered here with the thought that every student will gain much from it. As you will see, it is not a speech ever to be presented to a public audience.

EXPLANATION OF THE SPEECH OF SELF-EXPLANATION AND FEAR CONFESSION
    This speech is absolutely unrehearsed. It requires a maximum of honesty, sincerity, understanding of the other fellow, and straight-from-the-heart truth. Without complete honesty and frankness, many benefits are lost.

    When your turn to speak is called or you volunteer, merely take the floor and honestly tell your audience about all the peculiar, strange, and queer feelings you have when you talk to them. If your knees are shaking, you say so and go even further - you let them shake while you show your audience, without exaggeration, how they shake. In other words, tell everything.

    You may be amused at your fears as you recount them. Your audience may be amused with you, but not at you. They undoubtedly have many of the same fears. After making known all your fears, the class will tell you voluntarily how they think you can overcome your various nervous tensions. After the class suggestions, it will be your turn again. You will honestly tell them how you feel at that moment. You will likely be surprised to find yourself calm, greatly relaxed, and poised. If not, you probably will not have told the group all your fears and will still be trying to hide certain feelings which you hope your audience will not recognize. If you feel "pretty good," then it is likely that you have told everything and no longer are trying to hide a great number of normal nervous reactions. Throughout this experience you will remain standing.

SUGGESTED TOPIC FOR SELF-EXPLANATION AND FEAR CONFESSION
    You need no specific topic for this speech. Just tell how you feel before speaking, when speaking, and after you finish a speech. Also tell what you think really causes your fears.

HOW TO PREPARE A SPEECH OF SELF-EXPLANATION AND FEAR CONFESSION
    You should think of all the many sensations and thoughts and insignificant reactions that have flashed into your mind during your past speeches. In order not to overlook anything, write out a list of these bothersome gremlins and study them carefully so that you may orally trade stories with other class members. If something funny has happened to you because of stage fright, plan to tell the group about it. You will enjoy a good joke on yourself and so will they. It will be good mental hygiene.

    Your best preparation is to give yourself a definite "set of mind" in which you make a decision to tell all without reservation.

HOW TO PRESENT A SPEECH OF SELF-EXPLANATION AND FEAR CONFESSION
    This should be the simplest, most undramatic and sincere discussion you have made. It should come straight from the heart from start to finish - nothing more, nothing less. Your style should be you talking with a group of friends who will reciprocate. You do not need any notes unless they comprise a simple list of the fears and sensations you want to talk about.

    The order of the speech should be these three steps:
1. Describe all your fears and sensations.
2. Ask your audience to tell you informally how they think you can improve yourself.
3. After the audience conclude their remarks, tell them exactly how you feel at the moment; then retire to your chair.

-17-

IMPROVE YOUR VOCABULARY

Trepidation - (trĕp'i-dā'shun) n. A vibration or trembling, especially when from fright. A state of alarm or trembling, terror, fear, dread, panic, etc. Example: The speaker refused to give up despite much trepidation. Use this word five times daily for several days until it is yours. It is a good word to know. You can use it in describing your fear when speaking.

Love - Love may be everywhere, but you can best describe its shades of meaning with useful synonyms. Here are a few examples: affection, attachment, attraction, charity, devotion, fondness, friendship, liking, regard, tenderness, affinity, etc. Use these synonyms. They will make your conversation more interesting.

BIBLIOGRAPHY FOR THE SPEECH OF SELF-EXPLANATION AND FEAR CONFESSION

Buehler, E. Christian, and Linkugel, W. A., Speech Communication, Harper & Row, Publishers, 1969, pp. 74-81.

Jensen, J. Vernon, Perspectives on Oral Communication, Holbrook Press, Inc., 1970, Chapter 3.

McAuley, Jack G., Speech, the Essential Elements, Burgess Publishing Company, 1968, pp. 21-25.

Oliver, Robert T., and Cortright, R. L., Effective Speech, Holt, Rinehart and Winston, Inc., 5th ed., 1970, pp. 51-57, 288, 318.

Ross, Raymond S., Speech Communication, Prentice-Hall, Inc., 2d ed., 1970, Chapter 2.

Samovar, Larry, and Mills, Jack, Oral Communication, Message and Response, Wm. C. Brown Company, Publishers, 1968, pp. 15-16.

Verderber, Rudolph F., The Challenge of Effective Speaking, Wadsworth Publishing Company, Inc., 1970, pp. 55-56.

Williams, Barbara, Purposeful Communication, Kendall/Hunt Publishing Company, 1970, Chapter 8.

OUTLINE YOUR FEARS

Make no outline of your speech. Merely list here all the feelings, fears, and sensations you have before you make a speech, while you are speaking, and after you close a speech. Prepare to hand the list to your instructor when you rise to tell about yourself.

1.

2.

3.

4.

5.

6.

7.

8.

9.

10.

_____

(Signature of Student)

Chapter 8

THE SPEECH TO INFORM

This speech is due:
Time limits: 4-5 minutes.
Speaking notes: 10-word maximum limit.
Sources of information: Two are required, preferably three. For each source give the specific maga-
    zine or book it was taken from, title of the article, author's full name, date of publication, and the
    chapter or pages telling where the material was found. If a source is a person, identify him com-
    pletely by title, position, occupation, etc. List these on the outline form.
Outline your speech: Prepare a 72-150 word complete sentence outline. Designate the exact number of
    words in your outline. Use the form at the end of this chapter.

PURPOSE OF THE SPEECH TO INFORM

No one knows how many speeches are given each year. Neither does anyone know exactly what kinds of speeches are presented. We do know, however, that of the millions and millions of talks, many of them are made specifically to inform people - to tell them something they will find beneficial to include in their knowledge. While no one can foretell accurately what kind of speeches you may be called upon to present in the future, it is a safe bet that you will speak many times to inform people. Because so many speeches are informative in nature, you are offered here the opportunity to become acquainted with the informative speech.

EXPLANATION OF THE SPEECH TO INFORM

The speech to inform people provides them a clear understanding of the speaker's ideas upon a subject. It also arouses interest in the subject because the material which is presented is relevant to the lives of those who hear it. It is incumbent upon the speaker to provide this relevant material with its accompanying interest if he is to inform intelligently. To accomplish the ends of informative speaking, one is obliged to select a subject of interest to himself and his listeners. This can be done by an apt analysis of the audience - in this case your classmates. You as the speaker are charged further with the serious responsibility of knowing what you are talking about, knowing more about it, in fact, than anyone in your audience does. For this reason, your talk demands that you study not one but several (no less than two) sources of information. Under no consideration should you be satisfied to glance hurriedly through an article in a popular magazine, jot down a few notes, toss the periodical aside, and rush off to a "coffee drink," content with the world and a "sloppy" job of acquiring knowledge. This kind of preparation does not even begin to prepare you to give an informative discourse.

Occasions for the informative speech are many. They occur on the lecture platform, in the pulpit, in the classroom, at business meetings; in fact wherever you find reports being made, instructions given, or other ideas being presented by means of lectures and discussions. The point to bear in mind is that any time information is disseminated, an occasion for an informative speech arises.

SUGGESTED TOPICS FOR SPEECHES TO INFORM

1. Marriage customs.
2. Peculiar customs.
3. Jet propulsion.
4. Hunting.
5. Sports (how to play a certain game).
6. How to dance.
7. Boat racing.
8. Swimming.
9. Rescuing a drowning person.
10. Musical instruments.

11. What makes an airplane fly.
12. How a bill becomes a law.
13. New inventions.
14. Precious stones.
15. History of anything.
16. How to get along with people.
17. Mud driving.
18. How to make something.
19. Card tricks.
20. Speaker's choice.

HOW TO CHOOSE A TOPIC

Study the above list carefully. Select something that interests you and that is appropriate to the audience you are to address. Be sure that you can find information about the topic you select. Do not put off choosing a topic.

HOW TO PREPARE A SPEECH TO INFORM

To prepare for this speech, or any speech, you must know and follow certain fundamentals of preparation. These consist of the following steps: (1) choose your subject; (2) analyze the occasion; (3) diagnose the audience; (4) gather your material; (5) organize and support your main points with evidence; (6) word your speech by writing it out in full, in part, or by rehearsing it from an outline; (7) practice aloud.

If you wish to organize your thoughts logically, you should decide early what objective you hope to attain and what reaction you want from this particular audience. Next, if you wish, you may divide your discourse into three conventional parts: an introduction, the body, and the conclusion. To be more effective, some speakers break down their talks by using various combinations of the following steps: (1) gain attention; (2) make your audience want to hear your ideas; (3) present your ideas; (4) tell why this material is important to your listeners and how it affects them; (5) ask your audience to study the topic further or to take some action on it. The time required for any one division of a speech varies greatly; however, more time is given to the presentation of ideas than any other division of the speech.

The wording of your talk may be accomplished either by writing it out in full from the outline, or by considerable practice. In any event, rehearse before a mirror as many times as necessary (usually about four) to fix the proper steps and the order of their content, along with desirable stage appearance and bodily action. Do not memorize the words.

The use of notes is somewhat a matter of opinion. If you are adequately prepared, you will not need notes. You will talk extemporaneously, which is the most commanding method known. If you must refer to notes, they should be either short sentences, phrases, or single words which have a particular meaning to you. Whatever notes you hold in your hands should be brief, concise, meaningful, and entirely familiar. A glance at your notes should be sufficient for you to gather their full meaning so that you may speak fluently yet logically. The notes should be on a piece of paper the size of a postal card or larger.

One other point is important. The information you present must be accurate. For accuracy of information, acceptable sources of information written by reliable and competent authorities must be consulted. Your audience should know where you get your material. What is more, you are the person to identify these sources and authorities. You are expected to go even further in this matter of giving information: you are expected to offer your conclusions and views and evaluations of your information. All this entails the neat assimilation of all you have pulled together - that is, your entire speech.

A few hints might well be offered at this point. First, have only two or three main points to your speech. Buttress these well with examples, illustrations, analogies, and facts. Second, do not be afraid to inject humor and anecdotes into your thought to add interest. Be sure these additions are suited to your subject and audience. Third, be sure your speech moves ahead. Do not allow the speech to drag or become stalemated. And, last, bend plenty of effort toward an interesting introduction and an equally effective conclusion.

OUTLINE YOUR SPEECH

Outlining your speech is necessary if you wish to secure organization, logical order of material, coherence, and unity. Without these rhetorical qualities, your thoughts will be a jumbled mass of words with little direction or definite goal. An outline is to the speaker what a map is to a person taking a trip; it shows him where he is going and how to get there.

After neatly constructing a 75-150 word sentence outline, be prepared to hand the outline to your instructor when you rise to speak. He will undoubtedly wish to follow this while listening to your speech. He may write suggestions on it for your improvement. Remember that this outline is not to be used while you are speaking. State <u>two</u> or three sources of information.

Read at least two references on outlining. Ask your instructor for assistance.

HOW TO PRESENT A SPEECH TO INFORM

Use an easy, energetic presentation. Be enthusiastic and original in what you have to say. Use your hands to demonstrate how to do things. Draw pictures, exhibit charts, in fact, do whatever is necessary to make your ideas understood and interesting. Take stage properly, utilize expressive bodily action, maintain direct eye contact, observe time limits, and stop when your speech is finished. Your conclusion should be as strong and appropriate and as well prepared as your beginning remarks.

IMPROVE YOUR VOCABULARY

Empennage - (ĕm'-pĕ-nāj') n. The tail assembly of an airplane, dirigible, or flying machine. Know this word. It is important to the aircraft industry and the air age. Example: The empennage was damaged when the plane landed.

Pretty - This word is used so often it has lost much of its charm. You can improve your speech by employing synonyms in its place. Here are a few suggestions whose use depends on what you are talking about: music, for example, might be plaintive, moving, thunderous, bewitching, captivating, stirring, exquisite, magnificent, haunting, disturbing, rollicking, tantalizing. A girl may be graceful, buxom, lovely, comely, dainty, blooming. A house can be artistic, elegant, original, attractive. A dress may be becoming, rich, etc., a rug handsome or a flower delicate. It is a good idea not to label everything "pretty" indiscriminately.

BIBLIOGRAPHY FOR THE SPEECH TO INFORM

Buehler, E. Christian, and Linkugel, W. A., Speech Communication, Harper & Row, Publishers, 1969, pp. 103-104, 226-229.

Culp, Ralph Borden, Basic Types of Speech, Wm. C. Brown Company, Publishers, 1968, pp. 33-38.

Gilman, Wilbur E., and Others, An Introduction to Speaking, The Macmillan Company, 2d ed., 1968, Chapter 4.

Hance, Kenneth G., and Others, Principles of Speaking, Wadsworth Publishing Company, Inc., 2d ed., 1969, Chapter 16.

McAuley, Jack G., Speech, The Essential Elements, Burgess Publishing Company, 1968, pp. 35-44.

Monroe, Alan H., and Ehninger, Douglas, Principles of Speech Communication, Scott, Foresman and Company, 6th brief ed., 1969, Chapter 10.

Oliver, Robert T., and Cortright, R. L., Effective Speech, Holt, Rinehart and Winston, Inc., 5th ed., 1970, Chapter 18.

Ross, Raymond S., Speech Communication, Prentice-Hall, Inc., 2d ed., 1970, Chapter 8.

Samovar, Larry, and Mills, Jack, Oral Communication, Message and Response, Wm. C. Brown Company, Publishers, 1968, Chapter 2.

Strother, Edward S., and Huckleberry, A. W., The Effective Speaker, Houghton Mifflin Company, 1968, pp. 49-52.

Verderber, Rudolph F., The Challenge of Effective Speaking, Wadsworth Publishing Company, Inc., 1970, Part 3.

Williams, Barbara, Purposeful Communication, Kendall/Hunt Publishing Company, 1970, Chapter 4.

INFORMATIVE SPEECH

By R. Denise Cumbie

A DECISION THAT IS ALL YOURS

The little pang of unknown something that you will probably feel when you walk off the stage on the night of your high school graduation is just a reminder that you have, or will shortly, make a decision that will have a great effect on your life and future happiness. For after all the lofty speeches and the struggle with your hot awkward academic gown, you will depart from your comfortable high school environment into the stinging cold of "out there." Will you go into it naked and defenseless or will you gird yourself in the warmth of self knowledge and understanding?

Whether by accident or design, all humans are endowed with at least one unabductable possession; this is your individuality. Every person on this earth is a different, unique individual and therefore it is important that you know yourself before making a decision with the gravity of a lifetime hanging in balance. Forcing yourself into someone else's mold will not make things easier for anyone, least of all yourself. The crux of the matter is that the person who knows you best must be yourself.

Not everyone who earns a high school diploma is what the guidance counselors call "college material." And still from a larger number of capable prospective college students who enter an undergraduate course of study, about 50% will never complete four years of college work. Of the 50% who do stay to graduate, 75% will have changed their major at least two times, thereby losing time and money in the process. Why are these statistics so high? There is a number of reasons; barring tragic circumstances, most reasons stem from the fact that students do not fully understand their capabilities and capacities. Someone once said, "If you don't know who you are, college is an expensive place to find out."

How can you begin to make the preparation for your career or vocational decision? We all know grades are fairly important, and so are the batteries of pre-college and aptitude tests, but there has to be within yourself, a healthy respect for your talents and failings. For example, if you do not read and comprehend well, you would not be happy as an English literature major. If you were not proficient in the use of numbers, you would be a poor engineer. Examine yourself and your intrinsic and covert motives for deciding on your career. If you want to become a game warden, a plumber or an autobody repair man, take the appropriate steps to become one. Do not try to cast yourself in another mold. I know of a family of somewhat snobbish people who were horrified when one of their sons broke the line of Harvard men to become an air conditioning specialist. He was good at his work and he enjoyed it. The other two sons went to Harvard with high hopes and probably low self knowledge. One flunked out and is now a forest ranger and happy. The other is a rather mediocre lawyer on the skids. Be what you want to be; not what Aunt Hilda thinks you should be. Long after Aunt Hilda is gone and forgotten you will have to reckon with yourself.

Analyze what your expectations in a career will be, economically and emotionally. Consider the area of the country or world where your job is in the greatest demand. Our air conditioning specialist would find his job incompatable with his environmental placement if he lived in Greenland. Correlate your own temperament with probable working conditions. A woman who cannot stand children's screaming and romping about would make a poor kindergarten teacher's aide. Consider your financial limitations since most students are limited in some way as to choice and location of college or training school. Check guides and information catalogues to find out what school is right for you.

A better source of information comes "right from the horse's mouth" so to speak. You will probably get a clearer picture of the profession from an actual practitioner who is satisfied with his choice of profession than from an advisor or counselor. There is probably a wealth of material right in your own home town public library. Do not depend on anyone but yourself to gather all the information you feel is necessary to come to a final decision. Do not delay! The more time you allot yourself, the more carefully your decision will be considered. If you need more time than the summer after high school graduation, join the service or get an interesting job or take a vacation, but do not just follow the crowd or your Aunt Hilda to an institution that will not satisfy your needs. You will be taking up a seat that someone who has made his decisions might need, and almost anyone will regard this as a selfish or wasteful act.

You, and only you, will know on that last night of high school pomp and circumstance whether that pang you feel is excitement or fear of what lies beyond your high school diploma.

SPEECH OUTLINE

Construct a neat, complete sentence outline on this sheet, tear it out, and hand it to your instructor when you rise to speak. He may wish to write criticisms of the outline and speech in the margins.

Type of speech:_____ Name:_____

Number of words in outline:_____ Date:_____

Purpose of this speech: (What do you want your audience to learn, to think, to believe, to feel, or do because of this speech?)_____

_____

TITLE:

INTRODUCTION:

BODY:

CONCLUSION:

Instructor's comments may concern choice of topic, development of ideas, organization, language use, personal appearance, posture, physical activity, sources, and improvement.

(Write sources of information on back of sheet)

SOURCES FROM LITERATURE

(Fill out source requirements completely.   Write "none listed" if an author's name or copyright date is not listed.)

1.   Author's name _____

   Title of book or magazine used _____

   Title of article in above book or magazine _____

   Chapter and/or pages read _____

   Date of above publication _____

2.   Author's name _____

   Title of book or magazine used _____

   Title of article in above book or magazine _____

   Chapter and/or pages read _____

   Date of above publication _____

3.   Author's name _____

   Title of book or magazine used _____

   Title of article in above book or magazine _____

   Chapter and/or pages read _____

   Date of above publication _____

INTERVIEW SOURCES

1.   Person interviewed _____ Date of interview_____

   His position, occupation, and location _____

   Why is he a reliable source?   Be specific _____

   _____

2.   Person interviewed _____ Date of interview_____

   His position, occupation, and location _____

   Why is he a reliable source?   Be specific _____

   _____

PERSONAL EXPERIENCE OF SPEAKER

1.   Tell (1) when, (2) where, and (3) conditions under which you became an authority on subject matter in
   your speech _____

   _____

   _____

Chapter 9

THE SPEECH TO STIMULATE OR AROUSE

This speech is due:

Time limits: 4-5 minutes.

Speaking notes: 10-word maximum limit. (Try speaking without them.)

Sources of information: Two are required, preferably three. For each source give the specific magazine or book it was taken from, title of the article, author's full name, date of publication, and the chapter or pages telling where the material was found. If a source is a person, identify him completely by title, position, occupation, etc. List these on the outline form.

Outline your speech: Prepare a 75-150 word complete sentence outline. Designate the exact number of words in your outline. Use the form at the end of this chapter.

PURPOSE OF THE SPEECH TO STIMULATE OR AROUSE

It is an accepted truth that people need to be stimulated or aroused if they are to be concerned about a proposition or problem that is laid before them. Often a speaker appeals to his audience to do something, to change their minds, to give consideration to an idea, but he does not stir them sufficiently to make them willing to be more than mildly interested. As a speaker it is to your advantage to learn the methods and approaches that cause audiences to be stimulated by speech. This assignment will provide an experience for the speech to arouse or stimulate so that you will be fully aware of the importance of this type of speech.

EXPLANATION OF THE SPEECH TO STIMULATE OR AROUSE

The speech to stimulate an audience is one that does just that - it stimulates. If its purpose is fulfilled, it touches the emotions and influences the intellect of the audience sufficiently that they feel impelled to adopt new attitudes and/or take action suggested by the speaker. The basic features of this speech are these: use of vivid language, obvious sincerity and enthusiasm on the part of the speaker, and appeals to basic drives that all persons possess. Much of the stimulation is achieved by utilizing catchy slogans, concreteness, specific examples, illustrations, and facts. Contrast is stressed by playing the big against the little, the bad against the good, the money that can be earned against that which will not be earned, the sick against the well, . . .

Best known occasions for the speech to stimulate are anniversary memorials, dedications, commencement exercises, religious gatherings, conventions, rallies, pep meetings, sales promotions, and between halves situations in which a coach arouses his men to a high pitch of fury accompanied by a will to win.

The speech demands that the speaker himself be aroused and vigorous. It calls for enthusiasm, energy, force, power, and spirit - the quantity and quality depending upon the response sought from the audience. But most of all it requires that the speaker be sincere.

SUGGESTED TOPICS FOR A SPEECH TO STIMULATE OR AROUSE

Keep in mind that these topics are only suggested. They are intended to give you a few ideas so that you may make a selection from this group, or develop a topic of your own.

1. School anniversary
2. Memorial to a classmate
3. Dedication of a new athletic field, club house, etc.
4. Any kind of commencement
5. Patriotic meeting
6. Religious gathering
7. Convention of any kind
8. Promotional meeting - sales, political, sports, etc.
9. Rally of any kind
10. Any kind of campaign - Community Chest, Red Cross, Scouting, Salvation Army, election, etc.
11. Organization banquet

12. Political meeting
13. To raise funds for the Junior-Senior Prom
14. To gain a new school building or student union
15. To abolish final examinations
16. To gain support for the team
17. To provide housing for students
18. To secure a better social program for the school
19. To end war
20. To decrease crime
21. To end political corruption
22. A call for peace
23. Speaker's choice

HOW TO CHOOSE A TOPIC

Regardless of what kind of speech you present, it should always possess sincerity. Of all the many kinds of speeches there is none that demands _sincerity_ from the speaker more than the speech that is intended to stimulate or arouse. Therefore, in choosing a topic from the above list or in formulating your own topic, place sincerity foremost in your thinking. Do not try to find a subject that is suitable for the national congress or for presentation over a national radio network. Find a discussion suitable for your audience, in this case your classmates. It does not have to be something big, something startling or overwhelming. The occasion does not call for such a speech. It does call for a speech appropriate to your situation, your audience, one within the scope of your experiences, and, above all, one in which you are sincere.

HOW TO PREPARE A SPEECH TO STIMULATE OR AROUSE

Basically, you will prepare this speech according to the steps followed in preparing any speech. It is essential that you give more than passing attention to your purpose to stimulate or arouse. This purpose will be behind every statement you utter. It will be superimposed over your entire construction; hence it will receive first consideration.

Having made yourself keenly aware of your purpose, you will next set about achieving this purpose. Naturally, your attention turns to organization. We will assume that you have gathered your materials and are ready to arrange them under the various divisions of your organization. First, as always, you will think of your introduction. It may be that you will construct it or alter it after certain other parts of your speech are completed, but certainly you will give it close attention before you are ready to state that your speech is prepared. In arranging and organizing the main body of your remarks, the language will undergo no little scrutiny. Vivid phraseology, word pictures, graphic illustrations, all aptly told must be presented with words that contain acute meanings and definite associations in the minds of the listeners. You may also offer slogans and catchy phrases to make your ideas stick and remain with your hearers. You will also be concrete and specific by naming certain persons and definite places that the speech calls for. You will avoid the abstract and intangible when giving examples, illustrations, and facts. This does not mean that you are to employ needless detail, but it does mean that your ideas must be aimed to hit their mark and make a strong impact. If you do not do this, it will be like trying to drive a spike with a tack hammer. As was stated in the paragraph entitled "Explanation of the Speech to Stimulate or Arouse," you will use contrast as a means of clarifying your thoughts and pointing up their significance. And last, you will stimulate your audience because throughout your entire speech you will have appealed to the basic drives in people: security from enemies, saving or making money, keeping their homes intact, gaining recognition, enjoying social prominence, having a cleaner city or town, knowing new experiences . . . You will have touched your listeners' pride, their pocketbooks and bank accounts, their sympathies, their family and home affections - yes, even their fighting spirit. Once you have stimulated your audience, thoroughly aroused them, if the speech demands it, be sure to tell them what to do or what action to take, whether it be to think or perform. If you do not do this you will have generated power but failed to use it.

As usual, there is no better source of materials for a speech than the library. The librarian will gladly assist you in locating materials. Your instructor will advise you also in this matter. There may be persons on the faculty or friends you know who have special knowledge that you can use. Do not overlook interviews with them.

The last step in preparing this speech will be rehearsal. Be sure you rehearse enough that you know from memory the sequence of ideas, not words, that you plan to present. Practice before a mirror and/or friends until you feel competent to stand before an audience.

HOW TO PRESENT A SPEECH TO STIMULATE OR AROUSE
A forceful, dynamic, and energetic presentation should be used unless you are speaking on a solemn occasion involving reverence, devotion, or deep feeling. In such cases your voice and manner should be an animated and sincere projection of your ideas, accompanied by appropriate bodily action and gestures. On other occasions, indications should show that you are alive with your subject, full of it, and eager for others to share it. Above all, you must be sincere and earnest. Remember that your audience will reflect your activity and eloquence. They will be just as lively or solemn as you stimulate them to be.

The use of appropriate diagrams, charts, and demonstrations can add much to your speech.

IMPROVE YOUR VOCABULARY

Erratic - (ĕ-răt'ĭk) a. Having no definite course, wandering, departing from an accepted course in opinion or conduct, queer, strange or odd. Example: Are you erratic when you try to be different? Use this word several times daily during the next week. Make it yours.

Job - This word does too much overtime work. As a result it is less potent and meaningful than it should be. Try using one of the following synonyms in place of job. Here they are: task, duty, business, vocation, calling, undertaking, responsibility, service, profession, craft, trade, errand, position, chore, etc.

BIBLIOGRAPHY FOR SPEECH TO STIMULATE OR AROUSE

McAuley, Jack G., Speech, The Essential Elements, Burgess Publishing Company, 1968, pp. 35-44.
Oliver, Robert T., and Cortright, R. L., Effective Speech, Holt, Rinehart and Winston, Inc., 5th ed., 1970, Chapter 21.
Samovar, Larry, and Mills, Jack, Oral Communication, Message and Response, Wm. C. Brown Company, Publishers, 1968, Chapter 2.
Williams, Barbara, Purposeful Communication, Kendall/Hunt Publishing Company, 1970, Chapter 4.

SPEECH TO STIMULATE OR AROUSE

By Elmo Sackett

YOUTH'S MOST POWERFUL WEAPON

I'd like to talk with you for a moment about the one thing that young people know more about than anyone else. Yourselves. We've all heard of the younger generation, the older generation, the generation gap, the communication gap, and the credibility gap. Young people refer to older people as squares while the older generation thinks of the younger generation as long-haired hippies. The question I would like to ask is, how do you think of yourselves? Are you the beat generation, the hip generation, the turned on generation, the dropped out generation, or are you the generation with a cause?

I think most of you would like to think of yourselves as a generation with a cause. The cause may be anything from a stand against the longest war in our nation's history, to the improvement of living conditions in our nation's slums, or to the preservation of our great national resources. Unquestionably the young people of today are more concerned with the world around them than any previous generation. But, how do you show your concern? Do you riot in the streets? Do you picket? Do you participate in peaceful demonstrations? Or do you tune out and turn on? Do you avoid a personal involvement in a world in which you think you have no voice? Do you disassociate yourselves from the establishment and enter a downfilled world of drugs and drop-outs? Although any one of these methods can show your concern, there is another method that is much more effective and of greater lasting value.

Recently, young people between the ages of eighteen to twenty-one were given the most powerful weapon of change that our country has yet devised. That weapon is the right to vote. How this powerful force is put to work is up to each voter. Used properly, it can force change in virtually all elements of public life. Misused, abused, or worst of all, not used at all, it can lead to a society controlled by a select few. In nearly every country controlled by a totalitarian regime, the right to vote has been abolished. Too often the right to vote is left unused not because a totalitarian force disallows that fundamental right to its citizens, but rather, many citizens, even in a democratic society, allow this most precious civil right to go unused because of their own apathy.

At a western university recently, an all school election was held to elect student body officers. During that election only thirty per cent of the total student body voted. In other words, seventy per cent of the student body did not care enough to vote in an election that directly affected them. Is it any wonder that some people criticize the enfranchisement of eighteen to twenty-one year old voters in national elections?

Please don't misunderstand me, I am not opposed to student activists. I believe that young people should take an active part in letting their government know where they stand on particular issues. I am simply saying that the right to vote carries with it certain responsibilities on the part of the voter.

First, the right to vote carries with it a responsibility to be informed. In order to make a decision on political issues, the voter must completely understand those issues. He must be able to see both sides of an argument and then rationally and logically make his choice.

The process of being informed is not an easy one. The voter should read at least two newspapers daily. He should view at least one television newscast, both local and national, each day. He should subscribe to at least one weekly news magazine. Most of all, however, the voter should discuss his feelings with other people. He should take care that he does not spend all of his time talking with people whose opinions are the same as his own. Very little new insight can be gained by rehashing the same opinions.

Second, the right to vote carries with it a responsibility to be a legally bonafied voter. Each voter must be registered in his local precinct prior to a general election. See to it that you don't lose your right to vote because you are not a registered voter. Find out where to register and do so as quickly as you can.

Last, be sure to vote. The citizen who has the right to vote and does not use it loses his right to criticize political decisions. The power and the influence of young Americans between the ages of eighteen and twenty-one can only be felt if each one of you takes the responsibility to be an informed voter.

Remember that your vote will help to shape our nation's destiny.

SPEECH OUTLINE

Construct a neat, complete sentence outline on this sheet, tear it out, and hand it to your instructor when you rise to speak. He may wish to write criticisms of the outline and speech in the margins.

Type of speech:_____ Name:_____

Number of words in outline:_____ Date:_____

Purpose of this speech: (What do you want your audience to learn, to think, to believe, to feel, or do because of this speech?)_____

_____

TITLE:

INTRODUCTION:

BODY:

CONCLUSION:

<u>Instructor's comments</u> may concern choice of topic, development of ideas, organization, language use, personal appearance, posture, physical activity, sources, and improvement.

(Write sources of information on back of sheet)

SOURCES FROM LITERATURE

(Fill out source requirements completely. Write "none listed" if an author's name or copyright date is not listed.)

1. Author's name _____

   Title of book or magazine used _____

   Title of article in above book or magazine _____

   Chapter and/or pages read _____

   Date of above publication _____

2. Author's name _____

   Title of book or magazine used _____

   Title of article in above book or magazine _____

   Chapter and/or pages read _____

   Date of above publication _____

3. Author's name _____

   Title of book or magazine used _____

   Title of article in above book or magazine _____

   Chapter and/or pages read _____

   Date of above publication _____

INTERVIEW SOURCES

1. Person interviewed _____ Date of interview_____

   His position, occupation, and location _____

   Why is he a reliable source? Be specific _____

   _____

2. Person interviewed _____ Date of interview_____

   His position, occupation, and location _____

   Why is he a reliable source? Be specific _____

   _____

PERSONAL EXPERIENCE OF SPEAKER

1. Tell (1) when, (2) where, and (3) conditions under which you became an authority on subject matter in your speech _____

   _____

   _____

   _____

Chapter 10

TO CONVINCE AN AUDIENCE

This speech is due:

Time limits: 5-6 minutes.

Speaking notes: Try not to use any. <u>Know your material</u>.

Sources of information: Two are required, preferably three. For each source give the specific magazine or book it was taken from, title of the article, author's full name, date of publication, and the chapter or pages telling where the material was found. If a source is a person, identify him completely by title, position, occupation, etc. List these on the outline form.

Outline your speech: Prepare a 75-150 word complete sentence outline. Designate the exact number of words in your outline. Use the form at the end of this chapter.

PURPOSE OF THE SPEECH TO CONVINCE AN AUDIENCE

A speech to convince is used so widely that we are probably unaware of its frequency. Actually, very few persons do what someone else suggests unless they are convinced. The most common method used in convincing someone is a system of talking. The pattern of ideas employed is not always known to the person who uses it but, generally, the speaker uses certain techniques to gain conviction.

It is probable that you will be asked to present ideas and arguments at some future date. When this time arrives, you will find it a much easier task if you have had previous experience. This speech assignment will offer you excellent practice in the art of convincing an audience.

EXPLANATION OF THE SPEECH TO CONVINCE

The speech to convince is one which causes your audience to accept willingly your proposal through logic, evidence, and emotion. You must present sufficient logic and evidence to swing the audience to your belief. This usually means that you will also ask them to take the action which you suggest. It is usually wise and necessary to appeal to emotions that accompany attitudes and decisions which you desire from your audience. These basic emotions may be reached by certain basic appeals; such as, their wealth, love of country, self-preservation, desire for recognition, sex, desire for new adventure, loyalty, political beliefs, religion, and the like. This necessitates a thorough analysis of your audience so that you may base your appeal on their beliefs and attitudes. It also means that you must present your logic and evidence in such a way that it directs their thinking through channels they readily follow.

The speech to convince is utilized on many kinds of occasions. At most popular gatherings, such as: political meetings, lecture forums, charity drives, community drives, church services, and other civic gatherings, an effort is made to convince. Business meetings involve conviction at any time differences of opinion prevail. Decisions are reached by convincing someone. Any time that a debate is in progress, even though it be a formal argument between two rival schools, within a legislative body, among three farmers, or in court proceedings - the statements of the speakers involve persuasion through logic, evidence, and emotion. (Could it be that the last time you asked your father for the car you gave a most convincing argument containing much logic, considerable evidence, and some emotion by stating why you should have it?)

SUGGESTED TOPICS FOR SPEECHES TO CONVINCE

1. Eighteen years should be the national minimum age limit for marriage.
2. Every mentally able person should be compelled legally to attend school until he is seventeen years old.
3. All state colleges and universities should be tuition free.
4. No student should be permitted to play a role in more than two public three-act plays while he is in high school.
5. Schools should allow more holidays.
6. School boards should provide free yearbooks to all students.
7. All seniors with a four-year B average should be excused from final examinations.
8. School offices should be filled half with girls and half with boys.
9. Strikes should be prohibited by law.
10. Compulsory arbitration of all labor disputes should be established by law.

11. No president should be permitted to serve more than one term.
12. All soldiers should be paid at least three hundred dollars per month.
13. Liquor should be rationed nationally.
14. All high schools should have cafeterias.
15. Persons convicted of driving a car while under the influence of intoxicating beverages should pay a fine of at least one thousand dollars.
16. Athletes should be subsidized by the school.
17. Riding bicycles on sidewalks should be punishable by fine and/or jail sentence.
18. The atomic bomb should be outlawed in war.
19. All high schools and colleges should have courses pertaining to marriage.
20. Speaker's choice of a controversial subject.

HOW TO CHOOSE A TOPIC

Study the suggestions; then make your choice on the basis of suitability to you, your audience, and the occasion. Be sure you can secure at least two sources of information on your topic. Do not delay your choice of a topic. The sooner you make up your mind the better are your chances for preparing an excellent speech.

If you do not select one of the suggested topics, be extremely careful in the choice of a topic of your own. The points to watch are the way you word your topic and what you propose to convince your audience of. In wording your topic be sure you propose to your audience that they should adopt a certain debatable proposition. For example, if you decide to convince your listeners that "All school books should be free," notice the word "should." It implies "ought to be." So your purpose is to persuade your audience to believe this is a sound idea and it will be beneficial if carried out. You are not asking them to carry it out by standing behind a book counter and handing out free text books.

A sales talk is not a speech to convince because your purpose is to make your customer reach down in his pocket, pull out his money, and give it to you. This requires him to do something. Naturally a certain amount of convincing will precede your request for his money, but your actual purpose is to cause him to hand you one hundred dollars. You do not care whether he changes his mind or not, just so you get his money. We may conclude then that a speech to convince is not a sales talk, is not primarily to stimulate or arouse, but it is one in which your purpose is to change a person's mind about something on which there is definite disagreement.

Your topic must be a proposition which is specific and which offers a debatable solution to a controversial problem. It is not adequate to propose the subject "We should all drive more carefully." We agree on this already. To talk on such a broad topic would be merely to stimulate or arouse us. (See the chapter covering the speech to stimulate or arouse.) If you wish to do something to make us more careful drivers, suggest a definite and debatable solution, such as: "The legislature should pass a law limiting speed on the highways to sixty miles per hour," or "All persons who are convicted of traffic violations should be compelled to attend a driver's school for two weeks." These are proposals about which people disagree. We can readily say yes or no to them. We can debate them, but we cannot debate the subject that "We should all drive more carefully," since we agree on it.

Examine your topic closely to be certain you have a correct topic on which to base your speech to convince. If you are in doubt, consult your instructor.

HOW TO PREPARE A SPEECH TO CONVINCE

In preparing the speech to convince remember that your purpose is to swing people over to your beliefs so that they not only will think what you want them to think, but so that they will also do what you tell them to do. This is obviously not an easy task; however, it is not at all impossible. To achieve the "convincing effect," you need to look carefully into the organization of your speech. Briefly, it may be as follows:

1. Present a history of the problem. Discuss the events leading up to the present time that make the topic important. Tell why it is significant that the audience hear the discussion you are about to present. (Do not spend too much time on the history - you have other points to cover.)
2. Discuss the present day effects of the problem. Give examples, illustrations, facts, and views of authorities that clearly demonstrate the situation you are talking about. These are musts if you wish to be convincing.

3. Discuss the causes that brought about the effects you listed in point 2. Here again you must present examples, illustrations, facts, and views of authorities to prove your points. Be sure you show how the causes have and are bringing about the effects you mentioned. For example, if you say your car "upset" (effect) because of a blowout (cause) you must definitely establish this cause rather than permit your audience to believe that the car may have upset because the steering mechanism on the car suddenly broke.
4. List possible solutions to the problem. Discuss briefly the various alternatives that could be followed but show they are not effective enough to solve your problem. Give evidence for your statements; examples, illustrations, authorities' views, facts, and analogies.
5. Give your solution to the problem. Show why your solution is the best answer to the proposition you are discussing. Present your evidence and the reason for believing as you do. This must not be simply your opinions. It must be logical reasoning backed up by evidence.
6. Show how your proposal will benefit your audience. This is the real meat of your entire speech, if you have thoroughly fulfilled each preceding step up to this point. Here is that part of your speech where you must convince. You definitely have to show your listeners how they will benefit from your proposals; for example: How they will make more money, how they will be safer from an enemy, how they will live longer, how they will be happier, how they will get better roads, better schools, lower taxes, cheaper groceries, . . . In other words, your listener must see clearly and vividly that your proposal will help him.
7. What do you want your audience to do? Here is the proof of your effectiveness. You now will tell your hearers what you want them to do. If you have been convincing up to this point, they will probably go along with you; if not, you have "stumbled" somewhere in your speech. That is why it is very necessary that you develop your talk very carefully and completely. You may ask the audience to write to their congressman, to vote for or against a bill, to give money to charity, to attend a rally, to clean up their town, to declare war, to subscribe funds for a new church, . . .

If you do not care to follow the preceding organization of a speech to convince, here is one which accomplishes the same end but is described differently:
1. State your proposition in the introduction.
2. Present a history of the problem which brought up the proposal you are asking for adoption.
3. Show that your proposal is needed. Offer evidence which establishes a need for your proposal. No other proposal (solution) will do.
4. Show that your proposition is practical. Give evidence to prove that it will do what you say it will do. In other words, show that it will work.
5. Show that your proposition is desirable. This means to give evidence showing that what it will do will be beneficial rather than harmful. For example, concerning the desirability of military training people say, "Yes, military conscription will work, but it is undesirable because it will bring on a militaristic control of our government."
6. Conclude your speech with a final statement in support of your proposal.

Note: If you are opposed to a certain proposal, you may establish your point of view by offering arguments which show any one of the following to be true:
1. The proposition is not needed. (Give evidence.)
2. The proposition is not practical. (Give evidence.)
3. The proposition is not desirable. (Give evidence.)

Of course, if you can establish all three of these points, you will be more convincing than if you prove only one.

You should be warned that you will face untold difficulty from your audience if you fail to have the body of your speech properly organized and all your points supported by evidence. The best guarantee of success is careful preparation. In addition to a well-organized speech with its points supported by evidence, you must have a well-constructed introduction and a powerful conclusion. Besides these considerations in relation to the materials of the speech itself, your oral practice will determine whether or not you are actually prepared to present a convincing speech. Even though you possess volumes of evidence, clear-cut organization, and vivid language, you must deliver the speech confidently and well, without excessive use of notes, if anyone is to be very convinced that you yourself are convinced of your own proposal.

Materials for preparing your subject can be secured from your library. Encyclopedias, reader's guides, magazine and newspaper guides - all offer excellent sources. Check with your instructor and librarian for assistance.

HOW TO PRESENT A SPEECH TO CONVINCE

In general a frank, enthusiastic, and energetic presentation is desirable. A reasonable amount of emotion should be evident; however, it should not be overdone.

Your bodily action should suit the words you utter and be such an integral part of your overall presentation that no attention is directed toward it. Vigor and intensity should characterize your bodily action. You must show by your actions that you are convinced.

Your voice should reflect a sincere belief in your views, and through inflections and modulations, carry the ring of truth and personal conviction. Sufficient force should be utilized to convey sound and meaning to all who listen.

Naturally, your presentation must vary according to your audience, the occasion, the size of the room, its acoustics, and the type of meeting before which you present your speech. You would not speak to a small group of business men in the same manner that you would address a large political gathering.

If you use notes, restrict them to ten words on a paper at least three by five inches in size. Know them thoroughly. Do not try to hide them. Hold them high enough when looking at them that your head is not bowed. After the conclusion of your talk, remain standing at least two minutes to answer questions from your audience.

IMPROVE YOUR VOCABULARY

Languid - (lăn'gwĭd) a. Drooping from exhaustion, sluggish, tired, apathetic, listless, slow, weary, feeble, heavy, torpid, without energy. Example: A languid speaker is not convincing. Use this word in your everyday speech during the next week. Make it work for you.

Nice - Use a synonym for this adjective. Liven up your vocabulary with new words. Examples are: delightful, delicious, attractive, pleasant, fastidious, discriminating, hypercritical, pleasing, kind, delicate, dainty, alluring, refreshing, etc.

Note: The proper use of these synonyms for nice depends on what you are talking about such as time, place, or thing.

BIBLIOGRAPHY FOR THE SPEECH TO CONVINCE

Buehler, E. Christian, and Linkugel, W. A., Speech Communication, Harper & Row, Publishers, 1969, pp. 120-133, 230-233.

Gilman, Wilbur E., and Others, An Introduction to Speaking, The Macmillan Company, 2d ed., 1968, Chapter 5.

McAuley, Jack G., Speech, The Essential Elements, Burgess Publishing Company, 1968, pp. 35-44.

Monroe, Alan H., and Ehninger, Douglas, Principles of Speech Communication, Scott, Foresman and Company, 6th brief ed., 1969, Chapter 11.

Oliver, Robert T., and Cortright, R. L., Effective Speech, Holt, Rinehart and Winston, Inc., 5th ed., 1970, Chapter 19.

Ross, Raymond S., Speech Communication, Prentice-Hall, Inc., 2d ed., 1970, Chapter 9.

Samovar, Larry, and Mills, Jack, Oral Communication, Message and Response, Wm. C. Brown Company, Publishers, 1968, Chapter 2.

Verderber, Rudolph F., The Challenge of Effective Speaking, Wadsworth Publishing Company, Inc., 1970, Part 4.

Williams, Barbara, Purposeful Communication, Kendall/Hunt Publishing Company, 1970, Chapter 4.

NOTE: See page 34 for example of a speech to convince.

SPEECH OUTLINE

Construct a neat, complete sentence outline on this sheet, tear it out, and hand it to your instructor when you rise to speak. He may wish to write criticisms of the outline and speech in the margins.

Type of speech:_____ Name:_____

Number of words in outline:_____ Date:_____

Purpose of this speech: (What do you want your audience to learn, to think, to believe, to feel, or do because of this speech?)_____

_____

TITLE:

INTRODUCTION:

BODY:

CONCLUSION:

<u>Instructor's comments</u> may concern choice of topic, development of ideas, organization, language use, personal appearance, posture, physical activity, sources, and improvement.

(Write sources of information on back of sheet)

SOURCES FROM LITERATURE

(Fill out source requirements completely. Write "none listed" if an author's name or copyright date is not listed.)

1. Author's name _____

   Title of book or magazine used _____

   Title of article in above book or magazine _____

   Chapter and/or pages read _____

   Date of above publication _____

2. Author's name _____

   Title of book or magazine used _____

   Title of article in above book or magazine _____

   Chapter and/or pages read _____

   Date of above publication _____

3. Author's name _____

   Title of book or magazine used _____

   Title of article in above book or magazine _____

   Chapter and/or pages read _____

   Date of above publication _____

INTERVIEW SOURCES

1. Person interviewed _____ Date of interview_____

   His position, occupation, and location _____

   Why is he a reliable source?   Be specific _____

   _____

2. Person interviewed _____ Date of interview_____

   His position, occupation, and location _____

   Why is he a reliable source?   Be specific _____

   _____

PERSONAL EXPERIENCE OF SPEAKER

1. Tell (1) when, (2) where, and (3) conditions under which you became an authority on subject matter in your speech _____

   _____

   _____

   _____

Chapter 11

THE HECKLING SPEECH

This speech is due:
Time limits: 5-6 minutes.
Speaking notes: 10-word maximum limit.
Sources of information: Two are required, preferably three. For each source give the specific magazine
or book it was taken from, title of the article, author's full name, date of publication, and the chapter or pages telling where the material was found. If a source is a person, identify him completely by title, position, occupation, etc. List these on the outline form.
Outline your speech: Prepare a 75-150 word complete sentence outline. Designate the exact number of words in your outline. Use the form at the end of this chapter.

PURPOSE OF THE HECKLING SPEECH
A speaker never knows when he will be heckled by persons in his audience. Sometimes heckling occurs when it is least expected. At other times it does not develop when the occasion is ripe for it. But when heckling does come, a speaker should be ready to meet it whether it be mild or boisterous. This experience will provide practice in speaking while under the pressure of heckling from your audience. It should be valuable training for you.

Another reason why this assignment is given is that a student speaker often becomes aroused when under fire from his audience. He quite frequently discovers that he throws off his habitually meek speaking personality and suddenly faces his tormentors with a great surge of confidence and power - something he always possessed but did not use. This is a good feeling and inspires confidence in a speaker. However, because of the positive effect on him the student should not think that he must be stimulated always by questions and heckling in order to make a strong speech. This experience is intended primarily to make the student aware of his latent powers of expression so that he will use them in forthcoming speeches.

EXPLANATION OF A HECKLING SPEECH
The heckling speech is one that a speaker delivers while being subjected to heckling from his audience. Usually it supports or opposes a definite proposition. Normally, the speaker's purpose is to convince. A speech could inform or stimulate, but in either of these types of speeches, heckling is likely to be slight. The speaker selects one side of a contention which he will support and then does his best to justify his views. He presents argument and evidence that strengthen his stand. All the while he is doing this, the audience is free to heckle him in any way it sees fit. His problem is to control the volatile attention of his somewhat disturbing listeners, and at the same time successfully propound his ideas. It is necessary that the speaker possess positive self-control, retain his sense of humor, be fully prepared, and understand how to handle hecklers.

This type of speech is not encountered on any specific occasion. It arises somewhat unexpectedly. A speaker should be ready for it at any time.

SUGGESTED TOPICS FOR A HECKLING SPEECH
Note: Remember you are to take a side on one of these subjects, and that you are to uphold that side of the argument. You will have to work out the actual statement of your proposition.
1. Compulsory military training should be established in the United States.
2. Third or fourth terms for governors should be prohibited by laws.
3. National marriage laws with a minimum age limit, physical examination, and waiting period after applying for a license should be established by Congress.
4. National prohibition should be established by law.
5. National gambling should be legalized by law.
6. School dances should be free.
7. Girls should help pay the expenses of a date.
8. A woman should be elected President of the United States.
9. War should be declared only by a majority of the people.
10. The atomic bomb should be outlawed.
11. Hazing should be abolished on all college campuses.
12. There should be no clothing restrictions in public eating houses.

13. Married women should be prohibited from gainful employment.
14. The student newspaper should have no faculty control.
15. The Student Council should try all discipline cases.
16. Athletes should receive extra help from the school.
17. Students should be free to choose their own subjects.
18. Car tags should be free.
19. Picketing should be prohibited.
20. Speaker's choice of a proposition.

HOW TO CHOOSE A SUBJECT FOR A HECKLING SPEECH

When studying the above list of propositions, visualize yourself as being for or against one of the suggested topics. For this reason, select a subject upon which you hold a definite opinion and one which will also require you to secure additional information. Make your selection without delay so that you may give your subject adequate preparation.

HOW TO PREPARE FOR A HECKLING SPEECH

The purpose of the heckling speech is to convince your audience. At least we shall consider that your purpose for this particular occasion. Because you know now that you will be heckled, your secondary purpose will be to control your audience and put your ideas across.

The organization of this speech should be modeled after that of any Speech to Convince. Read the chapter bearing this heading for information on organization. Besides having your sequence of ideas well in mind, it will be wise for you to know this sequence so thoroughly you <u>cannot forget it</u>. Why? Under heckling pressure, loss of memory may be so overwhelming that you may stand blankly before your audience. If they can disturb you to this extent, they will be delighted no end. Such speechlessness need not trouble you if you are prepared for many interruptions. But you must not permit interruptions to cause you to forget the organization of your speech or to depart from it.

Prepare a complete sentence outline as indicated at the heading of this assignment.

HOW TO PRESENT A HECKLING SPEECH
Keep your head.
Your attitude should be one of firmness and good humor. Your firmness should not become officiousness or haughtiness. Your good humor should not permit you to be so sensitive to its presence that you laugh or turn to histrionics every time someone shoots a question at you or puts you on the spot. You should not be insensitive to a situation that demands a witticism or similar response from you. You should demonstrate enough flexibility in meeting your hecklers that you display the basic qualities of poise and self-confidence.

Your audience will be greatly pleased if they can disturb you or cause you to become so confused that you forget your speech or fly off into the wild blue yonder on a tangent, leaving your speech somewhere behind you. And your hecklers will try to accomplish these results. The question is: How can you avoid losing your poise? The answer can be stated in a few words. First, know your speech and know it well. Do not have a memorized talk, but have a memorized sequence of points which comprise your main ideas. Second, refuse to answer irrelevant questions that are nothing more than quips, pop-offs, or teasers. Simply state that such remarks are irrelevant, do not pertain to your speech, and hence cannot be answered. Third, whenever you are in doubt as to what your interrogator wants, ask him to repeat his question. Fourth, if you encounter a persistent heckler, you may sometimes silence him by a quick retort to some of his senseless chatter. For example, a college student was once speaking in defense of a certain race against which a strong prejudice existed. Suddenly one of his auditors yelled out, "Would you want your sister to marry a_____?" The speaker turned with a blazing eye and pointing his finger like a gun at the heckler, he thundered his reply, "I'd a thousand times she married a_____than a guy like you!" The heckler sank in his seat and did not speak a word during the remainder of the speech. Other hecklers became more cautious; the speaker continued his talk with relatively few interruptions. Afterward, he said that he had been waiting for that question, and that when it came he gave it all he had.

No one will criticize you for staying with your speech. For this reason, you should expect all kinds of interruptions, but not be disturbed by them. If the questions are legitimate, clear them up or tell the group that you will answer a certain question later in your speech when you discuss the point that has just been brought up. <u>Before you end your remarks, draw your thoughts together with a good conclusion.</u>

-32-

Throughout your speech, talk clearly, forcefully, and correctly. Be sure that everyone can hear you. While you are speaking, accompany your words with effective bodily actions and gestures. Look and act the way you feel - confident.

Observe these special hints: (1) be firm but flexible, (2) retain a sense of humor but do not interpret everything as something you should handle as if you were a comedian, (3) exhibit no anger and do not be afraid to stand up and face your audience vigorously and forcefully, (4) maintain self-control, (5) take advantage of opportunities offered by events occurring while you speak, (6) stay with your speech by refusing to be "jockied" out of position, and (7) keep your head.

HOW TO HECKLE
Interrupt the speaker at will, while you are either sitting or standing. Project such questions as: How do you know? Who's your authority? Where did you read that? What do you mean? Will you please explain_____? What is your evidence? Members of the audience may argue with the speaker (if he is naive enough to fall into such a trap), talk with each other, turn their backs on him, stand and address the audience, and the like.

These practices should not be overdone; however, the audience is obliged to see that each speaker knows, when he has finished his speech, that he has been through the fire; otherwise his experience will be weakened. Generously applaud each speaker when he concludes.

IMPROVE YOUR VOCABULARY
Chicanery - (shǐ-kān'-ẽr'ǐ) n. Questionable practice, trickery, sophistry, deceit. A person should not resort to chicanery to gain his point.

Anger - Use a synonym for this word. It will add color to your vocabulary. Here are several examples: animosity, displeasure, exasperation, fretfulness, fury, impatience, indignation, ire, passion, peevishness, pettishness, vexation, wrath, resentment, etc.

BIBLIOGRAPHY FOR THE HECKLING SPEECH

Buehler, E. Christian, and Linkugel, W. A., Speech Communication, Harper & Row, Publishers, 1969, pp. 225-226.
Hance, Kenneth G., and Others, Principles of Speaking, Wadsworth Publishing Company, 2d ed., 1969, pp. 70-72.
Ross, Raymond S., Speech Communication, Prentice-Hall, Inc., 2d ed., 1970, Chapter 11.

SPEECH TO CONVINCE

IN FAVOR OF THE AFFIRMATIVE

Frank L. Lundburg

There is an opportunity available to most high school students that is taken advantage of by comparatively few. It is sad too, for certainly if more students, particularly seniors planning to go to college, were to have some training in the fundamentals of debate, they would be better prepared for the future. The techniques and knowledge acquired from debating will help the student in almost every field of study; however, unfortunately, many students have some misconceptions about the activity.

When most people think of debate they think of the Senate or of the House of Representatives and of politicians discussing some particular piece of legislation, or perhaps they think of candidates airing their views before election day. What those people fail to realize, however, is that there is much more to debate than that. In reality most of life consists of making decisions and debating and reasoning in one form or another, and certainly, training in the basic concepts of argumentation and logic will help an individual later in life.

Now how does debating train a person to make decisions? The answer is found in looking at the goal of debate as stated by Arthur N. Kruger, Professor of English and Speech at Wilkes College. He tells us that "The paramount goal of academic debate is to train the student in the tools of argumentation, to train him how to construct logical arguments and to detect weaknesses or lapses from logical standards in the arguments of others."[1] "But," you may say, "I don't want to spend my time arguing about some topic of which I know very little". Therein lies the point: debating will teach you not to argue, in the common sense of the word, but rather will teach you to reason, and to draw significant conclusions from that reasoning and in learning to reason, you must do research -- to learn all about your topic. And in learning to do research on debate topics you get an added bonus. The abilities and techniques you acquire doing research for the debate topic will help you to gain information in many fields, and more important, to put that information to use in the form of clear concise reports and term papers.

But there is more to be gained from debate than just raw knowledge. Your method of thinking will change. You will learn to understand more about yourself and those around you, and in doing so, will mature. How is this true? First of all, debating teaches tolerance of differing points of view. By studying many sides of a question you are better able, and more likely, to want to see the position of a person whose ideas differ from yours. In presenting your particular side in a debate, too, you learn to think quickly and to have a logical answer for almost any situation. And by presenting your ideas orally in front of people you develop an awareness of your own abilities and limitations, and also an awareness of the abilities and limitations of those people around you. The rewards gained from such experience will only begin to manifest themselves in the classroom. Far more important than all the trophies or certificates is the knowledge that you, as an individual, will later in life, still be using these abilities, that you will be able to speak and conduct yourself with assurance and confidence, that you will be able to meet new challenges head on and will have an awareness and tolerance of ideas that are new and different.

Debating has paid off for many. A recent publication of the Pi Kappa Delta Speech Honorary[2] lists among its former members men who have indeed made good use of their training in high school and college debate. To name a few: Clinton P. Anderson, Senator from New Mexico and Chairman of the Committee on Interior and Insular Affairs; Chet Huntley, N.B.C. news broadcaster; George H. Mahon, Congressman from Texas and Chairman of the House Committee on Appropriations, one of the most powerful committees in the Congress; William L. Shirer, author of THE RISE AND FALL OF THE THIRD REICH. The list could go on and on. The point is that debate is more than just a static scholastic exercise. It is basic and dynamic.

Like the Biblical man who built his house on the rock, the high school student who acquires proficiency in debate will build a good foundation on which he can learn to communicate with his fellow-man. To debate is to consider and to understand issues and individuals, and if a person understands he will learn to think and to reason. And if a person learns to think and to reason and to impart this knowledge to others it will bring more than a small drop of order to a not so orderly world.

---

[1]Kruger, Arthur N.   Modern Debate - Its Logic and Strategy
New York, McGraw-Hill, 1960, p. 5.

[2]Fifty Famous Alumni of Pi Kappa Delta, The Forensic of Pi Kappa Delta
March, 1963, p. 27.

SPEECH OUTLINE

Construct a neat, complete sentence outline on this sheet, tear it out, and hand it to your instructor when you rise to speak. He may wish to write criticisms of the outline and speech in the margins.

Type of speech:_____ Name:_____

Number of words in outline:_____ Date:_____

Purpose of this speech: (What do you want your audience to learn, to think, to believe, to feel, or do because of this speech?)_____

_____

TITLE:

INTRODUCTION:

BODY:

CONCLUSION:

Instructor's comments may concern choice of topic, development of ideas, organization, language use, personal appearance, posture, physical activity, sources, and improvement.

(Write sources of information on back of sheet)

SOURCES FROM LITERATURE

(Fill out source requirements completely. Write "none listed" if an author's name or copyright date is not listed.)

1. Author's name _____

   Title of book or magazine used _____

   Title of article in above book or magazine _____

   Chapter and/or pages read _____

   Date of above publication _____

2. Author's name _____

   Title of book or magazine used _____

   Title of article in above book or magazine _____

   Chapter and/or pages read _____

   Date of above publication _____

3. Author's name _____

   Title of book or magazine used _____

   Title of article in above book or magazine _____

   Chapter and/or pages read _____

   Date of above publication _____

INTERVIEW SOURCES

1. Person interviewed _____ Date of interview_____

   His position, occupation, and location _____

   Why is he a reliable source? Be specific _____

   _____

2. Person interviewed _____ Date of interview_____

   His position, occupation, and location _____

   Why is he a reliable source? Be specific _____

   _____

PERSONAL EXPERIENCE OF SPEAKER

1. Tell (1) when, (2) where, and (3) conditions under which you became an authority on subject matter in

   your speech _____

   _____

   _____

Chapter 12

THE SPEECH TO ENTERTAIN

This speech is due:
Time limits: 5-6 minutes.
Speaking notes: None.
Sources of information: Two are required, preferably three. For each source give the specific magazine
    or book it was taken from, title of the article, author's full name, date of publication, and the chap-
    ter or pages telling where the material was found. If a source is a person, identify him completely
    by title, position, occupation, etc. List these on the outline form.
Outline your speech: Prepare a 75-150 word complete sentence outline. Designate the exact number of
    words in your outline. Use the form at the end of this chapter.

PURPOSE OF THE SPEECH TO ENTERTAIN

Many persons try to be entertaining when giving speeches. Some succeed and some do not. There
is a common misconception about the difficulty of presenting a speech to entertain: the idea is current
that the speech to entertain is a "breeze," that nothing is difficult about it, and that a series of risque
stories meet the requirements for a speech to entertain. This is far from the truth: a humorous speech
is one of the most difficult to present effectively. Because of this difficulty and for the reason that you
may be called at a future date to deliver a humorous speech, this assignment has been prepared.

EXPLANATION OF THE SPEECH TO ENTERTAIN

A humorous speech is one which entertains by utilization of humor. It may rely on words, anecdotes,
bodily actions, gestures, voice, speech construction, special devices, demonstrations, unusual situations,
pantomimes or a combination of any or all these factors.

Its purpose varies both in relation to the amount and type of humorous response the speech is
planned to elicit from the audience. Some speeches make listeners laugh gaily and loudly; others produce
only chuckles and snickers; and others bring forth only grins and smiles of amusement. It is important
for a student to understand that a humorous speech does not need to be uproariously funny to entertain. We
might be better understood if we were to call this speech a speech to amuse.

The special feature of a humorous speech is that it does not demand that a speaker do more than
catch the attention and interest of an audience and then hold these by developing a trend of thought or an
idea. The speaker is not required to make the audience feel that they are closely related to his subject
and that they must derive a moral or new philosophy from his remarks. Nor does he have to ask them to
take any action. It should be understood at this point, however, that a humorous speech may do more than
simply entertain. There is nothing to prevent its being informative, stimulating, or convincing, provided
none of these goals becomes the chief aim of the speaker. The chief aim of the speech is to entertain. An
idea may, and it is usually advisable that it should, be the main road which the speech travels. The humor
is achieved by hitting a few bumps, skidding around a bit, getting stuck in a mud hole, having a flat tire
and flirting with the farmer's daughter while you journey down the main highway. Thus, when you arrive
at your destination, you have traveled a straight road but you have had a pleasant time doing it.

The thought or ideas presented are the core of the speech around which humor is built. The overall effect is one in which the audience finds a definite trend of thought and philosophy presented delightfully
and entertainingly.

Occasions for humorous speeches are found ordinarily at dinners, club meetings, special assemblies, parties, and gatherings at which weighty discussions are inappropriate and out of harmony with the
mood of the occasion.

SUGGESTED TOPICS FOR A SPEECH TO ENTERTAIN

1. How to be serious
2. How to be funny
3. My great embarrassment
4. School life
5. Get rich quick
6. Pockets
7. Styles
8. Learning to fly
9. Hotels
10. Hospitals
11. He played football
12. Never say "no"
13. Shopping
14. Bring up father

15. How to get what you want
16. Gold is where you find it
17. I don't want to be rich
18. Sugar is sweet
19. The horse went away but the tractor came
20. Woman's most powerful weapon
21. Men
22. Children
23. Courting
24. Husbands are men
25. Sweethearts are human
26. A senator's life
27. If I were the teacher
28. After dinner speeches
29. Flattery versus praise
30. I predict
31. I am going to write a column
32. Words don't mean what they say
33. Why I read the comic strips
34. When time goes slowly
35. Where my money goes
36. Grandpa's first car
37. Grandma was a lady
38. Why people laugh
39. Wives are women
40. Speaker's choice

HOW TO CHOOSE A TOPIC FOR A SPEECH TO ENTERTAIN

In selecting a topic for a humorous speech, keep in mind the five necessary considerations that govern the selection of any speech topic, that is, the audience, the occasion, the speaker (you), the speech itself, and the surroundings in which the speech will be given. Your choice of a topic must be keyed to controlling factors. It is important to note that you may have a mixed audience with a widespread interest or taste. You must consider the probable speaking environment. Of course, since you will be the speaker, the subject that you choose must be one which you can present acceptably. The topic should be viewed from the standpoint of the time allowed for preparation, the availability of materials from which to build the speech, your own personality, your position in the community, your ability to present certain kinds of material and ideas, and your type of presentation. You should make your choice of topic with all of these considerations in mind.

One more point is significant. Do not postpone making your choice of subject. Take five minutes or so and choose carefully; be certain that you have the required information about all of the factors in the selection of a topic mentioned in the preceding paragraph. If you do not have the information, get it at once; then make up your mind. The student who leaves his choice of topic until the last minute does not leave much to his chances for giving a successful speech.

HOW TO PREPARE A SPEECH TO ENTERTAIN

As in the preparation of any good speech, in that of a speech to entertain, particular attention must be paid to organization of points, the arrangement of materials, and the rehearsal of the speech. The purpose, to entertain, should be clearly in mind; the purpose is assisted by a thorough understanding of the methods to be used for fulfilling this purpose. This type of speech requires a considerable study of references and some consultation with your instructor. In addition to the factors of good speech preparation previously studied, ample rehearsal is positively necessary. It is difficult to imagine anything more grotesque than a speaker's attempting to present a humorous speech and constantly referring to notes, because of his inadequate preparation of his speech.

The humorous speech should not degenerate into a series of unrelated funny stories, nor should it merely consist of the telling of one story. Exaggerations or episodes used as illustrations must apply to the theme of the speech or in some way assist the speaker in making his point. Only careful preparation and rehearsal will assure one that he is using his illustrations properly.

A few methods sometimes used to achieve humor are the following:
1. Telling a joke on oneself.
2. Telling a joke on someone in the group or some well-known person.
3. Making reference to the speech situation, local, state, or national situation.
4. Making reference to the occasion or other occasions.
5. Associating a speech with past incidents.
6. "Panning" members of the group, local, state, national, or world figures.
7. Exaggeration.
8. Deliberate underestimation.
9. Sudden change of thought.
10. Surprise thoughts.
11. After-thoughts tacked to the end of an otherwise serious statement.
12. Twisting ideas (do not overdo this).
13. Misinterpreting facts or figures (be clever about this).
14. Intentionally making errors (this must be skillfully done).
15. Intentionally placing oneself in a humorous situation.

16. Misquoting someone present or a well-known authority (be discreet).
17. Restating a well-known quotation to give it a humorous twist.
18. Pantomime.
19. Gestures poorly timed or timed too late.
20. Facial grimaces.
21. Using anecdotes.
22. Giving examples that are entertaining or that make an amusing point.
23. Impersonating a character that is used as an illustration (do not make your whole speech an impersonation).
24. Demonstrating or dramatizing a point (do this for purpose of illustrating to achieve humor).
25. Clever wording (concoct new words, apply certain words to new situations or give them new meanings, join two or more words together with hyphens then apply them in your speech).
26. Be quick to adapt your opening remarks to slips of the tongue of the toastmaster or other speakers. Do not overwork this device or it will become tiresome and trite; be appropriate.
27. Persons in public life, international situations, recent happenings in the news . . . all offer excellent opportunities for entertainment.

In actually setting up the speech to entertain you will follow the principles laid down for any speech: you will construct a clever and interesting introduction; you will develop your remarks point by point in logical order; you will bolster these points with examples, illustrations, facts, quotations from authorities, analogies, and conclusions, which you will draw from the material you present. Lastly you will have a conclusion to your speech which is appropriate to all you have said. It becomes evident that a speech to entertain simply does what every other speech does, and in addition, - this is important - it utilizes materials that in themselves carry and imply humor. The selection of these humorous materials, their arrangement in the speech, and the words used to present the ideas are what achieve the effect of entertainment.

Now, you ask, "How do I know my speech will be entertaining?" The answer is that you do not. The only assurance you can get is from your preparation. Frankly this is dependent entirely on your own effort and ability. It is difficult, very difficult, to select, to organize, to word, and to rehearse a speech to entertain, but you must do these preparations, nevertheless. Your own ingenuity and your own intelligence are the only assets you can have in preparing the humorous speech for presentation. Use these inherent personal resources well and you will have little to worry about. As far as this writer knows, there simply is no quick, easy way to prepare an entertaining speech - or any other for that matter. If any student is looking for a short cut, he will be wise to end his search and to apply himself in preparation, for that is what he will have to do in the end anyway; that is, if anything more than a mediocre speech is to be prepared for presentation.

HOW TO PRESENT A SPEECH TO ENTERTAIN

The humorous speech is characterized generally by a lively presentation. The speaker may be whimsical, facetious, gay, jovial, or he may present a mixture of these moods. He should be pleasant, of course. His entire bearing and decorum should reflect visibly the feelings and tenor of his remarks.

The speech should progress with a smooth forward motion. Delays and hesitations should be avoided, excepting those employed for a special effect. If laughter is incited, the speaker should carefully refrain from resuming his talk until he can be heard. Usually, this is at that moment just before all laughter has stopped. The speaker should never laugh at his own jokes or indicate that he knows he is funny. It is necessary, however, that he enjoy his audience and himself, and that this should be obvious.

One of the greatest dangers is that the inexperienced speaker will prolong his anecdotes, his jokes, or his whole speech. This may happen either because he enjoys himself so much that he forgets to keep moving or that he has improperly prepared his remarks. Then, too, nervousness may cause memory lapses and confusion. The principal point is, however, to hit the punch lines when they are hot and then to move on to the next ones. A speech, even an excellent one, is somewhat like ice cream - it is good and tickles the palate pleasantly if you do not eat too much of it at one time.

There is one last word of caution: watch your posture; use appropriate bodily actions and gestures; speak loudly enough to be heard by everyone; articulate well; and use good English.

IMPROVE YOUR VOCABULARY

Nasality - (nă-zăl'-ĭ-tĭ) n. The sound a person makes when talking through his nose. Example: The speaker's nasality was quite noticeable.

Smart - This word is often overused. You may add new enjoyment to your speech by using synonyms. Here are several: modish, trim, well-groomed, elegant, chic, fashionable, dashing, trig, etc. Give these synonyms a chance. They will do wonders for your conversation.

BIBLIOGRAPHY FOR THE SPEECH TO ENTERTAIN

Gilman, Wilbur E., and Others, An Introduction to Speaking, The Macmillan Company, 2d ed., 1968, Chapter 2.

Hance, Kenneth G., and Others, Principles of Speaking, Wadsworth Publishing Company, Inc., 2d ed., 1969, Chapter 17.

McAuley, Jack G., Speech, The Essential Elements, Burgess Publishing Company, 1968, pp. 35-44.

Oliver, Robert T., and Cortright, R. L., Effective Speech, Holt, Rinehart and Winston, Inc., 5th ed., 1970, Chapter 22.

Williams, Barbara, Purposeful Communication, Kendall/Hunt Publishing Company, 1970, pp. 175-181.

SPEECH TO ENTERTAIN

THE PLIGHT OF THE ONION

John E. Koch

Ordinarily, Ladies and Gentlemen, I am a very peaceful individual. It requires an event of great importance to stir my peaceful nature. Lately, such an event has come to pass. I must speak out in defense of my convictions, for silence would prove me a traitor not only to my own generation, but to generations to come. I cannot display indifference when the issue demands enthusiasm.

Just what is this issue that stirs the hearts of men to take arms against that sea of troubles and by opposing, end them? I do not feel that I am unique in being affected by this onslaught on human liberty. You, Ladies and Gentlemen, have also been touched by this debasement of our customs and traditions. Like the dark of nights, this creature has crept upon us, enveloping us in its deadly grasp, extinguishing the lamp of liberty and pinning the arms of the goddess behind her. What is this menace of which I speak that poses such a threat to all that we hold so dear? Is it a green-eyed fire-spouting monster from Mars, or a creature from the moon? No, it is not. It is one of our own kind. It is referred to as a scientist.

It will suffice to mention no names since we must judge them by their works. The intrusion of these people on our liberties has caused many to sound the call to arms; for when we are enveloped by that sea of troubles, we must fight back or swim.

The scene of attack is Idaho State University. There, a group of scientists as they call themselves, have been secretly experimenting, unbelievable as it may seem, to deprive the onion of its cooking odor. In some secret cache are hidden away thousands of odorless onions, the first of a line of odor-free American vegetables.

Picture the onion without its smell. A tired husband home from a weary day's toil would no longer have his appetite quickened by that tangy aroma drifting through the air. Take away the cooking odor of onions and you deprive millions of Americans of a familiar fragrance that signaled the secrets of the coming meal. To remove its odor is to destroy all that is dear to it -- its personality. The thought is enough to cause tears to come to one's eyes.

Although this be bad enough, the scientists will not stop here. They will not remain content with having removed the odor from the onion, but with their long tentacles they will reach out farther into the realm of life. What will be their next victim -- the smell of cooking cabbage, the grit of spinach, the hot of peppers, and soon the removal of color and taste? Will our diet become a mass of odorless, tasteless, colorless nourishment? It might, if we do not arise and take arms to prevent this calamity. I beg you to rally defenders to the cause of the onion. Go forward to loose the bonds from the hands of liberty, with the slogan, "Keep the odor in the onion; keep the onion out of college."

As Americans, we must demand the onion with its odor, the spinach with its grit, the pepper with its hot. Let us not sit here idly any longer -- Arise and carry that plea to all Americans. Keep the scientist out of the kitchen; keep the onion out of college.

SPEECH OUTLINE

Construct a neat, complete sentence outline on this sheet, tear it out, and hand it to your instructor when you rise to speak. He may wish to write criticisms of the outline and speech in the margins.

Type of speech:_____ Name:_____

Number of words in outline:_____ Date:_____

Purpose of this speech: (What do you want your audience to learn, to think, to believe, to feel, or do
because of this speech?)_____

_____

TITLE:

INTRODUCTION:

BODY:

CONCLUSION:

<u>Instructor's comments</u> may concern choice of topic, development of ideas, organization, language use, personal appearance, posture, physical activity, sources, and improvement.

(Write sources of information on back of sheet)

SOURCES FROM LITERATURE

(Fill out source requirements completely. Write "none listed" if an author's name or copyright date is not listed.)

1. Author's name _____

   Title of book or magazine used _____

   Title of article in above book or magazine _____

   Chapter and/or pages read _____

   Date of above publication _____

2. Author's name _____

   Title of book or magazine used _____

   Title of article in above book or magazine _____

   Chapter and/or pages read _____

   Date of above publication _____

3. Author's name _____

   Title of book or magazine used _____

   Title of article in above book or magazine _____

   Chapter and/or pages read _____

   Date of above publication _____

INTERVIEW SOURCES

1. Person interviewed _____ Date of interview _____

   His position, occupation, and location _____

   Why is he a reliable source? Be specific _____

   _____

2. Person interviewed _____ Date of interview _____

   His position, occupation, and location _____

   Why is he a reliable source? Be specific _____

   _____

PERSONAL EXPERIENCE OF SPEAKER

1. Tell (1) when, (2) where, and (3) conditions under which you became an authority on subject matter in

   your speech _____

   _____

   _____

   _____

Chapter 13

AFTER DINNER SPEAKING

This speech is due:

Time limits: 3 minutes - This time limit is necessary in order that each person may be permitted to speak. Longer speeches may extend the time too much.

Speaking notes: None.

Hint: Although you are not required to prepare an outline or to read source materials, it will be wise to do both for your own benefit.

PURPOSE OF AFTER DINNER SPEAKING

One of the best ways to learn anything is actually to experience it. From the experience of preparing this speech assignment, you will gain first-hand knowledge of after dinner speaking. You will see how the program is arranged, how the order of serving is coordinated with the speeches, and how the toastmaster must carry on and keep events moving. You will acquire much other valuable information concerning after dinner speaking. You will learn it because you will help build the entire program and because you will be a speaker at the dinner.

This experience is proposed so that you may broaden your knowledge of the various types of after dinner speeches and their related activities.

NOTE TO INSTRUCTOR

If it is impossible to carry out the plan which is suggested in the following pages, a first alternative may be worked out in class. This alternative may be one in which students sit in a group that is rectangular in shape to simulate positions around a table at a banquet. Toastmasters should be placed at the head of an imaginary table, with the speakers seated as they would be, had a dinner just been completed. Insofar as possible, an after-dinner-speaking atmosphere and environment should be created.

A second alternative to a real banquet is one in which the students eat a light, inexpensive lunch in a suitable room somewhere in the school building. The food should be served so as to duplicate banquet and after-dinner-speaking conditions in so far as is practicable.

It is the writer's belief that a real after-dinner-speaking situation is the most desirable atmosphere of all for practice of after dinner speaking. Full explanations follow which may be applied to any of the suggested plans for supplying a proper background for this speech experience.

EXPLANATION OF AFTER DINNER SPEAKING

After dinner speaking is giving a speech following a meal at which a group has gathered. The speech may have a serious purpose or it may be designed to give entertainment and pleasure. The type of speech which you present depends on the purpose of your talk. The type of speech is governed also by the occasion, its objective, and the reason for your remarks. After dinner speeches require that the speaker follow closely all the rules of organization previously noted, particularly those for serious talks. Entertainment, as a motive, charges you with the responsibility of altering the organization of the speech to the extent that is necessary to make your ideas fulfill the purpose of entertaining.

Occasions for the after dinner speech are many. They may be business luncheons, club dinners, committee meetings, special breakfasts, promotional gatherings, campaign inaugurations, afternoon teas, socials, celebrations, anniversaries, or any one of a dozen other occasions.

SUGGESTED TOPICS FOR AFTER DINNER SPEECHES

1. When I get married
2. Courting in an airplane
3. My first date
4. Money and women
5. Three girl friends
6. Why men or women talk
7. If I were president
8. Now it can be told
9. Never ask why
10. Silence is not always golden
11. It happened this way
12. Parking as I see it
13. Christmas shopping
14. My first job
15. The first days are hardest
16. The fish that got away
17. How to hitch hike
18. Income taxes
19. How to win friends and their money
20. A successful moocher

21. Of all the sad words
22. I own a car but -
23. Tipping
24. Waitresses are human
25. Ten years from now

26. If I had a million
27. Tomorrow's opportunities
28. A better world for all
29. Gold is where you find it
30. Speaker's choice

Note: These topics should be suitable suggestions unless a particular theme is followed at the dinner. In this case, new topics should be chosen that are in keeping with the theme.

HOW TO CHOOSE A TOPIC FOR AFTER DINNER SPEAKING

Decide on the purpose of your speech. Be sure you can develop your topic to fulfill that purpose. Select something suitable and interesting to you, yet adapted to the occasion and audience. Do not put off deciding about a topic.

HOW TO PREPARE AN AFTER DINNER SPEECH

First of all, study this assignment carefully to learn fully the requirements of successful after dinner speaking. Follow previous information relative to speech organization, wording, and practice. Plan to use no notes. If you are a toastmaster, knowledge of and preparation for your task are the only assurances of a satisfactory performance.

The speaker's obligations: The preparation for this talk is no different from that of any other speech of the type you intend to present. Possibly your thoughts will be to entertain. If this is true, of course you will prepare a speech to entertain. Should you not be familiar with the requirements of this kind of speech, read how it is done in the section of this book entitled "The Speech to Entertain." Follow this procedure for any type of speech you wish to deliver whether it be the speech to convince, to inform, or to stimulate.

Having ascertained your subject and the manner in which you will treat it, complete the preparation of your speech carefully. Before you consider yourself fully prepared, find out all you can about the program, when you will speak, who will precede you, and who will follow you. Then be sure that your speech is in line with the occasion.

It is not necessary and certainly not always advisable that a speaker plan to tell a joke on the toastmaster, regardless of what the toastmaster may do in the way of introduction. If the occasion calls for humor, a person should be ready to meet it. If it is doubtful what to do, play it safe. Good taste never offends. As far as risque stories go, leave them at home. If you do not have a clean story that packs a wallop, you have not tried to find one. The world has a great storehouse of humor and clean stories for all who want them and these are excellent for after dinner speeches.

To complete the preparation of your after dinner speech, practice it aloud several times before a mirror. It is a splendid idea to ask a friend or friends to hear you in rehearsal. Before you accept their advice or criticisms too literally, give some thought to their suggestions and the reliability of their advice.

The toastmaster's obligations: The toastmaster has an important task. He must see that everything is ready to go; he must open the proceedings, keep them going, and close the meeting. Let us examine these duties separately. First, to arrange everything, he should arrive at the meeting place early, at least a half hour. He will then perform the following chores: (1) He will advise the waiters in detail as to how the meal is to be served; (2) he will note the arrangement of the banquet room and suggest any changes he desires; (3) he will inquire about a check room or other space for wraps and make certain it is available and ready for use; (4) he will locate rest rooms and be ready to direct persons to them; (5) shortly before serving time, he will personally count the plates and check place cards on the tables to be sure that the right number are available; (6) he will keep careful check on the persons as they arrive so that he will know when everyone is there; (7) he will indicate to the group when they are to go into the dining hall, that is, if they have been waiting in a lobby. If everyone has previously gathered in the dining room, he will be the first to seek his chair as a signal that others should follow suit; (8) his general duty will be to see that guests are welcomed by himself or another designated person, that they are introduced, their wraps properly disposed of, and that they are entertained and put at ease; (9) during the banquet he will constantly remain alert to see that all goes well, and (10) he will see that the committee pays for the banquet or makes definite arrangements to settle the account later. He will also see that a tip is left for the waiters.

Of course, when there are several toastmasters, these duties may be divided among them. Everyone should know specifically what he is to do and should carry out each obligation conscientiously.

In regard to the actual work of introducing the speakers, considerable information must be gathered and set up several days early. This includes these necessary items: (1) The names of the speakers; (2) their topics; (3) data concerning speakers that will be suitable to use when introducing them; and (4) the order of the speakers. All this must be drawn together at a toastmasters' meeting and definitely agreed on by mutual consent. The act of introducing the speakers requires ingenuity and planning. A toastmaster should learn early that he is not to make speeches. This pleasure belongs to the after dinner speakers. The toastmaster merely presents each speaker by giving him a short introduction. Thirty seconds usually suffices, sometimes less, but never more than a minute or two, at the maximum. At this banquet the thirty second limit should prevail. The introduction may be a clever statement or two about the speaker, his name, and his topic. A fitting anecdote is in order if the occasion demands it. After the speaker concludes his speech, the toastmaster should get on with the show and not take time out to offer a rebuttal to some remark made by the speaker.

Throughout the evening's performances, the toastmasters should be agreed on matters such as when and whom to applaud and any other activities or procedures that should be initiated by the toastmasters.

HOW TO PRESENT AN AFTER DINNER SPEECH

Your presentation should reflect the type of speech you deliver. Generally speaking, a simple organization, graphic word pictures, sufficient humor, lively and animated delivery, and a forward motion of ideas characterize after dinner speeches.

Voice and bodily action should be in harmony with the speech occasion and environment. The chances are that you will not need to talk loudly to be heard, nor will you be permitted much bodily action because of room accommodations and arrangement. Care should be exercised when rising to speak, or your chair may scrape noisily on the floor making you appear awkward. To prevent this, see that your chair is far enough from the table that you may rise freely without moving the chair. When the chairman, toastmaster, or president introduces you, rise and address him according to the position he holds; such as, "Mr. Toastmaster," "Mr. Chairman," and the like.

If during the program some person appearing ahead of you unknowingly steals your speech, the best thing for you to do when you speak is to refer to his remarks in support of your statements. You can go ahead then with your own thoughts and elaborate on them as is necessary and as has been planned.

Note: Keep your remarks in line with the occasion and purpose of your speech. "Ad lib" and improvise as the situation demands. Retain a sense of humor; use it if it is appropriate, and observe your time limits. Remember that the program committee allotted only a certain amount of time to you.

GROUP PLANS TO BE MADE

To make this experience real, you should by all means hold this meeting at a local hotel, cafe, or other place where the class can meet and eat without crowding. The atmosphere should be absolutely real, no make-believe.

In order to prepare successfully for this dinner, the following arrangements should be completed by separate committees:

Committee No. 1:

The reservation and menu committee. It should set a date for the luncheon and reserve a suitable place to hold it. Committee members should check carefully the size of the room and whether or not there will be extra charge for the use of the room. Serving facilities should be ascertained and assurance should be received that the group will not be disturbed by customers, if they are in a public eating house. It is to be noted also if there is lobby space in which to gather and check wraps before going into the dining room. At least three different menus and their respective costs should be investigated and submitted to the class. One menu should be adopted and a price limit established. The time the meal will be served should be announced. It may be a noon or evening function, but preferably an evening one.

Committee No. 2:

The decorations committee. This committee decides what, if any, decorations are to be used. A fund must be established to cover any costs. Expenditures must be kept within the limits of this fund.

Committee No. 3:

The toastmaster's committee. Approximately twenty-five per cent of the class will act as toastmasters. They should be elected by secret ballot. Each class member will write on a piece of paper as many names as there are to be toastmasters. If five is the number of toastmasters, then the five persons whose names are written the greatest number of times will be declared elected. They, in turn, will meet as a committee to decide the order in which they will preside and the order of those they will introduce. They will learn in advance the topic of each speaker, thus preventing overlapping talks. Each toastmaster should plan to introduce a series of speakers, after which he will present the next toastmaster who will continue in the same manner. The first toastmaster will open the meeting and introduce guests. This may be done just before starting to eat, or it may be done at the first part of the program following the dinner. The last toastmaster, after introducing his speakers, should make appropriate closing remarks and adjourn the meeting. It is often embarrassing to everyone present if the last toastmaster does not make it absolutely clear that the banquet is concluded.

This use of several toastmasters may be somewhat unconventional but this arrangement gives more persons the experience as toastmaster. It adds variety to the program, provides opportunity for originality, and generally enhances the experience. It also suggests a basis for comparison of ideas as to what makes a good toastmaster.

Committee No. 4:
The collection committee. It is the responsibility of this committee to collect in advance the proper amount from each class member. They will divide and deliver this money to each committee chairman whose group has incurred a debt which must be paid immediately following the dinner. Persons who have a plate reserved at the dinner but who do not come should expect to forfeit the price of the meal. Most hotels will charge for the places set.

Summary: Needless to say, all of the above committees must coordinate their efforts and work as a unit. Each reports its activities so all may know what progress has been made. It is likely your instructor will act as coordinator. It will be wise to seek his advice, besides reading numerous references pertaining to banquet procedure.

The group may or may not wish to invite guests. It is highly desirable that parents, friends, teachers, or dates be invited. This makes the affair a real banquet. While it is advisable to bring guests, those who do so should remember that they will be expected to pay for the guests' dinners.

Here are several points to investigate:

1. How early should you arrive? (A minimum of five minutes early.)
2. What clothes should you wear? (Hint - better make this dinner informal.)
3. What is the proper etiquette? (Good manners and willingness to make conversation - do not "freeze up.")
4. When and whom should you applaud? (Follow the toastmaster's lead.)
5. What are the toastmasters' duties? (To set the pace throughout the banquet.)
6. When should the food be served? Between speeches? Just how? (Hint - better settle this point definitely and be sure your waiters are correctly informed. It is desirable that speeches come after dessert has been finished.)
7. What should you do if you make a blunder? (The answer is, do nothing; go on.)
8. Supposing someone is late; what then? (Wait a few minutes then start the banquet.)
9. What if you should forget your speech? (Hint - do not ever memorize it. Have your main points in mind. Rehearse.)
10. How and when should you seat yourself? Where? (If there are no place cards, find your own seat.)
11. What should you do when the toastmaster dismisses the group? Linger? Just what? (Go home, unless other arrangements have been made.)

IMPROVE YOUR VOCABULARY

Facetious - (fȧ-sē'-shŭs) a. Given to wittiness or characterized by pleasantry; witty. Example: An after dinner speaker frequently makes facetious remarks.

O. K. - Use a synonym for this word. It is tired from too much use. Here are a few examples: agreeable, satisfactory, splendid, excellent, elegant, admirable, choice, exquisite, etc. Employ these synonyms wisely. They don't have the same application.

BIBLIOGRAPHY FOR AFTER DINNER SPEAKING

Gilman, Wilbur E., and Others, <u>An Introduction to Speaking</u>, The Macmillan Company, 2d ed., 1968, pp. 30-32.

Oliver, Robert T., and Cortright, R. L., <u>Effective Speech</u>, Holt, Rinehart and Winston, Inc., 5th ed., 1970, pp. 484-486.

Ross, Raymond S., <u>Speech Communication</u>, Prentice-Hall, Inc., 2d ed., 1970, pp. 241-245.

Samovar, Larry E., and Mills, Jack, <u>Oral Communication, Message and Response</u>, Wm. C. Brown Company, Publishers, 1968, pp. 200-201.

Strother, Edward S., and Huckleberry, A. W., <u>The Effective Speaker</u>, Houghton Mifflin Company, 1968, pp. 55-59.

AFTER DINNER SPEECH

THE TERRIBLE MENACE

Lloyd Guderjohn

Ladies and Gentlemen: I would like to advise you of a terrible danger that threatens America today. Yes, a menace that threatens the welfare of every man, woman, and child. I refer not to an attack by a foreign power, I am speaking not of subversive Communists. No, I am talking of a deadly device found within our own home and which is, I might add, an instrument of our own making.

Perhaps I frighten you with talk of a creature about to turn on its own maker like Frankenstein's monster or the hydrogen bomb; however, these creatures are mere playthings compared with the destructive possibilities of this horror. There is a vast number of these infernal devices. They are possessed by a highly developed organization and they are very definitely plotting the destruction of mankind. They present a threefold menace. They threaten our lives, our health and our safety. Who or what are these unspeakable horrors? How do they threaten our lives, our health and safety? What can we do to avoid this approaching doom?

Ladies and Gentlemen, this menace is none other than the common doorknob. You may find this shocking fact hard to believe. Yes, the doorknob constitutes a deadly menace. Firstly, they menace our lives. Have you ever noticed the position of the doorknob upon the door? Do you realize that it is located in such a position that if the door were to open suddenly, anyone who happened to be looking thru the keyhole would be struck a terrible blow? Yes! The doorknob threatens our very lives.

Secondly, a doorknob endangers our health. As you all know, when a person wants to enter a washroom to wash his hands he must first open the door. He grasps the knob and thereby rubs all the dirt off his hand and onto the knob. When he returns he picks up the dirt and germs again. So as you can see, washing does no good.

Thirdly, doorknobs threaten our safety. Can you imagine the confusion if the doorknobs should go on strike for shorter hours, or for whatever they should want to strike? Do you know that if they should go on strike, half of us would be locked out? Do you also realize that the other half would be locked in? The danger seems incredible and one can hardly believe that such a danger confronts us.

The doorknobs are very numerous. There are two on every door. Every room has at least two doors. This would make twenty in the average five-room house. If five people were living there they would be outnumbered four to one. In addition to this, doorknobs may be found where we work, in schools, and in hospitals. In addition, they are very highly organized. <u>They always work in pairs.</u>

As I have shown you, doorknobs are indeed a menace. To circumvent disaster there is only one thing we can do. We must gather every doorknob and destroy them all. Of course we would have to learn to get along without them and this would indeed be difficult. But the inconvenience suffered would be well worth the sacrifice.

Chapter 14

IMPROMPTU SPEAKING

This speech is due:

Time limits: 2-3-4 and 5 minutes. (Start with two minutes. Increase the length of speeches until a student can talk five minutes.)

Speaking notes: During the first two experiences you may use notes which designate a "method." After this, memorize your method and apply it as you speak.

PURPOSE OF THE IMPROMPTU SPEECH

This speech experience is for the purpose of further enlarging your speech knowledge. It is to expose you to impromptu speaking and to provide you with a rudimentary acquaintance with the difficulties and nature of unprepared discourse. Many students assume that impromptu speaking is easy. Nothing could be further from the truth. In reality impromptu speaking is extremely difficult. It is used effectively only by experienced speakers. There are methods, however, which if properly used, will enable a person to perform acceptably on the spur of the moment. This assignment will assist you in learning these methods.

EXPLANATION OF IMPROMPTU SPEAKING

Impromptu speaking is giving an unprepared talk. A person simply takes the floor, selects a subject, and begins. Various methods are used to conduct impromptu expression. A common procedure is one in which the speaker takes the floor after being asked to talk on a certain subject which he may or may not know much about. This is another method: one topic is suggested by each of several persons in the audience; a few seconds are permitted the speaker to choose from the list of topics the topic on which he feels himself best suited to expound; then he begins his conversation. Differences in the manner of selecting a topic are many; however, in any case, one fundamental principle is that the ideas voiced are unrehearsed and unprepared.

The purpose of presenting the speech is the same as that for any other type of speaking. The distinctive feature is the unprepared delivery and the suddenness with which a person is confronted with a speech situation. Impromptu speaking is often required at those times when a person is called upon without warning "to say a few words" at a luncheon, special meeting, social gathering, or other occasion.

SUGGESTED TOPICS FOR IMPROMPTU SPEECHES

Write three suggestions in the spaces below. They should be suitable to those who will be asked to use them as subjects. Avoid those such as: "What Did You Do Last Night?", "A Trip to Yellowstone Park," . . . Your instructor will ask you to supply a topic from time to time as needed during the class. Examples of suitable topics for impromptu speaking are: dancing, movies, what is your opinion about (1) labor, (2) prohibition, (3) gambling, (4) free school books, (5) traffic laws, (6) radio programs, (7) . . .

1. _____

2. _____

3. _____

HOW TO CHOOSE A TOPIC FOR IMPROMPTU SPEAKING

There is one general rule to follow in selecting your topic; that is, if you have a choice. This rule is: choose the one on which you are best fitted to speak. Consider your audience and the occasion when you are making a choice of topic.

HOW TO PREPARE FOR AN IMPROMPTU SPEECH

Naturally you cannot prepare for an unknown topic, but you <u>can</u> prepare a method of attack on surprise offerings from your audience. One system of doing this is to have in mind various orders by which to develop your ideas.

One order might be the <u>time sequence</u> in which events occur by the hour, day, month, or year, moving forward or backward from a certain time. This example will illustrate the principle involved: Topic - Houses: (1) Give the history of houses from a definite date; (2) Tell which part of the country houses were first built in and their subsequent westward movement with time; (3) Describe how with time the styles of houses change, 1620-1700-1775-1800, and the like.

A space order would take you from east to west, top to bottom, front to rear . . ; for example: take the topic, Houses.   Then develop the speech in space order, giving the items in this way: (1) Specify the location of houses and their types, starting in California and traveling east; (2) Locate various classes of houses found in a city, starting at a slum area and moving to the wealthy outlying districts; (3) Describe houses according to locations in various parts of the world.

Using causal order, you might discuss certain forces and then point out the results which follow. Use this example: Topic - Houses: (1) Eskimos live in igloos. Why? Give reasons (causes). Or you might mention that South Pacific tribes dwell in grass and mud huts. Why? Give reasons (causes). (2) Prefabricated houses are now being built. Why? Give the causes that led to their development. (3) There are many hundreds of styles of houses of different architecture. Why? Give causes for this great diversification.

A special order is one of your own devising. For example take the same topic - Houses. (1) Tell how to build a house or different kinds of houses. (2) Give the legal aspects of house construction – such as, wiring, sewage disposal plants, plumbing, type of dwelling in restricted areas, distance from street, . . . (3) How to contract for house construction, . . .

Another method which your writer has found effective is given below. It should be borne in mind that any method a speaker elects to use is not self-propelled. The person who applies the method will need to keep his wits about him and utilize only those portions of the device which are adapted to his particular speech, the occasion, his audience, and his own background and knowledge. He will find it necessary to literally memorize the points which follow. If he does this and then develops his topic in the order of the various headings, he will make a logical discussion.

  I. Why is this topic important to your audience? To you?
 II. Give a history of important events which will show the background and development of your subject.
III. What are the overall effects of your topic (such as, gambling) on your audience, the state, the nation, the world?
     A. What are the effects geographically?
     B. What are the effects politically?
     C. What are the effects economically?
     D. What are the effects socially?
     E. What are the effects religiously?
     F. What are the effects educationally?
     G. What are the effects morally?
     H. What are the effects agriculturally?
     I. . . . .
 IV. What caused these effects?   (Give as many causes as you can which will explain the effects you have enumerated. You may do this by discussing an effect and then by giving the cause of it immediately after.)
  V. What are the different solutions to the problems? (You have told what is happening (effects) and you have told what brought them about (causes).   Naturally, you must tell now what you propose to do about the problem or problems. Thus, you will have offered several different solutions.)
 VI. Discuss the advantages and disadvantages of each solution you propose.
VII. Select one or two solutions which you think are best. Tell why they are best.
VIII. How do you propose to take action on these solutions? How may you and your audience go about putting your solutions into practice?   Mention one or more ways to do this.
 IX. Conclude your speech.
     A. You may summarize.
     B. You may appeal to your audience.
     C. You may ask your audience to do a specific act. Example:
        (1) Write to your congressman, (2) vote against _____ ,
        (3) and others, according to your own desire.

HOW TO PRESENT AN IMPROMPTU SPEECH
     In presenting an impromptu speech your attitude is a deciding factor in determining your effectiveness. First of all, you must maintain poise. It does not matter how surprised you are, how difficult your

topic is. It does not make any difference what happens when you receive your subject or while you are speaking or after you have concluded your speech; you still must maintain poise. It is impossible to over-emphasize the importance of poise. Now you ask, how do you maintain poise? Here are a number of suggestions and answers. (1) Do not fidget around at your seat before you speak, just because you know you will soon be "on the spot." (2) When you are called on to speak, rise calmly and take your place before your audience. (3) If you know your topic when you take the platform, begin your remarks calmly, without hurrying (have some vigor and force), and be sure that you have a plan in mind by which you will develop your thoughts. Do not apologize to your audience in any way, by word or action. (4) If you do not know your topic when you rise to speak but are offered several choices after obtaining the floor, simply stand calmly before the group and listen carefully to the suggestions which are made. You should ask that a topic be repeated if you do not understand it. After you have received all of the proposed subjects, either stand calmly or walk calmly back and forth a few seconds while you decide which offering you will talk about. Ten seconds should be the maximum time taken to decide. Once your selection is made, decide immediately what method or plan you will use in developing it. This plan should have been committed to memory before you ever attended class or placed yourself in a position where you might be asked to give an impromptu speech. After you have chosen your method of development, you will make your introductory remarks by telling why the subject is important to your listeners. When you begin to speak, do not make any apology of any sort whatsoever. Get on with your speech.

In actually delivering an impromptu talk, it is wise not to start too fast but rather to pick up speed and power as you go along. Aside from this, you should observe bodily actions and gestures which are in keeping with the speech situation. Your voice should be filled with meaning and easily heard by all. Naturally, your articulation, pronunciation, and grammar will be of high standard.

There is little to fear from impromptu speaking if you follow a preconceived method of attack on your subject. The way to do this is to refuse to allow yourself to become panicky, to recognize that some nervousness is a good sign of readiness, and to realize that your audience will expect nothing extraordinary from you because they, too, will know you are speaking impromptu. Actually, they will be "pulling for you." So you see, if you go about your task with poise and determination, your chances of success are exceedingly good. We might add here that a well-rounded knowledge attained from a strong reading program will assist you immeasurably.

IMPROVE YOUR VOCABULARY

Indolent - (ĭn'dō-lĕnt) a. A liking for ease or idleness, avoidance of exertion, idle, lazy, slothful, languid. Example: Indolent persons dislike preparing interesting speeches.

Huh - Omit this. It is a vulgarism which enjoys an unwarranted usage. Use a more desirable synonym. Examples are: What? I didn't understand? Please? Pardon? Sir? Madam? Yes? etc.

BIBLIOGRAPHY FOR IMPROMPTU SPEAKING

Hance, Kenneth G., and Others, Principles of Speaking, Wadsworth Publishing Company, 2d ed., 1969, pp. 268-269.
Jensen, J. Vernon, Perspectives on Oral Communication, Holbrook Press, Inc., 1970, Chapter 2.
Monroe, Alan H., and Ehninger, Douglas, Principles of Speech Communications, Scott, Foresman and Company, 6th brief ed., 1969, pp. 11-12.
Ross, Raymond S., Speech Communication, Prentice-Hall, Inc., 2d ed., 1970, pp. 71-72.
Samovar, Larry, and Mills, Jack, Oral Communication, Message and Response, Wm. C. Brown Company, Publishers, 1968, pp. 201-204.
Williams, Barbara, Purposeful Communication, Kendall/Hunt Publishing Company, 1970, pp. 106-111.

Chapter 15

A SPEECH TO GAIN GOODWILL

This speech is due:
Time limits: 6-7 minutes. Observe your time limits!
Speaking notes: Do not use them - your speech should be in you, not on paper.
Sources of information: Two are required, preferably three. For each source give the specific magazine
     or book it was taken from, title of the article, author's full name, date of publication, and the chap-
     ter or pages telling where the material was found. If a source is a person, identify him completely
     by title, position, occupation, etc. List these on the outline form.
Outline your speech: Prepare a 75-150 word complete sentence outline. Designate the exact number of
     words in your outline. Use the form at the end of this chapter.

PURPOSE OF A SPEECH TO GAIN GOODWILL

     One type of speech being utilized many thousands of times each year is the kind that secures good-
will from an audience. The popularity and usefulness of goodwill speeches are not likely to decline, but
rather to grow. Your place in society may at any time demand that you join the parade of those who present
speeches designed to secure goodwill. Because this type of speech occurs so often, you should, by all
means, have experience with it. This assignment provides such an opportunity for you.

EXPLANATION OF THE SPEECH TO GAIN GOODWILL

     A speech to gain goodwill is one in which the purpose is to secure a favorable attitude toward the
speaker and for the group which he represents. Normally, this speech is presented to a friendly audience,
which necessitates the presentation of what might easily be called a speech to inform. This will be the apparent purpose, as far as the audience is concerned. However, the thought behind the presentation of information is this; by causing his listeners to understand and appreciate the group he represents, the speaker will secure goodwill from them.

     Occasions for goodwill speeches occur at luncheons, club meetings, special demonstrations, school
meetings, religious gatherings, conventions, business meetings, ... Any group that convenes to hear a
speaker give them information, whether it be a straight informative talk, an illustrated lecture, the showing of a film, or the demonstration of a new product, likely will be the recipient of a goodwill speech. One
might classify a goodwill speech as a very subtle or indirect sales talk.

SUGGESTED TOPICS AND AUDIENCES

     Construct a goodwill speech in which you represent a certain group on a definite occasion.
1. Represent a mining company to a civic club.
2. Represent an aircraft manufacturing corporation to a chamber of commerce.
3. Represent a car manufacturing company to a Lions Club.
4. Tell how your company makes ladies' hats - to a sorority.
5. Represent a washing machine company - to a group of women.
6. Represent an insurance company to a group of students.
7. Represent a college to a high school.
8. Represent a "baby food company" to a group of young mothers.
9. Represent a correspondence school - to industrial workers.
10. Represent a foreign country - to a college assembly.
11. Represent the United States - to a foreign country.
12. Represent a publisher - at a teachers' meeting.
13. Represent an implement company - at a rural gathering.
14. Represent a "salesmanship school" - to a group of businessmen.
15. Represent the Navy, Army, or Air Corps - to a student body.
16. Represent a city at another city.
17. Represent a church - before a civic group.
18. Represent a "sports club" at a college assembly.
19. Represent a farmer's organization - before a group of businessmen.
20. Speaker's choice.

HOW TO CHOOSE A TOPIC

     As always, choose a topic that has a compelling interest for you. Choose one you know something
about; one about which you can get more information. Make your selection without too much delay. Putting
off a decision that can be made now will not improve your speech.

HOW TO PREPARE A SPEECH TO GAIN GOODWILL

First of all, remember that your purpose is to secure goodwill. Keep this in mind. Second, do not forget that your remarks will be necessarily of an informative nature. We will assume that you have analyzed your audience and selected your topic.

Naturally, as soon as you have done this, you should gather your materials. Practically all large companies and corporations will gladly send you information if you will write for it. Many local business houses and Chambers of Commerce will provide pamphlets and brochures. Encyclopedias and Readers' Guides are excellent sources. If you are willing to show a reasonable amount of initiative, you will have no difficulty in locating materials to supplement your own knowledge. If you reach an impasse, ask your instructor for assistance.

After you have gathered your material, you will need to organize it logically so that it can be easily followed. You must decide on the order, the arrangement, the illustrations and examples, an effective introduction, and a strong conclusion. In other words, the entire pattern of your speech must be worked out carefully.

There are several characteristics of the goodwill speech which you should note. First, be sure you have interesting facts, new material - the novel or out of the ordinary subject-matter that the listeners have not heard before. Another point is that you should show a definite relationship between your corporation, institution, a profession and the lives of your listeners. They should be made to see that their happiness and prosperity are tied in with your activities or those which you represent. In making this point do not be so bold that you ask their approval or request their approbation. You should take it for granted that they already approve. And last, be sure you offer them a definite service. It may be in the form of souvenirs, samples, or an invitation to visit your plant, city, or institution. It could be special favors or accommodations to members of the audience, or merely the answering of questions they cared to raise at the conclusion of your remarks. Above all, remember that you are willing to help your audience - you are at their service. (Do not forget to practice this speech aloud before you present it to your audience.)

HOW TO PRESENT A SPEECH TO GAIN GOODWILL

This is a speech in which friendliness, good humor, and modesty count to a high degree. You will be talking about yourself and your organization. Bragging will have no place - bragging is out. The information that you present will have to be strong and interesting enough to do its own talking. You must be tolerant of your competitors and gracious in your appraisal of them. You must be careful about forcing your material on your audience. If you possess the necessary good feeling and friendliness for your auditors, they will reciprocate these attitudes.

Dress yourself for the occasion, give attention to your posture, be alert and eager to communicate. Talk to be heard and understood. Avoid unnecessary formality. Bodily action and gesture will be in order, as always, if they are used appropriately. Avoid being suave and bland; just be friendly and sincere.

IMPROVE YOUR VOCABULARY

Use the following word in your speech today and five times each day during the next week.

Laconic - (là-kŏn'ĭk) a. Expressing a great deal in few words; concise, terse. Example: He used a laconic manner of expression, in fact he was almost curt.

Funny - Omit this word. Do not use it for ten days. It is completely "fagged." Use a synonym to brighten your speech. Examples: laughable, absurd, comical, ludicrous, humorous, waggish, droll, whimsical, burlesque, etc. - or, odd, strange, singular, unique, wierd, eccentric, irregular, quaint, grotesque, freakish, etc.

BIBLIOGRAPHY FOR THE SPEECH TO GAIN GOODWILL

Culp, Ralph Borden, Basic Types of Speech, Wm. C. Brown Company, Publishers, 1968, pp. 69-74.
Monroe, Alan H., and Ehninger, Douglas, Principles of Speech Communication, Scott, Foresman and Company, 6th brief ed., 1969, pp. 285-287.

Note: See page 80 for a speech to gain goodwill.

SPEECH OUTLINE

Construct a neat, complete sentence outline on this sheet, tear it out, and hand it to your instructor when you rise to speak. He may wish to write criticisms of the outline and speech in the margins.

Type of speech:_____   Name:_____

Number of words in outline:_____   Date:_____

Purpose of this speech: (What do you want your audience to learn, to think, to believe, to feel, or do because of this speech?)_____

_____

TITLE:

INTRODUCTION:

BODY:

CONCLUSION:

__Instructor's comments__ may concern choice of topic, development of ideas, organization, language use, personal appearance, posture, physical activity, sources, and improvement.

(Write sources of information on back of sheet)

SOURCES FROM LITERATURE

(Fill out source requirements completely. Write "none listed" if an author's name or copyright date is not listed.)

1. Author's name _____

    Title of book or magazine used _____

    Title of article in above book or magazine _____

    Chapter and/or pages read _____

    Date of above publication _____

2. Author's name _____

    Title of book or magazine used _____

    Title of article in above book or magazine _____

    Chapter and/or pages read _____

    Date of above publication _____

3. Author's name _____

    Title of book or magazine used _____

    Title of article in above book or magazine _____

    Chapter and/or pages read _____

    Date of above publication _____

INTERVIEW SOURCES

1. Person interviewed _____ Date of interview_____

    His position, occupation, and location _____

    Why is he a reliable source?   Be specific _____

    _____

2. Person interviewed _____ Date of interview_____

    His position, occupation, and location _____

    Why is he a reliable source?   Be specific _____

    _____

PERSONAL EXPERIENCE OF SPEAKER

1. Tell (1) when, (2) where, and (3) conditions under which you became an authority on subject matter in

    your speech _____

    _____

    _____

Chapter 16

THE INTRODUCTION SPEECH

This speech is due:
Time limits: 1-2 minutes.
Speaking notes: None.
Sources of information: They may be fictitious or real.
Outline your speech: Prepare a 50-100 word complete sentence outline. Designate the exact number of
    words in your outline. Use the form at the end of this chapter.

PURPOSE OF THE INTRODUCTION SPEECH
    Many untrained speakers are asked to give introduction speeches. Some of the introductions are well done; far too many are haphazard and embarrassing, because the person making the introduction is untrained. This brings criticism upon the person who must present a speaker and it also weakens programs that feature lecturers. Of all the types of speeches you may make in the future, it is probable that one of them will be the introduction of a featured speaker. This assignment will provide an introduction speech experience.

EXPLANATION OF THE INTRODUCTION SPEECH
    An introduction speech is one in which a chairman or other person introduces a speaker to an audience. The purpose is to bring an audience and speaker together in the proper spirit. Several of the requirements are that: the speech should be short; it should make the audience and speaker feel comfortably acquainted; it should interest the audience in the speaker and his subject; it should put the speaker at ease, announce his subject, and give his name.

    The introducer should avoid attempts at being funny. He should never embarrass the speaker either by heaping too much praise upon him or by belittling him. The person introducing a speaker should not call attention to himself nor say or do anything to detract from what the speaker plans to say. The person who once said, "Get up, speak up, shut up," probably was thinking of the individual who makes introduction speeches; and the introducer can hardly go wrong if he follows this advice.

    Occasions for the introduction speech arise every time a speaker is introduced. They probably number in the millions annually.

SUGGESTED INTRODUCTION SPEECHES
    1. Introduce your college president to a high school audience.
    2. Introduce the student body president to the freshman class.
    3. Introduce a lecturer to the student body.
    4. Introduce a lecturer to your class.
    5. Introduce the mayor to a public gathering.
    6. A famous explorer visits your school. Introduce him.
    7. Introduce a missionary at a religious meeting.
    8. A war hero speaks. Introduce him.
    9. A noted aviator speaks. Introduce him.
    10. A great inventor speaks. Introduce him.
    11. A famous scientist will lecture. Introduce him.
    12. The governor visits your city and school. Introduce him.
    13. A high government official is the speaker. Introduce him.
    14. Introduce a commencement speaker.
    15. Introduce a baccalaureate speaker.
    16. Introduce the valedictorian to an audience.
    17. Introduce any lecturer to a civic organization.
    18. Introduce a Hollywood celebrity to your school.
    19. Introduce a foreign speaker.
    20. Speaker's choice.

HOW TO CHOOSE AN INTRODUCTION SPEECH
    Look over the list of suggestions above. If you like one of the ideas, select it at once. If not, you may have some other topic which you prefer. In this case, make up your mind without delay and start thinking about your speech. You will have to decide for yourself as to the type of imaginary audience and

occasion you will use. You will also find it necessary to arrive at some decision concerning the specific person you plan to introduce. Be sure that your speaker is a suitable one for the occasion. Above all do not attempt to be different by improvising a speech built around a classmate whom you place in an impossible or ludicrous position. This will defeat you as a speaker and will not meet the assignment.

HOW TO PREPARE AN INTRODUCTION SPEECH

In preparing this speech you may draw your information from four sources: the speaker, his subject, the audience, or the occasion. Not all of these may be necessary in every speech; however, they are all often suitable if not required sources. You will not need much material, but that which you have must be accurate and pertinent. As for the speaker, get his name and be absolutely certain you have it right. Know how to pronounce it correctly. Discover any background the speaker has that should be known by the audience. This may concern his education, special training, travel experience, special honors, membership in organizations, important positions he has held, books he has written, or any other notable achievements. Of course, if he is a famous and well-known person, little need be said, possibly nothing. An example of the latter is the introduction often heard: "Ladies and gentlemen, the President." However, almost all speakers require more to be said than do the President of the United States, a governor or other high state official. You should know the title of the speaker's subject. As with his name, you must have it right. But you should say nothing about the speech that will tend to "steel the thunder" of his remarks. You should inquire thoroughly into the personnel of your audience so that you may adjust your remarks to them. The occasion of the address should be well known to you. From the four sources just mentioned and a fifth, yourself, you will construct your introduction speech. Short though this speech is to be, what you say must really "count." Thus, you must organize and arrange it carefully, selecting those bits of information that are most important.

Before you set your ideas, you should confer with the person you are going to introduce and, in conference, arrive at a definite understanding regarding what you plan to say in your introduction speech. After this point is decided, then rehearse aloud until you are confident that you are thoroughly prepared.

HOW TO PRESENT AN INTRODUCTION SPEECH

When the moment arrives for you to introduce the speaker of the evening, rise calmly, take your place on the platform, pause until the assembly grows quiet, and then deliberately address the audience in your normal voice, yet speak loudly enough for all to hear. Avoid straining or using greater force than is needed. You may say, "Ladies and gentlemen," or use some other salutation or form of introduction appropriate to the audience and the occasion.

Your bodily action and gesture will be limited. There will likely be no necessity for using either more than moderately. Your voice should be well modulated, the words spoken clearly, and your pronunciation correct - especially that of the speaker's name.

Keep in mind your part of the occasion. People did not come to hear you or see you. You are only a convenient but necessary cog in the events surrounding the speaker. Your poise and confidence and appropriate but brief remarks are all that are expected or wanted from you. You may greet the audience and mention the occasion, extend felicitations, and note the fact that there is an exceptionally good audience (if there is). If there is a poor audience, do not remark about it and do not make any apologies.

At the moment you present the speaker, announce his name and subject somewhat as follows: "I am happy to present Mr. A. who will address you (or speak to you) on _____(mention the subject)." Then turn to the speaker with the words, "Mr. A." You may bow slightly or nod and take your chair when he rises and approaches the front of the platform.

If you are chairman of the assembly, it will be appropriate for you to express publicly the appreciation of the audience to the speaker at the conclusion of his address.

IMPROVE YOUR VOCABULARY

Ephemeral - (ē-fĕm'ẽr-ăl) a. beginning and ending in a short period of time, say one day, existing or continuing for a short time only, transient, passing, fleeting, evanescent, momentary. Example: The book had only an ephemeral utility. Use ephemeral in this speech and five times a day for the next week. Make it work for you.

Good - Omit this word. Good is a bad word to overwork. Add color to your vocabulary by using synonyms. Examples: palatable, delicious, tempting, delectable, luscious, excellent, commendable, delightful, stimulating, well-made, exquisite, superior, creditable, valuable, meritorious, etc.

BIBLIOGRAPHY FOR THE INTRODUCTION SPEECH

Culp, Ralph Borden, Basic Types of Speech, Wm. C. Brown Company, Publishers, 1968, pp. 61-63.

Gilman, Wilbur E., and Others, An Introduction to Speaking, The Macmillan Company, 2d ed., 1968, pp. 38-41.

Hance, Kenneth G., and Others, Principles of Speaking, Wadsworth Publishing Company, Inc., 2d ed., 1969, pp. 321-322.

Monroe, Alan H., and Ehninger, Douglas, Principles of Speech Communication, Scott, Foresman and Company, 6th brief ed., 1969, pp. 281-282.

Nadeau, Ray E., A Basic Rhetoric of Speech Communication, Addison-Wesley Publishing Company, 1969, pp. 269-271.

Oliver, Robert T., and Cortright, R. L., Effective Speech, Holt, Rinehart and Winston, Inc., 5th ed., 1970, Chapter 23.

Oliver, Robert T., and Others, Communicative Speaking and Listening, Holt, Rinehart and Winston, Inc., 4th ed., 1968, pp. 304-305.

Ross, Raymond S., Speech Communication, Prentice-Hall, Inc., 2d ed., 1970, pp. 233-235.

Samovar, Larry, and Mills, Jack, Oral Communication, Message and Response, Wm. C. Brown Company, Publishers, 1968, pp. 204-205.

Williams, Barbara, Purposeful Communication, Kendall/Hunt Publishing Company, 1970, pp. 181-182.

INTRODUCTION SPEECH

(Introducing Coach Bob Dunkin to a High School Lettermen's Banquet)

By Brent Peterson

Principal Norton, coaches and lettermen of Valley High School. Meeting this evening as a group of athletes we all recall during many basketball games a most unforgettable shot, the "dunk." The gigantic pivot-men made it look simple, nevertheless the excitement came in watching the little fellow leap and stuff the ball through the hoop. It is a privilege to have with us such a man who thrilled many spectators. A little six-foot guard through hard work perfected the thrilling shot and became known as "Dunker" to match his own name, Bob Dunkin.

Bob, a three-year basketball letterman at Northside High in Kennington, attended banquets similar to this one. Upon receiving the free throw trophy after making seventy-six per cent of his free throws, at the banquet his junior year Bob announced, "Next year I'll shoot over ninety per cent." The following year persistent Bob made ninety-two per cent of his free throws due to his consistent practice during the summer. Coach Dunkin remembers well his high school experiences and conducts summer basketball camps to develop the abilities of young ball players because he is interested in them.

A competitive college athlete said, "You must always give one hundred per cent effort; if you don't, someone, somewhere will and he will beat you." "Dunker" Dunkin made that statement and has always gone the extra mile in all his life's endeavors and has rarely been beaten. At State U, "Dunker" was all-conference twice, led the conference in free-throw shooting and his team to a berth in the NCAA post season tournament. As Northside High coach his team lost only five times in three years and was rated number one in the state for two years. He has continued as an outstanding coach motivating athletes to their best performance. His teams have won 131 and lost 21 games during his five years at Southern State College. He's a winner.

Bob Dunkin's life is the story of persistence, hard work and success. It has been said, "No chance, no destiny, no fate can circumvent or hinder or control the firm resolve of a determined soul." Athletes, I want you to meet and hear this determined man who will speak to you concerning the value of reaching your own potential. Coach Dunkin.

SPEECH OUTLINE

Construct a neat, complete sentence outline on this sheet, tear it out, and hand it to your instructor when you rise to speak. He may wish to write criticisms of the outline and speech in the margins.

Type of speech:_____ Name:_____

Number of words in outline:_____ Date:_____

Purpose of this speech: (What do you want your audience to learn, to think, to believe, to feel, or do
                          because of this speech?)_____

_____

TITLE:

INTRODUCTION:

BODY:

CONCLUSION:

<u>Instructor's comments</u> may concern choice of topic, development of ideas, organization, language use, personal appearance, posture, physical activity, sources, and improvement.

(Write sources of information on back of sheet)

SOURCES FROM LITERATURE

(Fill out source requirements completely. Write "none listed" if an author's name or copyright date is not listed.)

1. Author's name _____

   Title of book or magazine used _____

   Title of article in above book or magazine _____

   Chapter and/or pages read _____

   Date of above publication _____

2. Author's name _____

   Title of book or magazine used _____

   Title of article in above book or magazine _____

   Chapter and/or pages read _____

   Date of above publication _____

3. Author's name _____

   Title of book or magazine used _____

   Title of article in above book or magazine _____

   Chapter and/or pages read _____

   Date of above publication _____

INTERVIEW SOURCES

1. Person interviewed _____ Date of interview_____

   His position, occupation, and location _____

   Why is he a reliable source? Be specific _____

   _____

2. Person interviewed _____ Date of interview_____

   His position, occupation, and location _____

   Why is he a reliable source? Be specific _____

   _____

PERSONAL EXPERIENCE OF SPEAKER

1. Tell (1) when, (2) where, and (3) conditions under which you became an authority on subject matter in your speech _____

   _____

   _____

Chapter 17

THE SPEECH OF WELCOME

This speech is due:
Time limits: 2-3 minutes.
Speaking notes: Do not use them. Be prepared.
Sources of information: None required. They may be real or fictitious.
Outline your speech: Prepare a 50-100 word complete sentence outline. Designate the exact number of
     words in your outline. Use the form at the end of this chapter.
To the teacher: It is a good practice to assign welcome speeches and speeches in response to a welcome
     to pairs of students because the latter speech is dependent upon the former.

PURPOSE OF THE SPEECH OF WELCOME

A speech of welcome is of sufficient importance that you should know how it is organized and what
it should do. It occupies a high place in speechmaking; upon its effectiveness hinges much of the success
of your public relations among groups that convene daily throughout the land. You may be asked to give a
speech of welcome in your own community at any time. It is not enough that you pass the request off lightly or refuse to assist in promoting goodwill because you do not know how to present a speech of welcome.
This assignment will provide the experience that will show you how to prepare and present a good speech
of welcome. Study it carefully.

EXPLANATION OF THE SPEECH OF WELCOME

A speech of welcome is one made to a single individual or to a group of individuals with the purpose
of extending greetings and promoting friendship. The person being welcomed should be made to feel that
he is sincerely wanted and that his hosts are delighted to have him among them. The warmest kind of hospitality should be expressed in the welcoming speech. Its genuineness should be so marked that the hearer
enjoys a spirit of gladness because he is the guest of a gracious host. The speech is characterized by
brevity, simplicity, geniality, and sincerity.

The occasions for the speech of welcome may be extremely varied. The occasion may be a recep-
tion for a distinguished visitor, for a native son returning, or for a total stranger. It may welcome home
a citizen from foreign travel, missionary work, diplomatic service, or business enterprise. It could welcome a school official, the new minister, or a county officer. If the occasion is to honor an organization,
the welcome may be for a delegation - such as an advertisers' club, a chamber of commerce, a booster
club, or a group of county, city, school, or community representatives. In some cases, the welcome may
be a special gesture to a conference or convention. But, whatever the occasion, the speech of welcome
plays a prominent part.

SUGGESTED SPEECHES OF WELCOME

Study the occasions listed below to discover which one interests you most.

1. Welcome a distinguished visitor.
2. A native son returns home.
3. A stranger visits a local civic organization.
4. A prominent citizen returns from foreign travel.
5. A successful diplomat pays your city a visit.
6. A missionary returns from foreign service.
7. A new minister comes to town.
8. A newly elected school superintendent arrives in your city.
9. A banquet is held for the new teachers.
10. A state official visits your community.
11. The governor stops over a few days on state business.
12. A neighboring city sends a friendly delegation.
13. A booster club visits your city.
14. An advertisers' club comes to your community.
15. A neighboring chamber of commerce is your guest.

16. A nearby city sends a delegation to study your community's excellent school system, water works, fire department . . .
17. An organization holds a convention in your city.
18. An important conference meets in your city.
19. A candidate for governor stops in your community.
20. Speaker's choice.

HOW TO CHOOSE A SPEECH OF WELCOME
Select the occasion that interests you most. Decide definitely the organization you will represent and what position you will hold in the organization. Select one that you know something about or one about which you can secure information. Do not procrastinate in making your decision. Study the list and make your choice or else set up your own occasion if none of the above suggestions suits you. The important point is do not put off your choice of occasion until the day before your speech is due.

HOW TO PREPARE A SPEECH OF WELCOME
First, fix your purpose in mind: you are to make your guests glad to be there. They should admire your hospitality. Next, get your information and set up your speech. Some suggestions follow. You may need to explain the organization which you represent. If so, mention its character, the work it is doing, and points of interest about it, including future plans. Pay a tribute to your guests for their work and tell of advantages gained by their visiting you. Note who the guests are, where they are from, and whom they represent. Explain briefly what their coming means and comment on the common interests your organization holds with them. You should speak of the occasion - its present enjoyment and its future importance. Express anticipated pleasant associations and mutual benefits which are to be derived from the meeting. Invite your guests to feel at home and participate fully in your community. Speak for those whom you represent.

Keep in mind the fact that not all of the above material is always needed in a speech of welcome. You will use only that which is appropriate and you will also adjust it to meet the occasion, whether it be for an individual or for a group of individuals.

Do not say too much or too little. There are plenty of the right thoughts to be expressed in a speech of welcome. Plan to make your remarks brief and to include the appropriate material. Considerable thought and organization will be required. Practice aloud until you have thoroughly mastered your material. Do not memorize the speech word for word.

HOW TO PRESENT A SPEECH OF WELCOME
Let the occasion govern your presentation. If it is formal, act and speak appropriately. If it is informal, adjust yourself and your remarks accordingly. In either case be sincere and genuine. Feel what you say. Give your guests a degree of hospitality and warmth of welcome which they will remember; however, do not overdo it and spoil the effectiveness of the speech. Portray the same gentility and friendliness that is present when you open the door of your home to a friend and invite him in.

Speak loudly enough to be heard. Use your normal voice. Speak clearly, pronounce all names distinctly and correctly, and smile pleasantly as is fitting.

Let your bodily action be appropriate to the occasion, the mood, and your remarks.

Your language should be simple, vivid, appropriate, and devoid of slang and redundancy.

Be brief in time used but complete in your welcome.

IMPROVE YOUR VOCABULARY
Succinct - (sŭk-sĭnkt') a. Succinct speech is compressed and frequently carries the impression of crispness. Concise, terse, short, brief, summary, laconic. Example: The speaker used rather succinct remarks when he became aroused. Use succinct in this speech and five times a day for the next week. Put it to work for you.

Hunch - Omit this word for a week or two. Use a synonym that enjoys more color and power. Example: premonition, intuition, presentiment, forewarning, omen, prevision, hallucination, etc.

BIBLIOGRAPHY FOR THE SPEECH OF WELCOME

Culp, Ralph Borden, Basic Types of Speech, Wm. C. Brown Company, Publishers, 1968, pp. 66-67.

Gilman, Wilbur E., and Others, An Introduction to Speaking, The Macmillan Company, 2d ed., 1968, pp. 38-42.

Hance, Kenneth G., and Others, Principles of Speaking, Wadsworth Publishing Company, Inc., 2d ed., 1969, pp. 324-325.

Kruger, Arthur N., Effective Speaking, A Complete Course, Van Nostrand Reinhold Company, 1970, pp. 558-561.

Monroe, Alan H., and Ehninger, Douglas, Principles of Speech Communication, Scott, Foresman and Company, 6th brief ed., 1969, pp. 282-283.

Oliver, Robert T., and Cortright, R. L., Effective Speech, Holt, Rinehart and Winston, Inc., 5th ed., 1970, Chapter 23.

Williams, Barbara, Purposeful Communication, Kendall/Hunt Publishing Company, 1970, pp. 185-186.

SPEECH OF WELCOME

By Nancy Ennis

Mayor Johnson, Mr. Raleigh, Commissioner Top, Ladies and Gentlemen. We are extremely honored to have with us today Atomic Energy Commissioner Frank Top who flew in from Washington D.C. early this morning in order to preside over a special meeting to preserve the Atomic Energy Commission (AEC) in Idaho. The meeting is scheduled for late tomorrow afternoon and is of vital importance to the future of Idaho, specifically the southeastern area. As most of us know, it has recently been under consideration to move the AEC desert site out of Idaho. This would, of course, greatly hinder the development and growth of businesses in the surrounding areas, since hundreds of AEC employees and their families would be forced to move. Commissioner Top has come here to talk with our various leaders and listen to our pleas. He will then fly back to Washington and take our stand in the discussions there.

In honor of Commissioner Top's visit several activities have been arranged, starting this afternoon with a small gathering of local AEC officials and their wives. Immediately following this event, a tour of the Power Burst Facility (PBF) project, directed by W. D. Ennis, will be taken, then a grand scale tour of the desert site will wind up today's activities.

Commissioner Top, a former Idahoan himself, will be given the key to the city in a public presentation to be held this evening, and he and his lovely wife, Jean, will be escorted to some of our town's high spots afterwards.

Idaho is always happy to welcome one of her own, and the various civic groups are planning a big AEC picnic scheduled for tomorrow noon at the TAUTPHUS Park picnic grounds. The Picnic is open for all AEC employees, their families and friends. Hopefully, Jean, Commissioner Top's lovely and charming wife will fry up a batch of her famous fried chicken. Everyone has heard so much about it and looks forward to at least a small sample.

Following our picnic, the meeting to discuss the AEC's future in Idaho will be held lasting several hours then exactly at 9:00 P.M. at the Country Club, a formal dinner dance is to be given in honor of Commissioner Top and his family. It is open to the public and everyone is welcome. It is hoped that Commissioner Top will be persuaded to give a small talk on some of the decisions he reached at the previous meeting. The evening will be climaxed by an award presented to Commissioner Top in token of Idaho's appreciation for his interest in the state's welfare.

The next two days will be busy, but Idaho wishes to welcome you, Commissioner Top, and to say thank you for coming.

SPEECH OUTLINE

Construct a neat, complete sentence outline on this sheet, tear it out, and hand it to your instructor when you rise to speak. He may wish to write criticisms of the outline and speech in the margins.

Type of speech:_____   Name:_____

Number of words in outline:_____   Date:_____

Purpose of this speech: (What do you want your audience to learn, to think, to believe, to feel, or do because of this speech?)_____

_____

TITLE:

INTRODUCTION:

BODY:

CONCLUSION:

<u>Instructor's comments</u> may concern choice of topic, development of ideas, organization, language use, personal appearance, posture, physical activity, sources, and improvement.

(Write sources of information on back of sheet)

SOURCES FROM LITERATURE

(Fill out source requirements completely. Write "none listed" if an author's name or copyright date is not listed.)

1. Author's name _____

    Title of book or magazine used _____

    Title of article in above book or magazine _____

    Chapter and/or pages read _____

    Date of above publication _____

2. Author's name _____

    Title of book or magazine used _____

    Title of article in above book or magazine _____

    Chapter and/or pages read _____

    Date of above publication _____

3. Author's name _____

    Title of book or magazine used _____

    Title of article in above book or magazine _____

    Chapter and/or pages read _____

    Date of above publication _____

INTERVIEW SOURCES

1. Person interviewed _____ Date of interview_____

    His position, occupation, and location _____

    Why is he a reliable source? Be specific _____

    _____

2. Person interviewed _____ Date of interview_____

    His position, occupation, and location _____

    Why is he a reliable source? Be specific _____

    _____

PERSONAL EXPERIENCE OF SPEAKER

1. Tell (1) when, (2) where, and (3) conditions under which you became an authority on subject matter in your speech _____

    _____

    _____

    _____

Chapter 18

THE RESPONSE TO A SPEECH OF WELCOME

This speech is due:

Time limits: 1-2 minutes.

Speaking notes: None. This will be impromptu on many occasions. When it is prepared it is so brief that no notes are needed.

Sources of information: None required. They may be real or fictitious.

Outline your speech: If this is a prepared response, construct a 40-75 word complete sentence outline. Designate the exact number of words in your outline. Use the form at the end of this chapter.

To the teacher: It is helpful to assign students in pairs to give speeches of welcome and response since the latter is dependent on the former. It is a good technique to assign impromptu as well as prepared response speeches. This can be accomplished by a mixed assignment or two separate assignments.

PURPOSE OF THE RESPONSE TO A SPEECH OF WELCOME

Throughout the land many organizations meet on various occasions when visitors are in attendance. Sometimes they just drop in as members of a national fraternal group. At other times they come, representing a similar organization, or they are guests at a convention at which a certain society may be host. On such occasions the visitors are welcomed by a speech. It is of course natural that a response to the welcome be made. Because you may at some time be asked to respond to a welcome speech, it is wise to study a speech of response. The purpose of this assignment is to acquaint you with this type of speech.

EXPLANATION OF THE RESPONSE TO A WELCOME

The speech in response to a welcome is simply a reply to the felicitations expressed by a host. Its purpose is to cement goodwill and friendship, and express these mutual feelings that exist between the groups. It is short, brief, courteous, and friendly. Often, the response is impromptu in nature - which places a burden of doing fast thinking and uttering logical thoughts on the person who presents it. It also demands sincerity and cordiality of manner from the speaker. Naturally, this implies ability and art in the speaking process.

Occasions for this speech occur any time a welcome is given, although a response speech is not always necessary. These occasions may be at conventions, meetings of civic, religious, educational, fraternal, and business organizations, and the like.

SUGGESTED SPEECHES OF RESPONSE

1. Respond to a Rotary Club welcome.
2. Respond to a Lions Club welcome or any other civic organization.
3. You are with a booster train; respond to your welcome.
4. You are a mayor visiting another city. Respond.
5. You are chief of police new to a city. Respond to your welcome.
6. You are a visiting student. Respond to a student council welcome.
7. You are a government official. Respond to a Farm Bureau welcome.
8. You are a student at a religious convention. Respond for your school.
9. You visit a neighboring school athletic council. Respond.
10. You are a teacher visiting another school. Respond to the principal's welcome.
11. You are a debater at a tournament. Respond for your squad.
12. Visit a new chapter of your fraternity. Respond to the president.
13. Visit a business similar to your own. Respond to the board of directors.
14. You are a new church member. Respond to a welcome at a dinner.
15. You are a new citizen. Respond to a welcome for newcomers at a dinner.
16. You join a new organization. Respond to their welcome.
17. You are a Hi-Y representative at a convention. Respond to a welcome for all representatives.
18. Visit a foreign country. Respond to a welcome at one of their schools.
19. You are a 4-H club member visiting a similar club. Respond to their welcome.
20. Speaker's choice.

HOW TO CHOOSE A TOPIC FOR A RESPONSE SPEECH

If you have been in a situation similar to one of those mentioned above, why not select it for your response? If not, choose a response situation that you believe you would enjoy. Your choice should hold an interest for you. Regardless of how apathetic you may be at the moment choose a topic for your response. Do not put off your choice of a topic, thinking it will be easier later on. As the time approaches for your speech, you may become panicky because you do not know what you will talk about. Such feelings of insecurity are to be expected if you have not selected your response-speech situation early enough.

HOW TO PREPARE A SPEECH OF RESPONSE

First, keep in mind the purpose of your talk, namely, to express your appreciation of the hospitality extended you and to strengthen mutual feelings of friendship. Second, follow an organization that permits use of good speech construction. Include an introduction and conclusion. Make your entire speech brief.

In general you will make the occasion of the welcome overshadow your own personality. Compliments proffered you may be adroitly yet easily directed to the occasion. More specifically, your remarks may be developed in the following manner. Address the host and those associated with him; acknowledge his greeting of welcome and the hospitality of the organization; and express sincere thanks for their courtesies. Extend greetings from your organization and show how the occasion is mutually advantageous to the host and your group. Explain briefly what your organization is, what it stands for. Mention the benefits to be derived from the attitude of mutual helpfulness and enjoyment which are prevalent at this meeting. Predict future pleasant associations with the host organization, showing this acquaintance to be only a beginning of a long-lasting cooperation and friendship. Mention in conclusion that you have been made to feel most welcome and at home. Thank your hosts again for their hospitality, extend best wishes, and then be seated.

This speech may have to be impromptu. Because of the frequent possibility of impromptu speeches of response, you should set up a basic sequence of ideas which you can use in replying to any speech of welcome. Of course, if you are designated ahead of time to present the speech, you should carefully organize and rehearse your speech until you have it well in mind. Under either circumstance, you can be prepared if you give attention to the points presented in the preceding paragraphs.

HOW TO PRESENT A RESPONSE SPEECH

Your attitude and demeanor must be a happy combination of appreciation and friendliness. Your remarks must have the qualities of sincerity and gratitude. The only way to reach these ends is to demonstrate them through appropriate bodily actions and a simple understandable language. There is no call for ostentation, sarcasm, bragging, or for any attempt to show off your personal qualities.

When you are presented by your host, rise politely, smile pleasantly, and begin your response. Avoid scraping your chair if you are at a table, or playing with the dinnerware if it lies before you. Maintain your poise by observing an alert posture. Make yourself heard by all but do not shout or speak overly loud. Adhere to the policy of brevity but do not give the appearance of having nothing to say. When you have finished the speech, sit down. Remember that you are still under observation.

Here are a few additional suggestions:

Be sure that your speech is appropriate to the audience and the occasion. If the occasion is formal, conduct yourself accordingly; if it is not formal, adjust yourself to this situation.

Have a few serious thoughts in your speech, even though gaiety fills the air. Do not resort to telling nothing more than a series of stories or anecdotes.

Do not apologize or attempt the trite pose of your being surprised. You should know that as a guest you are subject to being called on at any time. Accept your responsibility and meet it as a mature person by having something worthwhile to say.

IMPROVE YOUR VOCABULARY

Invidious - (ĭn-vĭd'i-ŭs) a.   Tending to cause ill will or envy, likely to offend, disagreeable, un-
justly and irritatingly discriminating, hateful.   Example: The invidious distinctions between
classes in America is a national problem.

Mighty - Try not to use mighty for several days. You probably rely on it too much. Liven up your
speech with synonyms. Examples are: extremely, overwhelmingly, highly, inordinately, im-
moderately, exasperatingly, preposterously, excessively, enormously, remarkably, notably,
signally, incredibly, stupendously, etc.

BIBLIOGRAPHY FOR THE RESPONSE TO A SPEECH OF WELCOME

Culp, Ralph Borden, Basic Types of Speech, Wm. C. Brown Company, Publishers, 1968, pp. 68-69.
Gilman, Wilbur E., and Others, An Introduction to Speaking, The Macmillan Company, 2d ed., 1968,
pp. 38-42.
Monroe, Alan H., and Ehninger, Douglas, Principles of Speech Communication, Scott, Foresman
and Company, 6th brief ed., 1969, pp. 282-283.
Oliver, Robert T., and Cortright, R. L., Effective Speech, Holt, Rinehart and Winston, Inc., 5th ed.,
1970, Chapter 23.
Williams, Barbara, Purposeful Communication, Kendall/Hunt Publishing Company, 1970, pp. 185-187.

RESPONSE TO A SPEECH OF WELCOME

By Craig W. Wallin

Miss Ennis, Mayor Johnson, distinguished members of the Chamber of Commerce, ladies and
gentlemen. When Jean and I boarded the plane this morning in Washington, I said this was going to be a
good day. Your sincere kindness and true Western hospitality have really proved it so, and we both thank
you.

I only regret that my return to the great state of Idaho carries with it the dark cloud of what the
future may bring . . . the closing of the Atomic Energy Commission's facility in this area. I realize what
storms this cloud could cause, thus I have come to gather evidence for our case of preservation. It is both
enlightening and encouraging to view the faces of you people, obviously and genuinely concerned about the
welfare of this fine community's todays and tomorrows. I assure you, we are both united in our cause.
Your interests are high, as evidenced by this fine turn out this morning. My interests are exemplified by
the fact I am here.

You have made my return to Idaho a proud and memorable experience. I hope to meet most, if not
all of you personally in my brief but important stay in your city, and I imagine I will with all the activities
you have planned. I don't mind telling you either, I'm looking eagerly forward to the picnic. Again I
express deepest appreciation from Jean and myself.

SPEECH OUTLINE

Construct a neat, complete sentence outline on this sheet, tear it out, and hand it to your instructor when you rise to speak. He may wish to write criticisms of the outline and speech in the margins.

Type of speech:_____ Name:_____

Number of words in outline:_____ Date:_____

Purpose of this speech: (What do you want your audience to learn, to think, to believe, to feel, or do because of this speech?)_____

_____

TITLE:

INTRODUCTION:

BODY:

CONCLUSION:

Instructor's comments may concern choice of topic, development of ideas, organization, language use, personal appearance, posture, physical activity, sources, and improvement.

(Write sources of information on back of sheet)

SOURCES FROM LITERATURE

(Fill out source requirements completely. Write "none listed" if an author's name or copyright date is not listed.)

1. Author's name _____

   Title of book or magazine used _____

   Title of article in above book or magazine _____

   Chapter and/or pages read _____

   Date of above publication _____

2. Author's name _____

   Title of book or magazine used _____

   Title of article in above book or magazine _____

   Chapter and/or pages read _____

   Date of above publication _____

3. Author's name _____

   Title of book or magazine used _____

   Title of article in above book or magazine _____

   Chapter and/or pages read _____

   Date of above publication _____

INTERVIEW SOURCES

1. Person interviewed _____ Date of interview_____

   His position, occupation, and location _____

   Why is he a reliable source? Be specific _____

   _____

2. Person interviewed _____ Date of interview_____

   His position, occupation, and location _____

   Why is he a reliable source? Be specific _____

   _____

PERSONAL EXPERIENCE OF SPEAKER

1. Tell (1) when, (2) where, and (3) conditions under which you became an authority on subject matter in your speech _____

   _____

   _____

   _____

Chapter 19

PRESENTING A GIFT OR AWARD

This speech is due:
Time limits: 1-3 minutes.
Speaking notes: None.
Sources of information: None required. They may be real or fictitious.
Outline your speech: Prepare a 50-75 word complete sentence outline. Designate the exact number of words in your outline. Use the form at the end of this chapter.

PURPOSE OF THE SPEECH EXPERIENCE OF PRESENTING A GIFT OR AWARD
Many centuries ago, ancient peoples presented gifts and awards. The practice continues today without abatement. Every time the occasion of presenting a gift or award occurs, someone must make the presentation speech. It is not easy to make a public presentation graciously, to handle the situation with ease, and to utter thoughts that symbolize the spirit of the event. Yet, at any time you may be designated to perform this task. When this necessity does arise, you should know something about making a presentation speech. This assignment will tell what to do and say on such an occasion.

To the teacher: It might be wise to assign students in pairs, one to present an award, the other to receive it. This provides an excellent experience. See the following chapter.

EXPLANATION OF THE PRESENTATION SPEECH
A presentation speech is one made in conjunction with the presentation of an award or gift. It is short, sincere, and commendatory of the recipient. It requires tact and good taste because of divided attitudes towards the recipient of the award. Too much nor too little should be said about the recipient, because others, no doubt, are just as worthy of the award or gift as he is. Intense rivalry may have been present in seeking the award. Feelings and emotions may have been high. To understand the tenor of the audience, to avoid embarrassing the winner, and to use a language appreciated by all or even a majority requires a simple yet artistic quality of speech.

Occasions for this type of speech vary. One of these occurs when a prize is won in a contest. Here the prize is known beforehand; for this reason there is no surprise relative to what it will be. There will be partisan desire, expectancy, uncertainty, and even divided opinion among the judges regarding the winner. This poses a delicate problem for the speaker who makes the presentation - which may be formal. Emphasis will be placed upon interest, the careful consideration of the judges, and their delicate position.

Another occasion is one in which an object is given to an organization, such as a school, church, city, society, or other group. It is likely that the whole atmosphere will be formal. The procedures, plans, and persons who participate will be known long before the actual donation takes place. There will be no surprise. The speech will be pointed to emphasize the symbolism or utility of the gift.

A third occasion involves awarding a medal or other recognition for service. The surprise element may or may not be present. Depending on the occasion and the type of recognition, much emotion may be present. The ceremony and speech should not make it difficult for the recipient. The deed will obscure the gift, although tribute will be paid the one who is honored. During times of national crisis or emergency, this is a frequent occasion for presentations.

A fourth kind of award is one made in appreciation of service. Surprise is often present. There is no rivalry, but rather good fellowship and possibly a little sadness. Examples of this kind of award are the retirement of a president or other official from a society, a school or civic organization, the leave taking of a pastor, or the departure of any prominent citizen from community or group service. Here, emphasis is placed on the happy side of joyful fellowship. Some regret for the departure is expressed, but hope for the future is given a prominent place.

SUGGESTED TYPES OF PRESENTATION SPEECHES
Construct a short speech around one of the following occasions:
1. Present a scholarship.
2. Present a cash prize to an essay contest winner.
3. Present a cup to a beauty contest winner.
4. Present a cup to the winner of·a tournament.

5. Present a cash prize to the winner of a sales contest.
6. Present an organ to a church.
7. Present a set of books to a library.
8. Present a swimming pool to a city.
9. Present $5000 to the college to apply on a new building.
10. Present a safe-driving award.
11. Present a medal for good conduct.
12. Present a medal for meritorious service during a fire.
13. Present a medal for outstanding leadership in the community.
14. Present an award for making a new scientific discovery.
15. Present an award to a retiring school official.
16. Present an award to the oldest employee in a business.
17. Present an award to an employee with the longest tenure.
18. Present an award to a minister who is leaving.
19. Present an award to the head of a business firm.
20. Speaker's choice.

HOW TO CHOOSE A TOPIC

Study the above list carefully. The suggestions represent different occasions for gifts or awards. Choose one that you would like to present by visualizing the occasion and ceremony. Make your choice without long delay so that you may adequately prepare your speech.

HOW TO PREPARE A PRESENTATION SPEECH

In preparing this speech, make certain that you are fully aware of the occasion and any particular requirements governing it or the presentation. Keep in mind that it is an honor to present a gift or award, that it is not an opportunity to make a speech on your pet subject. By all means observe proper speech construction.

In preparing your talk, there are several predominating thoughts to bear in mind. First, do not overpraise the individual or the person. Overpraise will do more harm than good. Second, it is desirable to pay deserving tribute to the recipient, if wise restraint is exercised. Third, be careful not to over-emphasize the gift or its value. Stress instead the work or merit which the award signifies. Let glory abide in achievement, not in the material object.

Briefly, your specific organization of ideas may fall into the following sequence: Make appropriate remarks to the audience; let these remarks refer to the occasion that brought them together. Relate a short history of the event that is now being fittingly culminated. Give the immediate reasons for the award and show that, regardless of its value, the award is only a token of the real appreciation for the service rendered or the esteem felt for the recipient of the award.

As for the recipient, recount his personal worth and tell how this worth was recognized or discovered. If you personally know him, mention the fact that you are intimately aware of his service or merit.

Next, explain the character and purpose of the gift or award. Should the object be a picture or statue, the custom is to have it veiled until the speech is concluded or nearly concluded; then at the proper moment withdraw the veil. If the gift or award is to be presented to an organization, the ceremony will go more smoothly if someone is informed ahead of time that he is to represent his group in receiving the gift.

Prepare your ideas by rehearsing aloud until you have them thoroughly in mind. Do not memorize your speech but be sure to know what you are going to say.

HOW TO PRESENT A PRESENTATION SPEECH

Your attitude and manner must convey the sincerity behind the entire occasion. There must be no ostentation, show, or flamboyancy in your speech or actions.

Be sure that the award or gift is available and ready to be presented. When the moment arrives for you to transfer the award or gift to the donee, call him to the platform. If he is already there, address him by name so that he may rise in response. Then, in a few words properly chosen, present the gift by summarizing the reasons for the presentation. Mention the appropriateness of the award and offer the recipient good wishes for the future. After the recipient has accepted the object, permit him time to thank you or make other remarks to you or to the people gathered around. An acceptance speech will be in order.

A few technicalities to observe are these: Be sure you stand so that the audience can see and hear you. Do not stand in front of the gift. Let the audience see it. Near the conclusion of your speech, when you are ready to make the presentation, pick up the gift or award, being particular to hold it so that it is clearly visible to everyone. Stand at an angle with your side slightly toward the audience. Hand the gift to the recipient by using the hand nearest to him (the upstage hand). He will in turn accept it with his upstage hand. If it is a medal you wish to pin to his coat, stand with your side to the audience while pinning it on. Should the object be a picture, statue, or other material which cannot be transferred from hand to hand, it will of course be unveiled or shown at the moment of presentation.

Be sure you speak loudly enough to be heard by all, especially when you are turned partially away from the audience.

IMPROVE YOUR VOCABULARY

Summary - (sŭm'a-rĭ) a. Done at once without delay or formality, executed quickly. Example: The man was dealt a summary punishment. Use this word five times a day for the next week so that you can add to your verbal tools.

Interesting - Try omitting this word. You probably work it too much. Use a synonym. Examples are: amusing, entertaining, diverting, fascinating, unusual, curious, exceptional, unique, remarkable, fantastic, bizarre, exotic, unconventional, etc.

BIBLIOGRAPHY FOR PRESENTING A GIFT OR AWARD

Culp, Ralph Borden, Basic Types of Speech, Wm. C. Brown Company, Publishers, 1968, pp. 63-64.

Gilman, Wilbur E., and Others, An Introduction to Speaking, The Macmillan Company, 2d ed., 1968, pp. 38-43.

Hance, Kenneth G., and Others, Principles of Speaking, Wadsworth Publishing Company, Inc., 2d ed., 1969, pp. 325-326.

Monroe, Alan H., and Ehninger, Douglas, Principles of Speech Communication, Scott, Foresman and Company, 6th brief ed., 1969, pp. 282-285.

Oliver, Robert T., and Cortright, R. L., Effective Speech, Holt, Rinehart and Winston, Inc., 5th ed., 1970, Chapter 23.

Ross, Raymond S., Speech Communication, Prentice-Hall, Inc., 2d ed., 1970, pp. 236-237.

Williams, Barbara, Purposeful Communication, Kendall/Hunt Publishing Company, 1970, pp. 182-183.

SPEECH PRESENTING A GIFT OR AWARD

(Mayor of the community is the speaker)

By Jacque Larson

Fellow members of our community and guests. We have come together this afternoon for the summation of a task we undertook a month ago. As a group we felt the need to assist a fellow citizen and his family who have been a great asset to our community. They are very friendly people with a gift for laughter even when times are bad. They are always ready to help others in time of need thus we are privileged to return their kindness when they need it most.

As we all know their home was destroyed by fire one month ago leaving the family destitute, and although everyone was very generous at that time now is when they again need help. For this reason it was through cooperation of the community that a fund drive was held to raise money for a new home and I am pleased to say your cooperation was magnificient.

Mr. Smith, would you please step forward.

(Mr. Smith walks to the front)

You were the victim of unfavorable circumstances which the community has recognized. We would like you to accept this check for five hundred dollars which will aid in purchasing a new home for your family. This is just a small token of our appreciation for being good neighbors and fellow community members. If we cannot help one another in time of need what good are neighbors?

Mr. Smith, would you say a few words please and then introduce your family.

SPEECH OUTLINE

Construct a neat, complete sentence outline on this sheet, tear it out, and hand it to your instructor when you rise to speak. He may wish to write criticisms of the outline and speech in the margins.

Type of speech:_____ Name:_____

Number of words in outline:_____ Date:_____

Purpose of this speech: (What do you want your audience to learn, to think, to believe, to feel, or do because of this speech?)_____

_____

TITLE:

INTRODUCTION:

BODY:

CONCLUSION:

<u>Instructor's comments</u> may concern choice of topic, development of ideas, organization, language use, personal appearance, posture, physical activity, sources, and improvement.

(Write sources of information on back of sheet)

SOURCES FROM LITERATURE

(Fill out source requirements completely. Write "none listed" if an author's name or copyright date is not listed.)

1. Author's name _____

   Title of book or magazine used _____

   Title of article in above book or magazine _____

   Chapter and/or pages read _____

   Date of above publication _____

2. Author's name _____

   Title of book or magazine used _____

   Title of article in above book or magazine _____

   Chapter and/or pages read _____

   Date of above publication _____

3. Author's name _____

   Title of book or magazine used _____

   Title of article in above book or magazine _____

   Chapter and/or pages read _____

   Date of above publication _____

INTERVIEW SOURCES

1. Person interviewed _____ Date of interview_____

   His position, occupation, and location _____

   Why is he a reliable source? Be specific _____

   _____

2. Person interviewed _____ Date of interview_____

   His position, occupation, and location _____

   Why is he a reliable source? Be specific _____

   _____

PERSONAL EXPERIENCE OF SPEAKER

1. Tell (1) when, (2) where, and (3) conditions under which you became an authority on subject matter in

   your speech _____

   _____

   _____

   _____

Chapter 20

ACCEPTING A GIFT OR AWARD

This speech is due:
Time limits: 1-2 minutes.
Speaking notes: None. Your remarks will be impromptu or, if not, then very brief.
Sources of information: None required. They may be real or fictitious.
Outline your speech: If this is not impromptu, prepare a 50-75 word complete sentence outline. Designate the exact number of words in your outline. Use the form at the end of this chapter.

PURPOSE OF THE SPEECH OF ACCEPTANCE OF A GIFT OR AWARD

Because untold numbers of presentation speeches for gifts and awards are made every year, we are justified in assuming that almost as many acceptance speeches are made by the persons who are honored with the awards. The custom is as old as the centuries. The recipient is not always told in advance that he will be honored by a gift or award; hence he can be embarrassed if he does not know how to accept the honor with simple sincerity. This speech experience will provide you a definite background for such an event; for this reason it is important.

To the teacher: It is a practical experience to assign this speech in conjunction with the one entitled "Presenting a Gift or Award." See the preceding chapter.

EXPLANATION OF THE ACCEPTANCE SPEECH

A speech made by the receiver of a gift or award is a sincere expression of his appreciation of the honor accorded him. It should establish him as a friendly, modest, and worthwhile individual to whom the people may rightfully pay tribute for merit and achievement. Its purpose should be to impress the donors with his worthiness and to make them happy in their choice. To do this will demand a gentility and nobleness that springs naturally from the heart of the receiver. There can be no artificial or hollow remarks uttered by a shallow mind.

It should be noted that in some instances no speech is necessary; the only essential propriety being a pleasant "thank you," accompanied by an appreciative smile. To do more than this when it is not appropriate to do so is awkward. However, when a speech is in order, it must be propitious. The recipient himself must decide on each occasion whether or not a speech is wanted or needed.

Occasions for acceptance speeches arise, potentially, every time an award or gift is presented. They occur in schools, clubs, societies, civic and religious organizations, business houses, government offices, . . . Any of these groups may wish to honor a member of their organization, another organization, or someone else for service, merit, achievement or winning a prize. Possibilities for presentations and their accompanying speeches are unlimited.

SUGGESTIONS FOR ACCEPTANCE SPEECHES
1. Accept a scholarship.
2. Accept a prize for writing poetry.
3. Accept a cup for winning a swimming contest.
4. Accept a prize for raising superior livestock.
5. Accept a prize for winning a golf match.
6. Accept a donation for a church.
7. Accept a donation of funds for the new ball park.
8. Accept a new cabin for the Boy Scouts.
9. Accept a cup for the debate team or some other team.
10. Accept a medal for saving a life.
11. Accept a medal for rescuing a drowning person.
12. Accept a medal for outstanding community service.
13. Accept a prize for a new invention.
14. Accept an award for long service on a particular job.
15. Accept an award for outstanding performance of duty.
16. Accept a prize for your school for winning a contest.
17. As captain of your basketball team accept a championship award.
18. Accept a birthday gift.
19. Accept a retirement award.
20. Speaker's choice.

HOW TO CHOOSE A TOPIC FOR AN ACCEPTANCE SPEECH

Study the above suggestions. Select the one you would like most to receive. Do not delay making a choice.

HOW TO PREPARE AN ACCEPTANCE SPEECH

This speech will necessarily be impromptu on some occasions; hence little preparation can be made other than by formulating a basic pattern of ideas about which you will speak. If you are warned or informed early that you will receive a gift or award, then, of course, you should certainly prepare a speech. In this case all the principles of good speech construction and organization should be followed. However, in either case, there are several important points to be noted: First, utilize simple language, without show or sham. Second, express in your initial remarks a true sense of gratitude and appreciation for the gift. If you are really surprised, you may say so; however, the surprise must be genuine. If you are not surprised, omit any reference to your feeling. No one will be moved by an attempt at naivete. Next, you should modestly disclaim total credit for winning the award. Give credit to those who assisted you in any way, for without them you could not have achieved your success. Praise their cooperation and support. Do not apologize for winning. Do not disclaim your worthiness. Inasmuch as you were selected to receive a tribute, be big enough to accept it modestly and graciously, but not grovelingly. Your next point may be the expression of appreciation for the beauty and significance of the gift. Its nature and kind will determine what you say. Do not overpraise it or over value it. Observe suitable restraint. In no manner should you express disappointment. Conclude your remarks by speaking of your plans or intentions for the future, especially as they may be connected with the award or gift or work associated with it. As a final word you may repeat your thanks for the object or recognition.

HOW TO PRESENT AN ACCEPTANCE SPEECH

Your attitude must be one of sincerity, friendliness, appreciation, modesty, and warm enthusiasm. Conceit and ego must be entirely lacking. You should be personal, if the award is for you. If you represent a group, use the pronoun "we" instead of "I."

When the donor speaks to you, either come to the platform or rise and step towards him if you are already there. Should you approach from the audience, move forward politely and alertly. Neither hurry nor loiter. Let your bearing be one of appreciation for what is to come. Arriving on the platform, stand near the donor but avoid viewing the award anxiously or reaching for it before it is extended to you. Do not stand in front of it. In accepting the award stand slightly sideways toward the audience, reach for and receive the object in the hand nearest the other person (this will be the upstage hand); in this way you avoid reaching in front of yourself or turning your body away from the audience. After receiving the object, hold it so it remains in full view of the audience. If it is too large to hold, place it in an appropriate spot on stage, step to one side and begin your speech; that is, if a speech is in accord with the proceedings and occasion. If you return to a seat in the audience, carry the gift in your hand, do not stuff it into a pocket if it is a small object.

Now as to the speech itself. Observe all the elements of acceptable stage presence. Be dressed appropriately, maintain an alert and polite posture, speak clearly and distinctly and loudly enough to be heard by all. If your speech is impromptu, you will not be expected to possess the fluency of one who was forewarned of the occasion. Insofar as is possible, let your manner express an undeniable friendliness and appreciation for the honor being accorded you. This sincerity is the most important part of your speech. It will have to be evident in your voice, your bodily actions, your gestures, the look on your face, everything about you. Be sure to express no shame. Do not be afraid of a little emotion; just control it so that you are not overcome by it. Make no apologies for your speaking. Avoid awkward positions that are indicative of too much self-consciousness. Do these things and your acceptance will be genuine and applauded by all who see and hear you.

IMPROVE YOUR VOCABULARY

Anomaly - (ȧ-nŏm'ȧ-lĭ) n. Deviation from the ordinary, irregularity, unnaturalness, abnormality, singularity, uniqueness, peculiarity, strangeness. Example: The sudden volcanic eruption was a great anomaly of nature. Use this word five times a day for the next week so that you may claim it for your own.

Mad - Let's use synonyms for this overworked language slave. Examples are: deluded, frustrated, insane, frenzied, annoyed, disappointed, chagrined, dismayed, irritated, disconcerted, confused, cross, peevish, ill-natured, touchy, crusty, testy, irascible, furious, enraged, etc.

BIBLIOGRAPHY FOR ACCEPTING A GIFT OR AWARD

Culp, Ralph Borden, Basic Types of Speech, Wm. C. Brown Company, Publishers, 1968, pp. 65-66.

Gilman, Wilbur E., and Others, An Introduction to Speaking, The Macmillan Company, 2d ed., 1968, pp. 38-43.

Hance, Kenneth G., and Others, Principles of Speaking, Wadsworth Publishing Company, Inc., 2d ed., 1969, pp. 326-327.

Monroe, Alan H., and Ehninger, Douglas, Principles of Speech Communication, Scott, Foresman and Company, 6th brief ed., 1969, pp. 282-285.

Oliver, Robert T., and Cortright, R. L., Effective Speech, Holt, Rinehart and Winston, Inc., 5th ed., 1970, Chapter 23.

Williams, Barbara, Purposeful Communication, Kendall/Hunt Publishing Company, 1970, pp. 183-185.

SPEECH ACCEPTING A GIFT OR AWARD

(A five hundred dollar check is accepted)

By Barbara Clifford

Mayor Chandler, and fellow members of the community. It is very difficult to express the appreciation I feel in my heart for what you people are doing today. It is true that we have suffered an unfortunate circumstance. However, it is living in a community such as this and having neighbors like you people that give us the strength to work and keep our faith in spite of unfortunate happenings. We are planning to start construction of a new home shortly and this check for five hundred dollars will be of untold assistance. I want you to know we will think of you as each nail is driven and as each room is completed. When our house is finished and we can enjoy the comfort and warmth you have helped us obtain we most certainly will ask you to join us in a house warming celebration that you, our good neighbors, will have made possible. We thank you all with sincere and heart-felt feelings. At this time I would like to introduce my family who, I know, share in everything I have said here today. My wife, Mary, son Glen, and daughters Susan, Carolyn and Denise. Again, I say thank you and we hope we will be able to repay your kindness in some small way as time goes along.

SPEECH OUTLINE

Construct a neat, complete sentence outline on this sheet, tear it out, and hand it to your instructor when you rise to speak. He may wish to write criticisms of the outline and speech in the margins.

Type of speech:_____ Name:_____

Number of words in outline:_____ Date:_____

Purpose of this speech: (What do you want your audience to learn, to think, to believe, to feel, or do because of this speech?)_____

_____

TITLE:

INTRODUCTION:

BODY:

CONCLUSION:

Instructor's comments may concern choice of topic, development of ideas, organization, language use, personal appearance, posture, physical activity, sources, and improvement.

(Write sources of information on back of sheet)

SOURCES FROM LITERATURE

(Fill out source requirements completely. Write "none listed" if an author's name or copyright date is not listed.)

1. Author's name _____

   Title of book or magazine used _____

   Title of article in above book or magazine _____

   Chapter and/or pages read _____

   Date of above publication _____

2. Author's name _____

   Title of book or magazine used _____

   Title of article in above book or magazine _____

   Chapter and/or pages read _____

   Date of above publication _____

3. Author's name _____

   Title of book or magazine used _____

   Title of article in above book or magazine _____

   Chapter and/or pages read _____

   Date of above publication _____

INTERVIEW SOURCES

1. Person interviewed _____ Date of interview_____

   His position, occupation, and location _____

   Why is he a reliable source? Be specific _____

   _____

2. Person interviewed _____ Date of interview_____

   His position, occupation, and location _____

   Why is he a reliable source? Be specific _____

   _____

PERSONAL EXPERIENCE OF SPEAKER

1. Tell (1) when, (2) where, and (3) conditions under which you became an authority on subject matter in

   your speech _____

   _____

   _____

   _____

Chapter 21

THE FAREWELL SPEECH

This speech is due:

Time limits: 4-5 minutes.

Speaking notes: Do not use any for this speech.

Sources of information: None required. They may be real or fictitious.

Outline your speech: Prepare a 75-150 word complete sentence outline. Designate the exact number of words in your outline. Use the form at the end of this chapter.

PURPOSE OF THE FAREWELL SPEECH

Many times a person finds himself the guest of honor in which his business or social friends entertain him at a farewell party; or they may simply "call a group together" as a final gesture of their esteem and admiration for him. The guest of honor is invariably asked to say a few words as a last expression before he leaves. Too often, what he says may be only a mumbling of incoherent remarks, because he has never had a previous experience of this kind and does not know what is appropriate at such a time. This speech assignment will give you an experience that will point the way when you are called upon to make a farewell speech.

EXPLANATION OF THE FAREWELL SPEECH

A farewell speech is one in which a person publicly says goodbye to a group of acquaintances. It should express the speaker's appreciation for what his acquaintances have helped him accomplish and for the happiness they have brought him. It may be given at a formal or informal gathering, a luncheon or a dinner. Frequently, on this occasion, the guest of honor will receive a gift from the group. A common informal party occurs when "the boss," a superior, or some other leader calls an informal meeting following the day's work, at which time the person who is leaving will receive commendation, favorable testimonials, and possibly a gift. He will, too, be expected to "say something." The formal occasion is, of course, much more elaborate and is surrounded by formalities from start to finish.

Occasions for the farewell speech are of one general kind - leave taking. Situations may vary greatly; however, a few of the usual ones are the following: retirement after years of service in a certain employment; taking a new job; promotion to a different type of work that demands a change in location; concluding service in a civic or religious organization; leaving school; or moving to another community for any reason whatsoever.

The occasion, whatever its nature, should not be treated with too much sadness. It should be approached with true sincerity and honesty. Feelings of deep emotion may be present, and if so, they should be expressed in a manner in keeping with the occasion and all persons present.

SUGGESTED OCCASIONS FOR A FAREWELL SPEECH

1. Leaving school.
2. Going off to college.
3. Joining the Armed Services.
4. Moving to a new location - any reason.
5. Taking a new job elsewhere.
6. Retiring from employment after twenty years.
7. Retiring from a church position.
8. Retiring from a civic position.
9. Going back home after completing a year's job.
10. Leaving a community where you were "stationed" on a job.
11. Just married - moving away.
12. Going to Hollywood to try your hand at motion pictures.
13. Going on a two year's tour around the world.
14. Going to Africa to do research on tropical diseases.
15. Leaving for South America to hunt oil.
16. Leaving for the South Pole on a trip of exploration.
17. Going to New York to become an actor.
18. Going to Central America to survey jungle lands.
19. Leaving on a rocket for the moon.
20. Speaker's choice.

HOW TO CHOOSE A TOPIC

First of all, is there any one of these topics that really compels your interest? If so, select it. If not, choose the one that interests you most. Perhaps no suggestion suits you. In this event think of situations similar to some of those mentioned and then formulate your own topic. Do not postpone your selection because you cannot make up your mind. Get a topic now; begin thinking about its organization and development. Above all things, do not try to excuse yourself from making a selection now or in the very near future. This will only mean less time in which to prepare your speech.

HOW TO PREPARE A FAREWELL SPEECH

Remember that this is a special occasion and that old friends are honoring you. Remember, too, that there may be an atmosphere of considerable sentiment and emotion, or there may be one merely of friendly gaiety. This means you must carefully analyze your audience, their probable mood, and the general atmosphere. If you are likely to be presented a gift, plan your remarks so that you may accept it graciously. Sincerity must dominate your utterances whatever they may be.

Farewell speeches usually follow a well-defined pattern with appropriate variations which the speaker deems necessary. It is advisable to begin your talk by referring to the past, the time when you first arrived and why you came to the community. A bit of humor of some interesting anecdotes may be in good taste. The way you were made welcome or to feel at home might be an excellent recollection. Continue your thoughts by pointing out how your ideals and those of the audience, though not completely attained, inspired you to do what you did, that work remains still to be done. Express appreciation for their support of your efforts which made your achievements possible. Commend the harmony and cooperation that prevailed. Tell them that you will always remember your associations with this group as one of the outstanding events in your life. Speak next of your future work briefly but sincerely. Explain why you are leaving, and what compelled you to go into a new field or location. Show that your work just completed will act as a background and inspiration to that which lies ahead. Continue by encouraging those who remain, predict greater achievements for them, praise your successor if you know who he is, and conclude with a genuine expression of your appreciation for them and a continued interest in their future. Remember, if you received a gift, to give a final word of thanks for it.

In your speech omit any and all references or allusions to unpleasantries or friction that may have existed. Do not make the occasion bitter or sad. Be happy and leave others with the same feeling. Smile. Make sure that a good impression will follow you.

Organize and practice this speech far enough in advance that you can conscientiously present it as representative of your best work.

HOW TO PRESENT A FAREWELL SPEECH

In this speech fit your manner to the mood of the occasion and audience. Do not go overboard in solemnity, emotion, or gaiety. Be appropriate. Use a friendly and sincere approach throughout. Adjust your introductory remarks to the prevailing mood; then move into your speech. Speak loudly enough to be heard by all. Use bodily action suitable to the audience, the occasion, the speech, the environment, and yourself. Be sure that your language is appropriate to the five requirements just recited. Avoid ponderous phrases, over-emotionalized words and tones, redundancy, and flowery or florid attempts at oratory. Let everything you do and say, coupled with a good appearance and alert posture, be the evidence that you are genuinely and sincerely mindful of their appreciation of you at your departure.

IMPROVE YOUR VOCABULARY

Fatuity - (få-tū'ĭ-tĭ) n. Easily "taken in," stupidity, folly, self-complacency, dullness, imbecility. Example: A smart person seldom exhibits fatuity. Use this word in this speech and five times a day for the next week. Make it yours. You can.

Blue or down in the dumps - Omit these words. Too many people have overworked them. Give them a rest for at least a week. Use one of the following synonyms to add power to your vocabulary: melancholy, morose, dejected, distressed, pensive, despondent, disconsolate, doleful, gloomy, wretched, miserable, etc.

BIBLIOGRAPHY FOR THE FAREWELL SPEECH

Culp, Ralph Borden, Basic Types of Speech, Wm. C. Brown Company, Publishers, 1968, pp. 78-79.

Gilman, Wilbur E., and Others, An Introduction to Speaking, The Macmillan Company, 2d ed., 1968, pp. 38-42.

Monroe, Alan H., and Ehninger, Douglas, Principles of Speech Communication, Scott, Foresman and Company, 6th brief ed., 1969, pp. 283-285.

Oliver, Robert T., and Cortright, R. L., Effective Speech, Holt, Rinehart and Winston, Inc., 5th ed., 1970, Chapter 23.

Williams, Barbara, Purposeful Communication, Kendall/Hunt Publishing Company, 1970, pp. 187-189.

FAREWELL SPEECH

(This speech follows a gift presentation at a dinner in a semi-formal atmosphere.
The occasion is the departure of a high school teacher to assume a new position elsewhere.)

Superintendent Herr, students, and guests. I often wondered in times past what I would say if ever my students and fellow faculty members did something for me as elegant as you have done tonight. I thought it would be easy to say thanks and goodbye -- perhaps like leaving your last class Friday afternoon knowing Monday morning was only forty-eight hours away. But Monday morning won't come again here.

Two years ago I came to Medicine Lodge to teach in my first high school after three years as a grade school teacher. I'll always remember that first junior-senior hayrack ride picnic. Besides the roasted weiners -- some of them thoroughly cremated -- that ball game was real football. It was the first time in my life I ever saw soft ball players tackled while running bases. There were other things I saw and learned that evening to really start my education, my liberal education. They say the modern age moves faster, young people want to do things in a hurry. And I learned in a hurry. Some of you students present tonight attended that picnic and I must say you taught exceedingly well -- and fast.

We all know that high school is not a picnic, not all the time. We know it is not all football and basketball or debate and drama. We know that quizzes and grades, study and recitation, homework and after-school jobs are a big part of high school. We know, too, that young men and women -- I don't think of you as boys and girls -- meet and learn to live and work and play together. We admit the dating and romances, and we admit the broken hearts. We admit the experience of maturing that goes with it. It is here we learn the darkness of cloudy days and the brightness of sunshine and I trust it is here we learn to accept the cloudy days as well as the sunshiny days. I must tell you candidly that you students helped impress this principle on me and I am indebted to you for doing it.

I am sure you students felt certain ideals regarding yourselves and your high school. There were things you wanted desperately to learn, things you wanted to do, approvals you longed for from your friends and the faculty. And sometimes these deep longings became driving forces in your behavior. But these same deep hidden hopes and dreams you held in your hearts were mine. I wanted the same things from you. And tonight I thank you for giving them to me as only high school students can give.

No one knows where or when your formal academic training will end. For some of you it will be graduation, for others it will be a college diploma, and some of you will go on to the doctoral level. But you will always continue to learn regardless of where you are or what you are doing. And I shall go with you in the sense that I will be in a new school learning new procedures, new rules, and teaching new students. If you and I have not accomplished all we wanted to accomplish here together we did accomplish much. It was your sheer exuberance, your unlimited energy, the songs in your hearts, and the laughter of love and hope and life's fullest enjoyments -- it was these things you gave me every day, it was these inspirations that I shall remember, these I shall never never forget -- and they will guide me always.

Next fall you will have a new teacher at my desk. You will be proud of him and he will be proud of you. Together you will continue to make Medicine Lodge one of the finest schools in the state.

I have been asked why I am leaving. Let me tell you it's one of the hardest things I have ever done. But teachers do move to new positions for reasons of salary and academic opportunity. In my case the salary will permit me to save enough to continue graduate study and at minimum expense because a university is located in the same city.

The wrist watch you gave me tonight is magnificent. See, I already have it on. That old one I wore was a carry-over from college days when I was on my austerity budget. You students must have observed its age and senility. So I do thank you for your generosity and choice of remembrance. Every time it ticks I shall think of one of you and if it ever stops I'll think of the time someone was tardy or I was late to class.

This dinner tonight, your kind remarks, and your good will are all something I shall cherish. They are the quality and kind that only a community high school can create. They are the true America, the real American youth, and that something we all live for. I give you my best wishes, my friendship, and my heart.

SPEECH OUTLINE

Construct a neat, complete sentence outline on this sheet, tear it out, and hand it to your instructor when you rise to speak. He may wish to write criticisms of the outline and speech in the margins.

Type of speech:_____ Name:_____

Number of words in outline:_____ Date:_____

Purpose of this speech: (What do you want your audience to learn, to think, to believe, to feel, or do because of this speech?)_____

_____

TITLE:

INTRODUCTION:

BODY:

CONCLUSION:

Instructor's comments may concern choice of topic, development of ideas, organization, language use, personal appearance, posture, physical activity, sources, and improvement.

(Write sources of information on back of sheet)

SOURCES FROM LITERATURE

(Fill out source requirements completely. Write "none listed" if an author's name or copyright date is not listed.)

1. Author's name _____

   Title of book or magazine used _____

   Title of article in above book or magazine _____

   Chapter and/or pages read _____

   Date of above publication _____

2. Author's name _____

   Title of book or magazine used _____

   Title of article in above book or magazine _____

   Chapter and/or pages read _____

   Date of above publication _____

3. Author's name _____

   Title of book or magazine used _____

   Title of article in above book or magazine _____

   Chapter and/or pages read _____

   Date of above publication _____

INTERVIEW SOURCES

1. Person interviewed _____ Date of interview_____

   His position, occupation, and location _____

   Why is he a reliable source? Be specific _____

   _____

2. Person interviewed _____ Date of interview_____

   His position, occupation, and location _____

   Why is he a reliable source? Be specific _____

   _____

PERSONAL EXPERIENCE OF SPEAKER

1. Tell (1) when, (2) where, and (3) conditions under which you became an authority on subject matter in your speech _____

   _____

   _____

   _____

Chapter 22

THE EULOGY

This speech is due:
Time limits: 5-6 minutes.
Speaking notes: 10-word maximum.
Sources of information: Two are required, preferably three. For each source give the specific magazine
    or book it was taken from, title of the article, author's full name, date of publication, and the chap-
    ter or pages telling where the material was found. If a source is a person, identify him completely
    by title, position, occupation, etc. List these on the outline form.
Outline your speech: Prepare a 75-150 word complete sentence outline. Designate the exact number of
    words in your outline. Use the form at the end of this chapter.

PURPOSE OF THE EULOGY
    This speech is assigned so that you may learn by doing and thus become familiar with the speech
of eulogy. Frequently a person is called upon to eulogize or praise someone. There are several ways to
do this. Of course, the type of eulogy you may be asked to present will depend on different aspects of the
speech situation. But whatever that requirement may be, you will be better prepared to do a creditable job
if you have had previous experience. This assignment will provide that experience.

EXPLANATION OF THE EULOGY
    The eulogy is a speech of praise that is delivered in honor or commemoration of someone living or
dead. Sometimes eulogies are presented for animals, particularly dogs, horses, and others. A more fanciful and imaginative eulogy would be one to inanimate objects, such as the sea or the mountains. Some
eulogies are written to trees and flowers, but these, too, are abstract and fanciful in nature.

    The purpose of a eulogy is to praise and evaluate favorably that which is eulogized; it commends
and lifts up the finer qualities and characteristics of the subject eulogized. It stresses the personality of
the person (or thing) that it concerns; it tells of their greatness and achievements, their benefits to society,
and their influence upon people. It is not merely a simple biographical sketch of someone. To illustrate
the point, imagine a eulogy of a great oak, in which the speaker tells the date on which the acorn sprouted,
and a later date when the tiny plant emerged from the soil; next the number in inches it grew each year
thereafter; and finally the number of leaves it developed in forty years. Compare this with the eulogy of a
person, and you can see why a biographical sketch is not a eulogy. Actually, it sounds like a scientific report on a man (or tree).

    Occasions for eulogies are many. For persons who are living, the speech may be given on a birth-
day, at a dinner in honor of an individual, at the dedication of a project someone has created and/or donat-
ed. Eulogies often appear at the formal announcement of a political candidate or at an inauguration. For
persons who are dead, not considering funeral tributes, eulogies are offered on birthday anniversaries or
in connection with notable events or achievements in individuals' lives. Sometimes eulogies in the form of
character studies are presented as evidences of good living. They become lessons of life.

SUGGESTIONS FOR EULOGIES
1. Franklin D. Roosevelt
2. Theodore Roosevelt
3. Thomas Edison
4. Henry Ford
5. Abraham Lincoln
6. Robert E. Lee
7. Ulysses S. Grant
8. Jefferson Davis
9. George Washington
10. Sam Houston
11. Robert G. Ingersoll
12. Louis Pasteur
13. Will Rogers
14. A friend
15. A buddy
16. A relative
17. General Patton
18. Ernie Pyle
19. Stephen A. Douglas
20. Speaker's choice

HOW TO SELECT A PERSON TO EULOGIZE
    First, it is essential that you eulogize someone whom you greatly admire and who, in your opinion,
is living or has lived a commendable life. This is necessary, because your eulogy must be completely
sincere. Second, select someone about whom you can secure adequate information. Third, do not select a
classmate or a town loafer, believing that your choice will be clever or smart. You will only embarrass

your classmate or make yourself appear immature. Not only that, but what you might say would not likely be a true eulogy. Finally, think twice before deciding to eulogize a tree, the sea, or the mountains, a dog, horse or other animal, because these are probably more difficult to eulogize than persons. At least, for the sake of experience, you will be wiser to select a person as a subject to eulogize.

HOW TO PREPARE A EULOGY

The purpose of eulogy is a set objective, regardless of the time, place or occasion. Since eulogies are laudations intended to stimulate an audience favorably towards the subject and to inspire them to nobler heights by virtue of the examples set by the person being praised, the speaker is not required to determine a purpose in preparing a eulogy.

Having selected the person to be eulogized, you should decide upon the method which you will use in developing the eulogy. Your method and whether or not the individual is living will determine the material that is necessary. Let us examine several different methods of constructing a eulogy.

First, you may follow a chronological order, that is, you will take up events in the order of their development. This will permit a study of the growth and orderly evolution of character in the subject. As you touch upon these broad and influential events in the subject's life, you will point to them as evidences of (1) what he accomplished, (2) what he stood for, (3) the nature of his influence upon society, and (4) his probable place in history. In building your speech chronologically do not end by composing a simple biographical sketch. If you do, you will have an informative speech but not a eulogy. It is not enough to list the significant happenings in a man's life chronologically and consider that you have built a eulogy. You must state how he reacted to the events in his life and what happened as a result of them. For example, if you were eulogizing Franklin D. Roosevelt (chronologically), you would recount, as one event, how he was stricken with infantile paralysis when a grown man, but you would not merely make a statement regarding the tragedy that befell him and then pass on. Rather, you would show how his illness became a challenge to him, how he resolved to live a great life despite a pair of useless legs, how he did overcome his handicap. You would show that, as a result of his sickness, he became more resolute, more determined, more kindly, and that today the nation honors him on his birthday and contributes millions of dollars to the fund for the aid of children afflicted with infantile paralysis. Other incidents should be given similar treatment.

A second method of developing a eulogy might well be labeled the period method. It is the one which covers the growth of an individual by treating different periods in his life. It is very broad and makes no attempt to enumerate the many events of his life with their attached significance. Instead of this, using Franklin D. Roosevelt again as an example, you could speak of him as he grew through: (1) boyhood, (2) college life, (3) early political life, (4) late political life.

In following this method you would attempt to bring out the same basic points mentioned above - namely, (1) what he accomplished, (2) what he stood for, (3) his influence upon society, (4) his likely place in history. Although this treatment is broad, it is quite effective.

It should be emphasized at this point that, regardless of which method you use, there are certain necessary points to be observed. A discussion of these follows. First, omit the unimportant events, the small things, and the insignificant details. Second, in developing your speech, point up the struggles which he made in order to achieve his aims. Avoid overemphasis and exaggeration when you are doing this. Third, show the development of his ideas and ideals. Fourth, describe his relations and services to his fellow men and indicate their significance.

It is not necessary to cover up an individual but rather to admit the human element in him. In doing this, mentioning the human element is enough. It need not be dwelt on nor apologized for. It can be shown that despite weaknesses or shortcomings a man was great. It can be shown that a man lived above these frailties of human nature. But whatever the qualities of your subject, be honest in your treatment of him. It is only fair to assume that the good in him outweighed the bad by far, or you would not have elected to eulogize him.

In constructing your speech, be sure you pay careful attention to your introduction and conclusion. Aside from these, do not neglect the logical organization and arrangement of the remainder of your talk. Actually, a eulogy is a difficult speech to prepare. However, if you go about it knowing what you wish to put into it, you should have no particular trouble. When you have the eulogizing speech ready for rehearsal, it will be advisable to practice it aloud until you have thoroughly mastered the sequence of ideas. Do not memorize the speech word for word.

Materials for eulogies may be found in Who's Who, histories, biographies, autobiographies, encyclopedias, newspapers, magazines, and similar sources. Consult your librarian for assistance.

HOW TO PRESENT A EULOGY

Your overall attitude must be one of undoubted sincerity. You must be a true believer in the man about whom you speak. Aside from your attitude, you will, of course, observe all the requirements of good speech. There should be no showiness or gaudiness in your presentation that will call attention to you instead of your ideas about the subject of your speech.

You will need to be fully aware of the occasion and atmosphere into which you will step when you deliver the eulogy. It is your responsibility to know what will be required of you in the way of carrying out rituals or ceremonies if they are a part of the program. Since you will be in the limelight, you should fit easily into the situation without awkwardness. Naturally you must adjust your bodily actions and gestures to your environment - and your audience. Your voice should reach the ears of all present. If you are sincere, well prepared, and mean what you say, the eulogy which you present should be inspirational to all who hear it.

IMPROVE YOUR VOCABULARY

Placid - (plăs'ĭd) a. Undisturbed, quiet, peaceful, gentle, unruffled, calm. Example: The placid stream was beautiful in the twilight. Use this word in your everyday speech at least half a dozen times. It has many applications that will add variety to your language.

Old - There is too much work thrown on this word. Use one of the suggested synonyms instead. Examples are: aged, ancient, antiquated, decrepit, elderly, hoary, immemorial, senile, venerable, time-worn, etc.

BIBLIOGRAPHY FOR THE EULOGY

Buehler, E. Christian, and Linkugel, W. A., Speech Communication, Harper & Row, Publishers, 1969, pp. 233-235.

Gilman, Wilbur E., and Others, An Introduction to Speaking, The Macmillan Company, 2d ed., 1968, pp. 38-44.

Monroe, Alan H., and Ehninger, Douglas, Principles of Speech Communication, Scott, Foresman and Company, 6th brief ed., 1969, pp. 189-191, 284.

Ross, Raymond S., Speech Communication, Prentice-Hall, Inc., 2d ed., 1970, pp. 237-240.

Williams, Barbara, Purposeful Communication, Kendall/Hunt Publishing Company, 1970, pp. 196-199.

EULOGY

THEY LABOR UNTIL TOMORROW

My parents are walking with slowed steps into the last sunset of a long evening. Together they have watched and waited sunsets more than half a century and now the sun hangs low. The night, when it comes, will be lighted by uncounted stars, each recalling days of doing, days of deeds, and love of life and living. The moon will shine through the mists of eternity as the glow of memory lingers after. It will be soft and warm and will light my way.

Our parents can give us life and they can love us. They can teach us truth and train us to be honest and humble. They can guide us to be self-sufficient and enterprising. They can imbue us with courage to do right, to abhor evil, and to so live that the life we leave behind will be exemplary. All this they did, and they were exemplary.

Courage and brave living were and are the moral fiber of my parents' lives. In the debacle of the great depression when financial failure, unemployment, sickness and the hand of death hovered over them they were never fugitives of fear. They knew it not. When land they lived on swirled in black clouds above them and when drought laid the land naked of crops and vegetation and cracked it open they did not flee from it nor did they abandon hope. When the years before them were bleak and barren and dry winds seemed interminable they looked each night to the west for the sign of rain.

I saw my father refuse money and aid when he was broken to disaster by blowing dust and the debts of others. I saw him in middle age assume an unbelievable burden helpless debtors placed on his shoulders to free their own. And in this same hour of horror death haunted his only daughter week after week from spring to summer. By his side in those days of doubt and torment my mother was his helpful, steady companion. Together they conquered uncertainty, calmly they waited, and with courage God gives only to kings and queens they saw life reappear in a wasted body and new hope whisper with each dawn.

Years passed as the family necessities were provided. Hands grew tired and calloused by labor, and unending work left its sign on their faces. In those times of distress there was never defeat. If it ever raised its voice my parents never let it show its form. The five children growing to adulthood knew no words touching despair nor did they hear them. "Things will be better next year," "We must work hard," "We'll wait a little while," "We'll do it later." These were the words. These were the courage. Never the admission that anything was wrong. And now since the years have hurried to yesterday I see their hope, I see their faith, and I know their sacrifice. I know their love and I shall never cease thanking God for them.

Man's religions teach him great principles of the ages and they teach him how to live with his fellowmen. My parents have never attended church often. They know well the charities of each day and not those on Sunday only. They live every day like Sunday and in their souls is peace of mind known only to those who live well. If God is righteousness, they are Godlike. If God is love, they are Godlike. If God is charity and hope, they are Godlike.

My parents have no wish for fame nor do they seek its fascination. They are not ostentatious. They are in their later years extremely busy. Almost a generation past the age when men retire, my parents are working each day giving to the world a new dignity to labor and hope eternal. And their children, impressed by the lifetime habit of work, attempt to emulate their example of more than a half century.

The sun is sinking low and soon twilight must mingle the light and shadows into the darkness of eternity. My parents approach the horizon with uplifted faces and the light of a new day shines on them. They will pass into the setting sun leaving only their labors behind. Two people will have lived for their children and for the world. No parents could do more and no parents will have lived better.

SPEECH OUTLINE

Construct a neat, complete sentence outline on this sheet, tear it out, and hand it to your instructor when you rise to speak. He may wish to write criticisms of the outline and speech in the margins.

Type of speech:_____ Name:_____

Number of words in outline:_____ Date:_____

Purpose of this speech: (What do you want your audience to learn, to think, to believe, to feel, or do because of this speech?)_____

_____

TITLE:

INTRODUCTION:

BODY:

CONCLUSION:

Instructor's comments may concern choice of topic, development of ideas, organization, language use, personal appearance, posture, physical activity, sources, and improvement.

(Write sources of information on back of sheet)

SOURCES FROM LITERATURE

(Fill out source requirements completely. Write "none listed" if an author's name or copyright date is not listed.)

1. Author's name _____

   Title of book or magazine used _____

   Title of article in above book or magazine _____

   Chapter and/or pages read _____

   Date of above publication _____

2. Author's name _____

   Title of book or magazine used _____

   Title of article in above book or magazine _____

   Chapter and/or pages read _____

   Date of above publication _____

3. Author's name _____

   Title of book or magazine used _____

   Title of article in above book or magazine _____

   Chapter and/or pages read _____

   Date of above publication _____

INTERVIEW SOURCES

1. Person interviewed _____ Date of interview_____

   His position, occupation, and location _____

   Why is he a reliable source? Be specific _____

   _____

2. Person interviewed _____ Date of interview_____

   His position, occupation, and location _____

   Why is he a reliable source? Be specific _____

   _____

PERSONAL EXPERIENCE OF SPEAKER

1. Tell (1) when, (2) where, and (3) conditions under which you became an authority on subject matter in your speech _____

   _____

   _____

   _____

Chapter 23

THE DEDICATION SPEECH

This speech is due:
Time limits: 3-4 minutes.
Speaking notes: This is a short speech - you do not need any. "Prepare to meet thy audience."
Sources of information: Two are required, preferably three. For each source give the specific magazine
     or book it was taken from, title of the article, author's full name, date of publication, and the chap-
     ter or pages telling where the material was found. If a source is a person, identify him completely
     by title, position, occupation, etc. List these on the outline form.
Outline your speech: Prepare a 75-150 word complete sentence outline. Designate the exact number of
     words in your outline. Use the form at the end of this chapter.

PURPOSE OF THE DEDICATION SPEECH

     You may not give a speech at dedication ceremonies for a long time, then again the occasion for a speech of this kind may arise sooner than you had thought possible. But regardless of when you are called on for this type of speech, one thing is sure, and that is that you must know its requirements. The dedication speech occurs on an occasion and in an atmosphere that requires very strict observance of certain aspects of speechmaking. This speech assignment is designed to give you an experience like the "real thing," so that you may do a creditable performance when the opportunity presents itself.

EXPLANATION OF THE DEDICATION SPEECH

     The dedication speech is one presented on commemorative occasions. It is generally brief and carries a serious tone. It employs excellent language, demands careful construction, fine wording, and polished delivery. Its purpose should be to commemorate, to honor an occasion, and to praise the spirit of endeavor and progress that the dedication symbolizes. The speech should thrill the audience with pride regarding their community, ideals, and progress. Occasions for the dedication speech usually involve a group enterprise. Common among these are occasions such as: erecting monuments, completing build-ings, stadiums, swimming pools, and baseball parks, or laying corner stones and opening institutions. Similar events considered as marks of progress are also occasions for dedication speeches. Lincoln's Gettysburg Address is one of the finest dedication speeches ever made.

SUGGESTED TOPICS FOR DEDICATION SPEECHES

     A speech of dedication for any one of the following should be suitable:

1. A new college.
2. Laying the corner stone for a new Student Union building.
3. A new library.
4. A new stadium.
5. A new baseball park.
6. A new courthouse.
7. A new city hall.
8. A new high school building.
9. A new swimming pool.
10. Laying the corner stone for a new auditorium.
11. A new city hospital.
12. A new city park.
13. Laying a corner stone for a new "Lodge" building.
14. A monument to a local citizen.
15. A monument as a historical marker.
16. A monument to honor the war dead.
17. A monument to a great race horse.
18. A monument to a national hero.
19. Laying a corner stone for a new church.
20. Speaker's choice.

HOW TO CHOOSE A TOPIC

This will involve a bit of imagination on your part; however, choose an occasion that you wish were actually true, really being enacted. Be sure you could be thrilled at such an occasion. Look over the topics again, then make up your mind. Do not put it off. Choose, and start your preparation.

HOW TO PREPARE A DEDICATION SPEECH

First, know your purpose. It must dominate this speech the same as the purpose dominates every speech. This means that you are to compliment the ideals and achievements which the dedicated structure symbolizes, thus setting it apart for a certain use or purpose.

These are the points to cover in your speech. Give a brief history of events leading up to the present time. Mention the sacrifice, the work, the ideals, and the service that lie behind the project. Next, explain the future use or work, the influence or significance that will be associated with the structure being dedicated. Place the emphasis upon what the object dedicated stands for (ideals, progress, loyalty) rather than upon the object itself.

The above thoughts will constitute your material. Now, organize your speech carefully, very carefully. Pay particular attention to the introduction, the conclusion - yes, everything in your speech. It must have order. To accomplish the organization of the speech you will first outline it. Wording it follows. Do this meticulously. Do not be grandiose or grandiloquent, but be understandable and simple in language. The speech is serious, not frivolous. Leave your humor at home.

You are now ready to practice. Do this orally. Rehearse aloud until you have definitely fixed the order of the speech in your mind. Avoid complete word for word memorization. You may memorize certain words and phrases, but you should not memorize the entire speech. When you have mastered an effective presentation, you will be ready to speak, and not before. Remember to include appropriate bodily action, gesture, and voice in your practice.

HOW TO PRESENT A DEDICATION SPEECH

The attitude of the speaker should be one of appropriate dignity. Emotion and sentiment should be properly blended to fit the noble sentiments that will be present. The adequacy and poise of the speaker should be obvious from his appearance, his bearing, and his self-confidence.

Bodily action must be keyed to the tone of the speech. The environment surrounding the speaker may permit much action or limit it severely. If a public address system is used, the speaker cannot move from the microphone. He can and should utilize gestures.

Whether speaking with the aid of a microphone or not, the voice should be full and resonant and easily heard. If the crowd is large, a slower speaking rate should be used. Articulation must be carefully attended, yet not so much so that it becomes ponderous and labored. Voice and action must be in tune, neither one overbalancing the other. The speaker must be animated, alive to his purpose, desirous of communicating, and capable of presenting a polished speech.

IMPROVE YOUR VOCABULARY

Use the following word in your speech today and also five times each day for a week. Make it yours, a valuable asset.

Altruistic - (ăl'trōō-ĭs'tĭk) a. An attitude that causes a person to be helpful because of a regard for the welfare of others. Example: The building being dedicated was made possible only by the altruistic efforts of several local citizens.

Get - Omit this word. Do not use it for a week, it is tired and overworked. Use a synonym. Examples: obtain, induce, attain, procure, acquire, achieve, take, secure, win, contract, gain, etc.

BIBLIOGRAPHY FOR THE DEDICATION SPEECH

Culp, Ralph Borden, Basic Types of Speech, Wm. C. Brown Company, Publishers, 1968, pp. 79-80.

Gilman, Wilbur E., and Others, An Introduction to Speaking, The Macmillan Company, 2d ed., 1968, pp. 38-44.

Monroe, Alan H., and Ehninger, Douglas, Principles of Speech Communication, Scott, Foresman and Company, 6th brief ed., 1969, pp. 283-285.

Oliver, Robert T., and Cortright, R. L., Effective Speech, Holt, Rinehart and Winston, Inc., 5th ed., 1970, Chapter 23.

DEDICATION SPEECH

THE BULL RUN GOLF COURSE DEDICATION

Fellow golfers and guests. Three brief years ago men stood on this green when it was a mound of earth in a cow pasture. The buffalo grass spread like a blanket into every gully and draw and onto every rocky ledge. Closing their eyes against a blinding July sun seven dreamers saw before them men and women, young people and old people, and strangers and newcomers playing golf on the ledges and in the swales and from many mounds rising gently on the prairie. They saw them in sunset and twilight, in dawn and sunrise and they saw them at noonday. In the vision they saw a club house and a well flowing clean cool water. Then the dreamers left the pasture and the cattle grazing the swale and returned to the small country town where they lived and worked.

There was talk and meetings were held, some on street corners, some in stores, some in barber-shops and pool halls, some in the post office and service stations, and finally in the local bank.

With a title in their hands and a nine hole plat on file the fairways and greens took shape and form. The farmer's tractors and plows can prepare a seed bed for wheat and corn or they can prepare cow pasture land for a golf ball -- and they did.

Beneath this morning July sun we are assembled as wheat farmers, as cattlemen and ranchers, as business men, and professional men, as wives and children to dedicate this golf course. Our words won't make the greens brighter nor will they smooth fairways to make our drives longer. But we can assure ourselves that imagination, dedication, and determination can create what we want and need as a community project. We can feel pride that we have before us on this Kansas prairie a golf course that would never have been born except for the powerful will of a small community that worked together for a common cause and will now play together for a common pleasure. Our children need not roam the alleys for excitement nor tease their friends for fun. When they tire of their rifles and fishing rods, they can come here to play and learn a game to enjoy for fifty years.

Tomorrow is forever and when it comes it is always the next day, yet we live for tomorrow. Our efforts to create a playground in a pasture are not ephemeral and they will not vanish in dust or darkness. Each evening's dew will refresh the greens and fairways and each ball that sails into the sky and drops in a swale will mark a new game for someone and a new day for the years ahead.

Fellow citizens the cow pasture is ready. Let's tee off.

GOODWILL SPEECH

By Steven Rigby

SO, YOU WOULD LIKE TO BE A DOCTOR

Many of you will be graduating from high school this May, and enrolling in premedical courses in colleges and universities next September. If I were to ask a few of you just why you think you want to be doctors, I would get many different answers in reply -- some good answers, some bad ones. But each of you, for one reason or another, feels that your goal should be medicine. You think that medicine has something to offer you and that you have something to offer medicine. On your list of priorities, medicine is number one.

Many of you see the years of study that lie ahead of you as a mysterious blur. You know, of course, that you will go to college for three to four years. You know that you will then go on to medical school -- if you're accepted -- for another four years, taking courses in anatomy, physiology and many other courses with long names. And then you will intern in a hospital for a year. You may even decide to specialize and go to school for a few more years. You realize that you have to invest a long period of time and a frightening amount of money, in order to complete your goal of becoming a medical doctor.

But just remember the practice of medicine has always meant something more than just another way to make a living, and that an education in medicine implies something more than the completion of certain science courses and the reading of certain textbooks.

A modern physician can look forward to various rewards for his contribution to medicine. Most doctors make a good living from their work. I am not going to list average incomes of doctors in their respective specialties as they are listed today because they probably will be quite different by the time you become a doctor. But, by and large, I think you would have to look for quite a while to find a doctor who is starving to death.

Certainly, a physician has a high degree of security. A doctor will never have to worry about finding a job; there has always been a shortage of doctors. He can expect to have a home of his own and a new model automobile. He will be able to provide a good education for his children.

On the other hand, it would be a mistake to have medicine as your goal because of the tangible rewards that are offered. There are many other occupations in which you can make much more money with much less effort, if that is your major concern.

Aside from income, there is a multitude of rewards that face the physician. A doctor most always enjoys respect in his community. There is no other profession which is held in as high esteem as the profession of medicine. A doctor is respected for merely being a doctor. He is often regarded as public property and is expected to take part in community progress. He may be consulted for completely non-medical community affairs.

Most important, the physician derives immense satisfaction from doing work that is worthwhile, work which is needed and received with much gratitude. He takes pride in doing work which few others can do, and doing it well. He finds satisfaction every day from the positive benefit that comes from his work.

But at the same time he must assume certain unusual responsibilities. Very often patients forget that doctors are people, as well as being doctors. A doctor must be available when he is needed. Even if that happens to be at two in the morning, he is still expected to accept the call. Most all physicians work hours that would astonish the average person. And they accept this as a way of life.

A doctor's home life is often a very trying situation, especially when he is establishing his practice. He may not see his wife and children regularly. It has been said that any woman who marries a doctor is either an idiot or a fool; if this is the truth, I know quite a few very charming idiots and fools who are willing to share their husbands with the numerous duties of a medical profession, duties which take the doctor away from home usually half the night and always at meal times.

This demand on a doctor's time is accepted by the profession as part of the game. This is the way a doctor lives, and that's all there is to it. If you don't think you would like this kind of life, you shouldn't be a doctor. There is no one the profession scorns more than the physician who shirks his duties, that is, puts his personal life above the life he must dedicate to his profession. The rest of the profession accepts this life -- why shouldn't he?

It is true that many doctors form group practices where they take turns being on call. This does eliminate some of the interruptions a doctor may encounter, but the responsibility still exists.

Who knows, by the time many of you become doctors the single practitioner working twenty hours a day may well be a thing of the past although I think the responsibilities will always be there. True, I think it takes a very special type of person to become a doctor, because the incentive must be there. The opportunities and rewards always outweigh the disappointments. If you have made up your mind to become a doctor, I want to congratulate you and wish you success, because I don't think you will ever regret your decision.

SPEECH OUTLINE

Construct a neat, complete sentence outline on this sheet, tear it out, and hand it to your instructor when you rise to speak. He may wish to write criticisms of the outline and speech in the margins.

Type of speech:_____ Name:_____

Number of words in outline:_____ Date:_____

Purpose of this speech: (What do you want your audience to learn, to think, to believe, to feel, or do because of this speech?)_____

_____

TITLE:

INTRODUCTION:

BODY:

CONCLUSION:

Instructor's comments may concern choice of topic, development of ideas, organization, language use, personal appearance, posture, physical activity, sources, and improvement.

(Write sources of information on back of sheet)

SOURCES FROM LITERATURE

(Fill out source requirements completely. Write "none listed" if an author's name or copyright date is not listed.)

1. Author's name _____

   Title of book or magazine used _____

   Title of article in above book or magazine _____

   Chapter and/or pages read _____

   Date of above publication _____

2. Author's name _____

   Title of book or magazine used _____

   Title of article in above book or magazine _____

   Chapter and/or pages read _____

   Date of above publication _____

3. Author's name _____

   Title of book or magazine used _____

   Title of article in above book or magazine _____

   Chapter and/or pages read _____

   Date of above publication _____

INTERVIEW SOURCES

1. Person interviewed _____ Date of interview_____

   His position, occupation, and location _____

   Why is he a reliable source?   Be specific _____

   _____

2. Person interviewed _____ Date of interview_____

   His position, occupation, and location _____

   Why is he a reliable source?   Be specific _____

   _____

PERSONAL EXPERIENCE OF SPEAKER

1. Tell (1) when, (2) where, and (3) conditions under which you became an authority on subject matter in

   your speech _____

   _____

   _____

Chapter 24

THE ANNIVERSARY SPEECH

This speech is due:
Time limits: 5-6 minutes.
Speaking notes: It is advisable to use none. Try it.
Sources of information: Two are required, preferably three. For each source give the specific magazine
      or book it was taken from, title of the article, author's full name, date of publication, and the chap-
      ter or pages telling where the material was found. If a source is a person, identify him completely
      by title, position, occupation, etc. List these on the outline form.
Outline your speech: Prepare a 75-100 word complete sentence outline. Designate the exact number of
      words in your outline. Use the form at the end of this chapter.

PURPOSE OF THE ANNIVERSARY SPEECH
      The experience of presenting an anniversary speech now will prove helpful to you at some later
time when you meet the real situation requiring knowledge of its structure and presentation. A speaker is
often disturbed, nervous, and ill at ease when speaking on an occasion that he has never previously experienced. His feelings of uncertainty probably spring from his lack of familiarity with the environment in
which he finds himself. In your case, having known what it is to give an anniversary talk at least once, you
should find future performances considerably easier and perhaps enjoyable. That is why you should do
your best with this assignment.

EXPLANATION OF THE ANNIVERSARY SPEECH
      The anniversary speech is one presented in commemoration of an event, a person, or occasion of
the past. Its purpose is to recall and remember the past so that we may more adequately serve the present and courageously prepare for the future. It will weigh the past, observe the blessings of the present,
and look to the future optimistically. Elements of loyalty and patriotism usually are contained in the remarks.

      Because this talk is similar to the dedication speech, its requirements of the speaker do not vary
noticeably from those for the dedication speech. The speaker should be a good man, both in character and
ability. He should be fully acquainted with the history, the present status of the anniversary, and future
plans as they pertain to it. You might think of the anniversary as a birthday celebration and incorporate
all the ideals and ideas associated with such a day.

      Occasions for anniversary speeches arise whenever the passing of time is marked by a pause in
which people lay aside their work long enough to note what has been accomplished. The remembrance of
Independence Day, landing of the Pilgrims, Armistice, Thanksgiving, Christmas, Labor Day, birthday of a
national, state, or local figure, are all examples of such occasions. Observance of the progress during a
certain number of years of a business firm, a school, a church, a city, state or nation, or any organization, may form the basis of an anniversary speech. During recent years, state centennials marked by re-
gional and state fairs have proved themselves worthwhile as anniversaries. Every day is the birthday of
somebody or something; hence every day is a potential anniversary, whether it is observed or not.

SUGGESTED OCCASIONS FOR AN ANNIVERSARY SPEECH
     1. Your school is a half century old.
     2. The County was organized seventy-five years ago.
     3. Today the state is 100 years old.
     4. Your city observes a birthday.
     5. It is Army Day.
     6. The Navy has an anniversary.
     7. Your church was established _____ years ago.
     8. Your lodge is now twenty-five years old.
     9. The fire department has been active _____ years.
   10. It is Armed Forces Day.

11. It is Labor Day.
12. It is Thanksgiving.
13. Your business is fifty years old.
14. Your business produces its one-millionth car, watch, washing machine.
15. It is Lincoln's birthday (or anyone's).
16. This bridge was built _____ years ago.
17. Radium was discovered _____ years ago.
18. The first airplane flight occurred _____ years ago.
19. The radio, telephone, sewing machine, etc., were invented _____ years ago.
20. Speaker's choice.

HOW TO CHOOSE A TOPIC FOR AN ANNIVERSARY SPEECH

If you have a particular loyalty or devotion, it would be advisable to construct your speech around it at an imaginary or real anniversary. Otherwise, select one of the above suggestions in which you have an interest. Be sure you are interested in the topic you select for your speech. Make your choice soon. Do not wait until the day before your speech is due. The longer you delay choosing your topic the greater are your chances for a weak and insipid speech.

HOW TO PREPARE AN ANNIVERSARY SPEECH

Remember that your purpose is to commemorate. Keep this purpose in mind constantly. Your thoughts must be constructed to achieve this end.

Second, the organization of your speech is important. Here you must observe all the characteristics of adequate speech composition. You should include the following points: Tell why you are especially interested in this anniversary. Show historically that the people and their ideals are responsible for the organization's celebration. Trace the development of these ideals. Anecdotes, stories, incidents, and humor are appropriate and impressive if properly used. The past should vividly live again for your audience. Turn next to the present; compare it with the past. Avoid references to or implications of partisan or class views. Speak broadly for all the people by utilizing a spirit of friendliness and goodwill. Bend your energies toward unity and interest for the common good. Speak next of the future. By virtue of a splendid past and a significant present, the future holds promises of greater things to be. Speak confidently on this thesis. Indicate that the cooperation of all persons directed toward a determined effort for a greater service to mankind is the goal all are seeking. Show the relationship of this anniversary to the welfare of the state and nation.

After having constructed your speech, be sure to rehearse it aloud until you have fixed the order of points in your mind. Do not memorize it. Practice bodily action and gesture while rehearsing, but be sure to avoid mechanical movements.

HOW TO PRESENT AN ANNIVERSARY SPEECH

Speak sincerely. If you cannot and do not mean what you say, you should not speak. Your bodily actions, your voice, your entire organism should evince sincerity. There should be no display either of voice or action. You should be easily heard by all and completely in their view. Your dress should be appropriate to the occasion. Observe your time limits.

IMPROVE YOUR VOCABULARY

Exigency - (ĕk'sĭ-jĕn-sĭ) n. Emergency, urgency: a situation which necessitates immediate action or remedy. Example: A resourceful person can meet a sudden exigency calmly. Use this word in this speech and five times a day for the next week. Make it yours.

Fine - Omit this word from your vocabulary for a week. It is tired to the point of insipidity. Give life to your conversation by using synonyms. Examples: excellent, tasteful, rare, enjoyable, superior, high-grade, pleasant, showy, subtle, refined, delicate, fashionable, etc.

BIBLIOGRAPHY FOR THE ANNIVERSARY SPEECH

Culp, Ralph Borden, Basic Types of Speech, Wm. C. Brown Company, Publishers, 1968, pp. 80-84.

Gilman, Wilbur E., and Others, An Introduction to Speaking, The Macmillan Company, 2d ed., 1968, pp. 38-44.

Oliver, Robert T., and Cortright, R. L., Effective Speech, Holt, Rinehart and Winston, Inc., 5th ed., 1970, Chapter 23.

Ross, Raymond S., Speech Communication, Prentice-Hall, Inc., 2d ed., 1970, pp. 237-240.

Williams, Barbara, Purposeful Communication, Kendall/Hunt Publishing Company, 1970, pp.189-190.

ANNIVERSARY SPEECH

A MOMENT FOR YESTERDAY

Fellow alumnae and guests. Twenty-five years ago we walked gaily and hurriedly from a red brick building on this soil where tonight stands a new high school. This auditorium covers the space that housed several classrooms and the principal's office, and unless I am mistaken I am standing on a spot right now where many of us stood - for various reasons on numerous occasions - in the principal's office. Perhaps it is significant that we are gathered here on this anniversary in the same place where we learned that law must be observed. We can rightfully say it was here many of us got our start in the right direction. And if we theorize a bit further it is possible that had the principal not exercised his authority and set us straight we might be detained elsewhere tonight in a place that lets you out after ten or twenty years.

That night twenty-five years ago was life's greatest achievement for most of us -- we had it made, and we knew it even though no one else was aware of it. Somehow a quarter of a century later looking back, I find myself disagreeing with the things I was so sure of then. I didn't have it made and I don't have it made yet. There was a group of people in this town called citizens who paid taxes to hire teachers to give us an exposure to education and to train us to make some contribution to this community and the state. It was their insistence that we have a good school then, that brings us back here tonight. And I am sure I represent every old grad present when I say we owe them a greater debt than we can ever repay.

Most of us were born in this county as the community's most recently admitted illiterates. It just happened we could neither read nor write nor speak the English language. We were potential criminals, potential Communists, potential everything bad or good, and we had no religion. The people of this community paid money in taxes and contributions to churches, Boy Scouts, Girl Scouts, and other organizations for eighteen years to make certain we learned to read and write, that we developed good character, and that we did not try to overthrow the democratic form of government. And again I say we owe them a debt of gratitude.

There were instances I must admit when the faith of the community was tested. There was the time when the cheer leader at a football game hit an opposing rooter over the head with his megaphone and the sheriff adjudicated the argument. I think we lost the game, too. On one occasion a billy goat somehow managed to climb the stairs to the second floor to the principal's office and was awaiting him when he unlocked the door. There was the time when a lovely milk cow wandered into the manual training shop through a locked door, all the work of magic, and to this day the community's finest detectives have not unraveled the mystery.

Twenty-five years ago was an age of dreams. Every male was going to become a millionaire and every girl was going to marry one. Looking around me tonight I must say I am not talking to a group of millionaires. Reports have it there might be one. But we enjoyed the dreams and we still enjoy them. Probably it concerns us more today that we dream of losing that extra fifteen pounds we accumulated while trying to find a million dollars. Or maybe it concerns us more that we meet the next payment on the house.

The ideas expressed most often to me by this anniversary class suggest a close relationship to ideas our parents had twenty-five years ago. They wanted a good school for their kids; a good place for them to grow up. They were thinking about us. And tonight we are thinking about our kids and we want good things and opportunities for them.

Last night in the cool of the evening I drove to the hill south of town. It was all so quiet there. The headstones were silent, the green mounds spoke no words, and I felt a deep emotional moment of sadness. The names of former friends and citizens identified on the gray marble seemed suddenly to cross the void of eternity. They were the faithful ones, they were voices that built the red brick high school where you and I made that perilous journey toward adulthood. They were the ones who gave us opportunity and a good community. I stood among them a long time and as twilight deepened their everlasting silence communicated to me. I felt a gratefulness to them I have never known before.

We are told the next quarter century will bring more change to the world than any comparable period in history. I look to it with anticipation and curiosity and I am sure you do. At that time we will all be nearly seventy years old - a wonderful age I'm sure. We'll be riding everywhere in our rockets and flying saucers. We'll be dialing on telephones we carry in our pockets and we'll be taking our annual vacations to the moon. It will all be so commonplace. And our great grandchildren will be reading about those machines people had a long time ago called cars or automobiles.

Some of us here tonight will work directly in the scientific areas that will develop the wonders of tomorrow. Some of us will have children and grandchildren who will casually go about their daily living in a world we dreamed about in this building so long ago - but only yesterday.

Our past governs us with an unseen hand to the end of time and place. We cannot escape its power and direction nor can we elude the destiny it forges for us.

I would like to propose a toast to those great people of this community who guided us through those high school days twenty-five years ago. And I would like to propose a toast to this group tonight for following the lead of those who gave us the will to do our best to make this world a better place to live.

I wish you all a rainbow in your window until we meet again.

SPEECH OUTLINE

Construct a neat, complete sentence outline on this sheet, tear it out, and hand it to your instructor when you rise to speak. He may wish to write criticisms of the outline and speech in the margins.

Type of speech:_____ Name:_____

Number of words in outline:_____ Date: _____

Purpose of this speech: (What do you want your audience to learn, to think, to believe, to feel, or do because of this speech?)_____

_____

TITLE:

INTRODUCTION:

BODY:

CONCLUSION:

Instructor's comments may concern choice of topic, development of ideas, organization, language use, personal appearance, posture, physical activity, sources, and improvement.

(Write sources of information on back of sheet)

SOURCES FROM LITERATURE

(Fill out source requirements completely. Write "none listed" if an author's name or copyright date is not listed.)

1. Author's name _____

   Title of book or magazine used _____

   Title of article in above book or magazine _____

   Chapter and/or pages read _____

   Date of above publication _____

2. Author's name _____

   Title of book or magazine used _____

   Title of article in above book or magazine _____

   Chapter and/or pages read _____

   Date of above publication _____

3. Author's name _____

   Title of book or magazine used _____

   Title of article in above book or magazine _____

   Chapter and/or pages read _____

   Date of above publication _____

INTERVIEW SOURCES

1. Person interviewed _____ Date of interview _____

   His position, occupation, and location _____

   Why is he a reliable source? Be specific _____

   _____

2. Person interviewed _____ Date of interview _____

   His position, occupation, and location _____

   Why is he a reliable source? Be specific _____

   _____

PERSONAL EXPERIENCE OF SPEAKER

1. Tell (1) when, (2) where, and (3) conditions under which you became an authority on subject matter in

   your speech _____

   _____

   _____

   _____

Chapter 25

THE NOMINATING SPEECH

This speech is due:

Time limits: 2-4 minutes. Keep your speech within your allotted time.

Speaking notes: Nobody wants to watch you use notes so you will remember how good the candidate is. Do
not use notes.

Sources of information: None required, however, you should be accurate in your statements regarding
qualifications of your nominee and the office he will fill.

Outline your speech: Prepare a 75-150 word complete sentence outline. Designate the exact number of
words in your outline. Use the form at the end of this chapter.

PURPOSE OF THE NOMINATING SPEECH

How many times have you heard the remark, "I wish I had nominated Henry Porter for president
last night; I almost did. He's a lot better man than Bill Johnson." But, the sad fact remains that Henry
Porter, well qualified and capable, was not nominated. Why? Probably because the person who wanted to
nominate him lacked the courage to get on his feet and also lacked the knowledge of what to say in order to
nominate him effectively. It is to be hoped that should you ever wish to nominate a capable leader, you
will have the courage to rise and speak and the knowledge to utter appropriate thoughts. This experience
should show you what to do and how to present an effective nominating speech should the occasion for one
arise.

To the teacher: It is a practical experience to assign students in pairs to present this speech and the
speech in which an office or nomination is accepted.

EXPLANATION OF THE NOMINATING SPEECH

A nominating speech is one in which a speaker places the name of another person before an assembly as a candidate for office. The speech is usually not long, most often lasting only a few minutes.
There are exceptions, of course. In presenting the candidate to the audience, the speaker tells why his
candidate is especially fitted for the office in question. All remarks made by the nominator should be expressed in such a way that they set forth, in an orderly manner, the reasons why the candidate should be
elected.

Before a speaker can make a nomination, the chairman of the assembly must announce that nominations for the_____office are in order. The speaker must be recognized by the chairman. This is accomplished when the speaker rises and addresses the chair by saying, "Mr. Chairman." At the time, the
presiding officer will give the speaker permission to speak either by calling the man's name, by nodding,
or by some other word or sign. Only then, will the nominating speech be in order.

Occasions for nominating speeches arise most often when officers for a society of any kind are
elected by a group of people. Many common occasions occur at meetings of political delegates, church
representatives, fraternity and sorority members, civic organizations, councils, charitable groups, business men, labor unions, school meetings, and many other assemblages or congregations.

SUGGESTED NOMINATING SPEECHES

Plan to nominate a candidate for one of the following positions:
1. Yell leader.
2. Class officer.
3. Student council president.
4. All-school representative.
5. Candidate for "outstanding student" award.
6. "Most popular student."
7. Who's Who.
8. Governor.
9. Mayor.
10. City council.

11. Representative.
12. Senator.
13. President of any civic organization.
14. Officer of a student legislature.
15. Most valuable athlete.
16. Boy Scout leader.
17. Candidate for "safety award."
18. Candidate for "good driving award."
19. Candidate for "good citizenship award."
20. Speaker's choice.

HOW TO CHOOSE A CANDIDATE FOR A NOMINATING SPEECH

First, you must have confidence in the ability of the person whom you nominate. Second, be sure that he will be acceptable as a candidate. Choose someone reasonably well-known with a good record. Make certain that if the candidate is elected he will do his work creditably.

HOW TO PREPARE THE NOMINATING SPEECH

The purpose of this speech is obvious. It is equally obvious that all of the elements of the speech should point in one direction: Elect This Candidate! A careful organization should be worked out in which you utilize an arrangement somewhat as follows. Name the office, set forth its specific requirements and indicate what its needs are. Once these points are established, show that your candidate has exceptional fitness to satisfy all the needs and demands of the office. Be specific. Mention his training, experience, abilities (especially those of leadership and cooperation with people), outstanding qualities of personality and character, and clinch your point with a statement to the effect that he is undoubtedly the person best fitted for the office. If your candidate is well-known, you may present his name at the conclusion of your speech. If he is not well-known, it will be advisable to offer his name earlier in your speech, mention it once or twice more at appropriate points; then conclude with it.

You should gather all your information, organize and arrange it as indicated above; then practice until you have it well enough in mind to make an effective extemporaneous delivery.

HOW TO PRESENT THE NOMINATING SPEECH

You must have confidence in yourself. The audience can and will sense this. The speaker may achieve the appearance of self-confidence by observing an alert, polite and erect (not stiff) posture. The use of appropriate bodily action and gesture will be evidence of poise and confidence. The words of the speech must be vivid, descriptive, and meaningful. They must be carried to your listeners in a voice that is heard clearly and distinctly without traces of straining. There must be a fluency and readiness of speech that fairly shout to your auditors that you know what you are talking about and that you want them to understand how important it is that the right man (your man) is elected for office. Your emphasis, spontaneity, and sincerity must be manifested by your entire organism. This will be shown by what you do, the way you look, and how you sound. You should avoid giving the appearance of being overconfident, overbearing, or conceited. Have a lively, energetic, unhesitant manner, as well as a pleasant, confident voice, an appropriate appearance, and a sincere desire to communicate; and then you will likely make a good speech.

IMPROVE YOUR VOCABULARY

Inexorable - (ĭn-ĕk'sō-rȧ-b'l) a. Not to be persuaded to change your mind or position; unyielding, relentless, inflexible, stubborn. Example: The student exhibited an inexorable tenacity and spirit in his efforts to overcome stage fright - and he was victorious. Use this word in this speech and five times a day for the next week. Make it yours. You can.

Cute - Omit this word. It occupies too much of your speaking time. There is nothing distinguishing about it except that you have probably used it too much. Here are a few synonyms. Try them: clever, shrewd, saucy, pert, impertinent, sprightly, etc.

BIBLIOGRAPHY FOR THE NOMINATING SPEECH

Culp, Ralph Borden, Basic Types of Speech, Wm. C. Brown Company, Publishers, 1968, pp. 99-101.

Gilman, Wilbur E., and Others, An Introduction to Speaking, The Macmillan Company, 2d ed., 1968, pp. 60-75.

Kruger, Arthur N., Effective Speaking, a Complete Course, Van Nostrand Reinhold Company, 1970, pp. 553-556.

Oliver, Robert T., and Cortright, R. L., Effective Speech, Holt, Rinehart and Winston, Inc., 5th ed., 1970, Chapter 23.

Ross, Raymond S., Speech Communication, Prentice-Hall, Inc., 2d ed., 1970, pp. 237-238.

NOMINATING SPEECH

By Virgil B. Loveday

(Note: The chairman recognized the speaker before he began his speech)

Mr. Chairman, and members of the student body. As you know, we are gathered here today to nominate student government officers. I have been asked to nominate the Student Body President for this year. I feel the one best suited for this position is someone who has had past experience in student government and has an understanding of how it works. For this reason I nominate Paul Kinney as Student Body President.

The qualifications set by the student body for this position as stated in the School Constitution are that the students nominated have at least a 2 point or "C" average in their academic studies and that they pass the "Student Citizenship Test" with a "C" or above.

I stated before that the main reason I feel Paul would make a good Student Body President is because of his past experiences in student government. In his Sophomore year he was a Senator and in his Junior year he was Vice-President of the Student Body. During the time he held these offices, student government became stronger and grew in membership. I think he has contributed to this fact enormously. His past efforts have proved this.

Most of you know him as a friend. You know that he has a pleasant disposition which is a desirable characteristic of a leader. You have seen him in action before and you know he wouldn't let you down. His reputation is one of honesty and dependability and he is known for his good judgement.

For these reasons I feel he would make an outstanding Student Body President and I urge you to support his nomination.

ACCEPTING A NOMINATION

By Laurie J. Montgomery

(Note: The chairman recognized the speaker before he began his speech)

Mr. Chairman, and members of the student body. I regard the nomination for office of Student Body President as an honor. At the same time, I wish to express my appreciation for the nominating speech given in my behalf and the opportunity to be a candidate running for this office.

Lack of proper facilities at the old school hampered our organizations and social functions in the past. Despite the handicaps we operated to the best of our abilities. Through student body efforts we presented the Samuel family with a $500 check to go into their little boy's operation fund. We started a scholarship program for a needy student which proved a success when we contributed a $300 scholarship at graduation. We worked together last year gaining recognition and admiration from our community. As a result, school spirit and enthusiasm started to rise.

Since the doors to our new school have opened, I believe our school spirit, enthusiasm, and endeavors will continue to rise. We will also surpass previous accomplishments.

A successful year and changes in our school program are open to us if we take the opportunity as students to work them out.

I accept the nomination as candidate for Student Body President. If elected -- I will do everything in my power to bring our dreams from the old school to working plans for student government in our new school. As leader representing our student body I would strive for more games, more dances, more activities in general, a school newspaper, and organize our South American School Project.

I truly appreciate the honor bestowed upon me today and thank you for the opportunity to speak with you.

SPEECH OUTLINE

Construct a neat, complete sentence outline on this sheet, tear it out, and hand it to your instructor when you rise to speak. He may wish to write criticisms of the outline and speech in the margins.

Type of speech:_____   Name:_____

Number of words in outline:_____   Date:_____

Purpose of this speech: (What do you want your audience to learn, to think, to believe, to feel, or do
                because of this speech?)_____

_____

TITLE:

INTRODUCTION:

BODY:

CONCLUSION:

Instructor's comments may concern choice of topic, development of ideas, organization, language use, personal appearance, posture, physical activity, sources, and improvement.

(Write sources of information on back of sheet)

SOURCES FROM LITERATURE

(Fill out source requirements completely. Write "none listed" if an author's name or copyright date is not listed.)

1. Author's name _____

   Title of book or magazine used _____

   Title of article in above book or magazine _____

   Chapter and/or pages read _____

   Date of above publication _____

2. Author's name _____

   Title of book or magazine used _____

   Title of article in above book or magazine _____

   Chapter and/or pages read _____

   Date of above publication _____

3. Author's name _____

   Title of book or magazine used _____

   Title of article in above book or magazine _____

   Chapter and/or pages read _____

   Date of above publication _____

INTERVIEW SOURCES

1. Person interviewed _____ Date of interview_____

   His position, occupation, and location _____

   Why is he a reliable source? Be specific _____

   _____

2. Person interviewed _____ Date of interview_____

   His position, occupation, and location _____

   Why is he a reliable source? Be specific _____

   _____

PERSONAL EXPERIENCE OF SPEAKER

1. Tell (1) when, (2) where, and (3) conditions under which you became an authority on subject matter in

   your speech _____

   _____

   _____

   _____

Chapter 26

ACCEPTING A NOMINATION OR OFFICE

This speech is due:
Time limits: 1-3 minutes.
Speaking notes: None.
Sources of information: Yourself.
Outline your speech: Prepare a 50-75 word complete sentence outline. Designate the exact number of
    words in your outline. Use the form at the end of this chapter.

PURPOSE OF THE SPEECH TO ACCEPT A NOMINATION OR AN OFFICE
Right now you may consider that you are the last person in the world who will ever be nominated for an office or elected to one. Because fate alters circumstances and changes men's minds, you may be among those to achieve the distinction of being asked to perform public service. On the other hand, you may openly seek nomination for public duty. Whatever the events that may place you on the rostrum at some future date, you should know beforehand something about accepting a nomination or an office. This speech experience will provide much useful information for you if you are ever to make a speech to accept a nomination or an office.

To the teacher: It is a practical experience to assign students in pairs to present the nominating speech
    after which this one is given.

EXPLANATION OF THE SPEECH TO ACCEPT A NOMINATION OR AN OFFICE
A speech in which you accept a nomination or an office is one in which you publicly recognize your own nomination or your election to an office. The speech is much the same for either occasion; hence it is unnecessary to make a distinction between the two as far as this discussion is concerned.

Your speech should firmly establish you as a man of ability, courage, and modesty. It should create confidence in you in the minds of the audience. Your purpose is to establish this confidence.

An occasion of this sort is potentially important. Anything you say may be used for you or against you. Hence it is essential to say the right thing. It is possible although a bit improbable that you could be nominated or elected and the situation be a total surprise to you. If this surprise should ever occur, you might be wise not to speak because of unpreparedness, for you could easily say the wrong thing. In such a situation, your own judgment will have to tell you what to do.

Occasions for accepting a nomination or an office may arise any time that candidates are selected or elections held. The selection of officers for private clubs, social and civic organizations, schools, churches, fraternal groups, and others offer occasions for the acceptance speech.

SUGGESTIONS FOR THE SPEECH ACCEPTING NOMINATION OR AN OFFICE
Accept nomination or office for one of the following:
1. Class president.
2. Student council president.
3. Student body president.
4. Official in a fraternity or sorority.
5. Official in a special organization.
6. Official in a farm organization.
7. Official in a church organization.
8. Official in a city government.
9. Official in a county government.
10. Official in a state government.
11. Official in a national government.
12. Official as a health executive.
13. Official in a corporation.
14. Official on a school board.
15. Official of a country club.
16. Official of a golf course.
17. Official of a charitable society.
18. Official of a taxpayers league.
19. Official of a booster club.
20. Speaker's choice.

HOW TO CHOOSE A SUBJECT

Study the above list; then make a selection for your speech. Base your decision on your own interest in the topic and in the suitability to your audience. Make your choice without too much delay so that you will have adequate time to prepare your speech. There is no good reason why anyone should make a late and hasty choice of a subject for this speech.

HOW TO PREPARE A SPEECH ACCEPTING A NOMINATION OR AN OFFICE

First of all, be sure to adhere closely to the rules for preparing and constructing any speech. Assuming that you know these, the next point to consider is the purpose of your speech. Your purpose is to establish yourself as a leader and to impress upon people the fact that you are a capable leader. The next logical step is to discover how to accomplish this end. To do this, you will generally speak somewhat as follows: In appropriate and well-chosen words you will express your appreciation and thanks for the honor conferred upon you. (Do not talk about yourself.) Speak of the organization and its importance. Commend its history, its achievements, and its principles. Explain how these have made it grow and how they will continue to operate in the future. You may refer to the names of great men of past fame in the organization and pay them tribute. You should promise to uphold their ideals. Finally, pledge your loyalty and support to the principles of the organization. State frankly that you accept the nomination or office with a complete realization of its responsibilities and that you intend to carry them out. It will be appropriate as a last remark to express again your appreciation of the honor conferred upon you.

A few points to keep in mind are these: Do not belittle yourself or express doubt regarding your fitness. This would be a perfect opening for your opponent and it would not build confidence among your supporters. Do not express surprise at your nomination or election; this is an old trick, worn out long ago and it has little truth or sincerity in it anyway. In no way should you "let the people down" by causing them to feel that they have made a mistake. Finally, avoid grandiloquence by using a simple and sincere language.

Rehearse your speech aloud until you have the sequence of ideas well in mind. Give particular attention to the introduction and conclusion.

HOW TO PRESENT A SPEECH ACCEPTING A NOMINATION OR AN OFFICE

Your attitude should be one of dignity, friendliness, sincerity, and enthusiasm. Your manner, your voice, your bodily actions and gestures should all reflect your attitude. Attention should be paid to your dress so that it is appropriate to the occasion, the audience, and yourself. It will be unwise to consider yourself a Lincoln by not being very careful about how your clothes fit.

When you rise to speak, it is likely that there will be applause. Wait until the applause subsides before you begin to speak. If the applause continues long, raise your hand to ask for silence and a chance to speak. Talk loudly enough to be heard by all, speak clearly and distinctly, and do not talk either too fast or too slowly. If your voice echoes, slow down. Try to make your ideas understandable, and you will be likely to present a good speech.

IMPROVE YOUR VOCABULARY

Graphic - (grăf'ĭk) a. A picturesque or vivid description is said to be graphic. Example: A good speaker will use graphic language to make his points clear. Use this word in this speech and five times a day for the next week. It is a good helper.

Dumb - Give this word a rest. Omit it. Try a synonym. Examples: uninteresting, stupid, uninspired, dull, asinine, irksome, monotonous, arid, inane, fatuous, maudlin, platitudinous, insipid, unimaginative, etc.

BIBLIOGRAPHY FOR ACCEPTING A NOMINATION OR AN OFFICE

Gilman, Wilbur E., and Others, An Introduction to Speaking, The Macmillan Company, 2d ed., 1968, pp. 60-76.

Oliver, Robert T., and Cortright, R. L., Effective Speech, Holt, Rinehart and Winston, Inc., 5th ed., 1970, Chapter 23.

Note: See page 88 for speech accepting a nomination.

SPEECH OUTLINE

Construct a neat, complete sentence outline on this sheet, tear it out, and hand it to your instructor when you rise to speak. He may wish to write criticisms of the outline and speech in the margins.

Type of speech:_____ Name:_____

Number of words in outline:_____ Date:_____

Purpose of this speech: (What do you want your audience to learn, to think, to believe, to feel, or do because of this speech?)_____

_____

TITLE:

INTRODUCTION:

BODY:

CONCLUSION:

Instructor's comments may concern choice of topic, development of ideas, organization, language use, personal appearance, posture, physical activity, sources, and improvement.

(Write sources of information on back of sheet)

SOURCES FROM LITERATURE

(Fill out source requirements completely. Write "none listed" if an author's name or copyright date is not listed.)

1. Author's name _____

    Title of book or magazine used _____

    Title of article in above book or magazine _____

    Chapter and/or pages read _____

    Date of above publication _____

2. Author's name _____

    Title of book or magazine used _____

    Title of article in above book or magazine _____

    Chapter and/or pages read _____

    Date of above publication _____

3. Author's name _____

    Title of book or magazine used _____

    Title of article in above book or magazine _____

    Chapter and/or pages read _____

    Date of above publication _____

INTERVIEW SOURCES

1. Person interviewed _____ Date of interview_____

    His position, occupation, and location _____

    Why is he a reliable source? Be specific _____

    _____

2. Person interviewed _____ Date of interview_____

    His position, occupation, and location _____

    Why is he a reliable source? Be specific _____

    _____

PERSONAL EXPERIENCE OF SPEAKER

1. Tell (1) when, (2) where, and (3) conditions under which you became an authority on subject matter in

    your speech _____

    _____

    _____

    _____

Chapter 27

THE INTERVIEW

This speech is due:
Time limits: 4- 6 minutes for report of an interview.
$\frac{1}{2}$- 2 minutes for role-played telephone appointment.
5-10 minutes for a role-played interview.
Speaking notes: 25-50 words for interview report.
Sources of information: List the person interviewed.
Outline your speech: Prepare a 75-150 word complete sentence outline. Designate the exact number of words in your outline. Use the form at the end of this chapter.
To the teacher: All students should complete in class: (1) the role-played telephone appointments for an interview and (2) role-played class interviews for a job or for information to report. Only those students who are "ready" by virtue of maturity should be assigned to interview local business men - and they should be well trained.

PURPOSE OF THE INTERVIEW EXPERIENCE

Of all the probable events in your life you can bet the interview in some form or another will be one. Perhaps you have already interviewed for a job or you are planning to do so. Unless you are that one person in a million you will be interviewed (briefly or extensively) before you are employed and whether or not you get the job, or any other favorable response, will depend on how you conduct yourself under interview circumstances. And if you are interviewing for other reasons, to gain information, for a report, to prepare a newscast, to prepare a legal brief for a case in court, or to sell an article, the maturity, skill, and judgment you exercise will bring success or failure. This experience will add to your chances for success, help put money in your pocket, and give the confidence needed to do well.

EXPLANATION OF THE INTERVIEW

An interview is talking with another person or a group with a specific purpose. It is planned except for impromptu interviews among business people and others often observed on the street, in a store, even in a home. Unplanned interviews possess characteristics of conversation while more formal interviews tend to proceed in an orderly manner. It is the latter we wish to discuss here since they impose restrictions on the parties involved such as (1) making an appointment - you don't walk into a place of business interrupting the manager from whatever he is doing; (2) there may be limited time for you to finish the interview; (3) you may have several separate meetings, all scheduled before you complete your interview purpose.

One common element in an interview is talk, thus if you can express yourself well things should go smoothly. If you cannot, you may have trouble. Another common element is your physical behavior, your appearance, your walk, your posture, subtle movements of your hands and feet, eye contact, facial expressions. Everything you say and do tells something about you and altogether it tells what you really are. It is your personality. Your thoughts and moods, attitudes and feelings, are all symbolized by your total behavior and you can't hide them. You are kidding yourself if you think you have secretly mastered an art of deceit and won't be discovered. Business executives or sales personnel are quick to detect a phony.

Since the interview situation often places the parties involved close together, perhaps in a small office, the interview permits many personal judgments and subconscious reactions. In effect the interview places all participants in positions of judgment with everyone revealing himself to other persons present. No one has yet invented a better way to formulate final evaluations of people whether it be a prospective employee or prospective boss.

Occasions for interviews occur in all kinds of employment, inquiries for information, sales situations, personnel work, special reports and surveys, and others.

Remember an interview may be conducted by a group such as when news reporters interview a governor or other official. In contrast to this a school board may interview a prospective teacher and the teacher may interview the board members. Or a single reporter might interview any executive or administrative group.

SUGGESTED INTERVIEW SITUATIONS
1. A school official.
2. A minister.
3. The mayor.
4. City official.
5. An internal revenue or state tax official.
6. An employment official.
7. A business man about his business.
8. A business man for a job.
9. A construction contractor for a progress report.
10. Conduct a survey by interviews. (Be sensible with survey.)
11. A school board for a job.

12. The city council about street improvement.
13. A board of directors about company policy.
14. A church board about church policies.
15. A religious group about their projects.
16. An insurance agent about insurance.
17. The city building inspector.
18. A fish and game official.
19. A chamber of commerce official.
20. A forest ranger
21. Student's choice of a suitable interview.

HOW TO CHOOSE AN INTERVIEW SITUATION

Select an area that interests you and one you can complete. Avoid a person or group too distant to reach or who cannot grant the interview within a short time or at a time you can meet. Make your choice and arrangements within twenty-four hours. Why so soon? You may learn that the person you want to interview is on vacation or ill, thus you will be forced to start anew. Also supposing you wait until several days before your report of an interview is due and your appointment is cancelled. You then run to your instructor begging mercy saying you don't have time to do it. You are the dawdler and procrastinator, not your instructor, and you should expect no special consideration. Make your decision at once and do a superior interview.

HOW TO PREPARE FOR AN INTERVIEW (THE INTERVIEWER)

1. Since you are the interviewer make an appointment and if it is made in person be prepared to conduct it on the spot should the interviewee suggest you do so. If your appointment is by telephone be pleasant and efficient by using a carefully prepared and rehearsed request constructed as follows: (a) make sure you are talking with the right person, (b) introduce yourself completely, (c) explain why you want the interview also suggesting the amount of time needed, the date, hour, and place. Do not apologize, (d) leave your name, telephone number, and ask to be called should it be necessary for the interviewee to change the appointment. Sometimes a secretary will take your appointment.

2. Regardless of whether you are interviewing for a job or to acquire information for a report you should acquaint yourself with background data about your interviewee. Examine biographical material in books of scholars, educators, renowned persons, scientific men, "Who's Who" compilations, and others or make inquiries about him.

   Now comes the crux of your interview preparation. <u>What is your purpose and what do you want to know</u>? You will determine the purpose first; second you will prepare a list of about ten lead questions and twenty specific inquiries that will bring out the information you want. <u>Do not read your list of questions verbatim while interviewing</u>. Memorize selected questions from it to be used as needed. You will refer to your list occasionally and originate other questions as the interview proceeds.

3. Dress neatly, carefully and appropriately. Avoid being conspicuous by your appearance. Casual school clothes are not suitable. Dress for an adult's approval who is used to seeing secretaries and other employees attired to meet the business world. Gaudy hair styles or fads (men or women) should be avoided like a plague. You can fail an interview before opening your mouth to speak if your clothes are shabby, dirty, outlandish, or your hair makes you look like a museum piece. Recently a personnel worker who interviewed job applicants for a large mercantile business told this writer that some applicants appeared for interviews without regard to their appearance seemingly with an attitude their appearance was a personal matter and none of the interviewer's business. They were not even considered and would have saved everyone's time by not applying.

4. Get the <u>correct</u> address and <u>exact</u> time for the interview. Be sure of this. Allow more time than needed to get there. You might have car trouble or traffic problems.

5. Study the background information and your list of questions. They should be partially memorized. Be sure you have your questions laid out with adequate space for writing responses to them or provide yourself with an additional notebook for recording the interviewer's answers. Also have a pencil or pen <u>that writes.</u>

6. Think of your approaching interview as enjoyable experience.

HOW TO CONDUCT AN INTERVIEW (TO ACQUIRE INFORMATION)

Arrive ten minutes early <u>at the office</u> of the interviewee, not the parking lot which is several blocks away. Inquire where to locate Mr._____, or tell the secretary, if one is present, who you are and that you are there to meet your appointment. When informed that Mr._____ is ready, go into his office, introduce yourself if the secretary fails to do this, shake hands if you are a man (use a firm grip but don't pump for oil or hang on in a death struggle), politely wait to be seated when invited or seat yourself if your judgment tells you it is appropriate. The host may be busy at his desk and request you to wait a moment. You may stand or sit politely, or look over the office furnishings and arrangements casually, but don't fidget or pace nervously. You might glance over your list of questions to refresh your memory. When your host is ready you may sincerely comment on the office, the view, or something of general interest as an opening remark.

Start your interview by explaining why you are there. State your questions courteously, tactfully, and directly. Initial opening questions may concern (1) history of the business, (2) the nature of the business such as products sold or services performed, (3) number of employees, labor practices, qualifications of employees, vacations, employee benefits, (4) advantages of this business, (5) etc. Do not press questions on any subject the interviewee obviously doesn't want to discuss. It's your obligation to direct the interview into the desired areas and bring the discussion back if it gets too far off the subject. Remember this is your interview. Bring the interview to a pleasant conclusion (perhaps by saying you have one more question), and do not overstay your time. Should the interviewee offer to show you his place of business, have a cup of coffee, or tour the grounds, accept graciously but don't forget that his time may be limited---don't overstay your invitation. Thank him when it seems appropriate and invite him to visit your school.

While the interview is underway take notes quickly and accurately. (Write clearly so you can read your notes later.) Listen attentively so you won't have to ask him to repeat, and should time run out request a later appointment to finish your interview. Thank the interviewee before leaving.

Be courteous at all times. Avoid random, nervous movements, any familiarities, excessive throat clearing, mumbling, and usually it's advisable not to smoke even if invited.

HOW TO INTERVIEW FOR A JOB

Let's suppose you must interview for a job. You will be the interviewee and the interviewer. Questions will be directed to you and you will ask questions about the work. Read again the preceding section on conducting an interview to refresh your thinking. Next, you should have a copy of your birth certificate with you, a complete transcript of your grades beginning with the ninth grade, also honors received, offices held, activities participated in, memberships, a record of your work experience, a list of at least three personal references with complete addresses and telephone numbers (a business man, minister, teacher or other influential person) and/or letters of recommendation. All of these may not be required but they should be available in neatly typed form and correct. A recent good small photograph is also advisable. Several extra copies of these records should be kept in your files. Before you are interviewed you may be required to fill out an application form and, if so, fill it out completely answering every question fully. Be neat and accurate. Omit nothing and don't assume that a stranger studying the form will be able to read your mind and fill in blank spaces.

When you go into the job interview conduct yourself as you would before any business or professional person. Greet the interviewer cordially, shake hands if appropriate, state your purpose and ask generally what positions are available unless you are applying for a particular one. So you will know what is expected of you ask about the qualifications, responsibilities, duties, and requirements of the offering. Most likely you will be asked questions about your experience, background, training and education. Answer these questions honestly and directly but don't belittle yourself. Suggest that the interviewer might like to examine summaries of your personal history, training, experience and recommendations you have with you. Sit politely while he reads them. Besides the job you are applying for he may be looking for someone to fill a special position he has not advertised and it's quite possible he would select you, especially if you conduct a superior interview showing alertness and intelligence. Or maybe he will try you out at something less important with the idea of moving you up if you are a superior worker. As the interview progresses you should be ready to talk and give answers or to wait with poise if anything unusual occurs. Sometimes interruptions are planned to test your reactions - the telephone rings, a secretary brings a message, an employee comes in. Or sometimes he asks a startling or unexpected question. Don't be surprised at anything - just respond intelligently and respectfully.

Before the interview ends, if you haven't been told, inquire about company policy concerning union membership, insurance, up-grading, salary or wages, vacations, sick leave, and other important matters. If it appears appropriate you might ask to be shown around the buildings or grounds where you would work. In all instances when you inquire avoid an attitude of distrust or suspicion - just be interested, courteous, alert.

Before the interview concludes ask when you will be notified about the job. If you receive a vague or indefinite answer ask if you may contact him or write him at a future date. It is only fair before you leave that you have his word you will be notified within a reasonable time. And if you do make a follow-up inquiry it is advisable to appear in person rather than telephoning unless you are asked to telephone.

When the interviewer indicates by words or rises from his chair indicating that the interview is ended bring your remarks to a close, thank him for his consideration, and leave. Sometimes it may be necessary for you to close the interview - you can stay too long.

Here's a hint: If you don't fill out an application form and you want the interviewer to remember you -- instead of a dozen other applicants even though he writes your name on a pad -- just as the interview ends hand him a three by five card, neatly typed, with your name, address, telephone number, age, sex, picture attached, education, work experience, and type of work you are interested in or qualified to do.

Assignment 1. (Appointment for job interview)   The instructor may develop the <u>Interview Assignment</u> as follows:

Two persons at a time sitting back-to-back eight to ten feet apart carry out an imagined telephone conversation. One is a businessman, the other a student seeking an appointment for an interview. A third person, appointed by the instructor, or a fourth person, also appointed, in the audience, may occasionally answer the telephone instead of the businessman. The extra two persons may be secretary, janitor, partner, etc., who take calls for the businessman when he is out or busy. The student must make his appointment even if he has to call back twenty minutes later. Don't overdo the role-playing -- and keep it realistic. The instructor may send the student outside the classroom while he sets up the appointment situation. The person seeking the appointment then enters the room, seats himself, and indicates he is calling by saying "ding-a-ling" until the phone is answered.

Note: If time permits, students should participate in Assignment 1 before doing Assignments 2 or 3.

Assignment 2. (The job interview)

Two persons role-play the job interview from five to ten minutes. The interviewee should enter the classroom door after the instructor has set up any special circumstances the interviewer will confront. The businessman, a secretary, or someone else will admit the student who will take it from there. This should not be rehearsed by the participants since a real interview is not rehearsed; however, the participants should be well prepared to conduct their individual parts and try to make the entire affair true to life.

Assignment 3.

The appointment and interview aspects of this assignment should be role-played successfully before any student is permitted to actually complete the interview with a businessman. Here's the assignment:

1. By telephone make an appointment with a business or professional man whom you do not know personally.

2. Complete an interview to l e a r n about the business, its general operations, policies (labor, products, organization, etc.), and future plans. Take notes. Prepare a five to six minute oral report of the interview and what you learned for the class.

The instructor should keep a list of all businessmen interviewed in order that future classes will not interview. the same ones too often. A letter of appreciation from the instructor to the businessman expressing gratitude for his cooperation is a good practice.

Assignment 4.

Students wanting work should conduct actual job interviews, then prepare five to six minute oral reports of their experiences for the class.

IMPROVE YOUR VOCABULARY

<u>Fallible</u> - (făl'ĭ-b'l) a. Subject to making errors or to being deceived. Subject to being erroneous. Subject to error. Example: Every man is <u>fallible</u> - also foolish if he thinks he is not.

<u>Pay</u> - Try using a synonym for this word. You will be surprised at the variety you can achieve. Here are a few examples: fee, hire, recompense, stipend, compensation, emolument, requital, remuneration, earnings, etc.

BIBLIOGRAPHY FOR THE INTERVIEW

Kruger, Arthur N., <u>Effective Speaking, a Complete Course</u>, Van Nostrand Reinhold Company, 1970, pp. 601-609.
Oliver, Robert T., and Cortright, R. L., <u>Effective Speech</u>, Holt, Rinehart and Winston, Inc., 5th ed., 1970, pp. 126-127.
Oliver, Robert T., and Others, <u>Communicative Speaking and Listening</u>, Holt, Rinehart and Winston, Inc., 4th ed., 1968, pp. 308-310.
Tacey, William S., <u>Business and Professional Speaking</u>, Wm. C. Brown Company, Publishers, 1970, Chapter 9.
Williams, Barbara, <u>Purposeful Communication</u>, Kendall/Hunt Publishing Company, 1970, pp. 65-66.

SPEECH OUTLINE

Construct a neat, complete sentence outline on this sheet, tear it out, and hand it to your instructor when you rise to speak. He may wish to write criticisms of the outline and speech in the margins.

Type of speech:_____   Name:_____

Number of words in outline:_____   Date:_____

Purpose of this speech: (What do you want your audience to learn, to think, to believe, to feel, or do
                           because of this speech?)_____

_____

TITLE:

INTRODUCTION:

BODY:

CONCLUSION:

Instructor's comments may concern choice of topic, development of ideas, organization, language use, personal appearance, posture, physical activity, sources, and improvement.

(Write sources of information on back of sheet)

SOURCES FROM LITERATURE

(Fill out source requirements completely. Write "none listed" if an author's name or copyright date is not listed.)

1. Author's name _____

    Title of book or magazine used _____

    Title of article in above book or magazine _____

    Chapter and/or pages read _____

    Date of above publication _____

2. Author's name _____

    Title of book or magazine used _____

    Title of article in above book or magazine _____

    Chapter and/or pages read _____

    Date of above publication _____

3. Author's name _____

    Title of book or magazine used _____

    Title of article in above book or magazine _____

    Chapter and/or pages read _____

    Date of above publication _____

INTERVIEW SOURCES

1. Person interviewed _____ Date of interview _____

    His position, occupation, and location _____

    Why is he a reliable source? Be specific _____

    _____

2. Person interviewed _____ Date of interview _____

    His position, occupation, and location _____

    Why is he a reliable source? Be specific _____

    _____

PERSONAL EXPERIENCE OF SPEAKER

1. Tell (1) when, (2) where, and (3) conditions under which you became an authority on subject matter in

    your speech _____

    _____

    _____

    _____

Chapter 28

THE SALES TALK

This speech is due:
Time limits: 5-6 minutes.
Speaking notes: Do not use notes when trying to sell something to an audience.
Sources of information: Two are required, preferably three. For each source give the specific magazine or book it was taken from, title of the article, author's full name, date of publication, and the chapter or page telling where the material was found. If a source is a person, identify him completely by title, position, occupation, etc. List these on the outline form.
Outline your speech: Prepare a 75-150 word complete sentence outline. Designate the exact number of words in your outline. Use the form at the end of this chapter.

PURPOSE OF THE SALES TALK

The sales talk is something you may be called upon to present much sooner than you now expect. It involves a situation in which you usually try to trade or sell a group of persons an article in exchange for their money. Sometimes this is a difficult task. Many persons have had little or no experience in this particular type of speaking and selling. This one experience is not intended to make a sales expert out of anyone, but certainly it will help the person who later finds it necessary to sell something to a group. That is why this assignment is made.

EXPLANATION OF THE SALES TALK

A sales talk is a speech in which you will attempt to persuade a group of persons to buy a product from you now or at a later date. In some instances, you will actually take orders at the conclusion of your remarks; in other cases, you will merely stimulate an interest in your goods so that prospective customers will buy from you later. But in either case, your purpose is to sell by stimulating the customer to want what you have and to be willing to part with his money to acquire the goods you have for sale.

The sales talk makes special demands on the speaker. He must be pleasing in appearance, pleasant to meet, congenial, and friendly. He must be thoroughly familiar with his product and be conversant with all matters pertaining to it, including many details. He should, by all means, be able and willing to answer questions regarding the production, the manufacturers (or the company sponsoring it, such as an insurance company), the cost, terms of selling, guarantees, repairs, cost of upkeep, and other such matters about his product. The speaker should know how to meet objections, questions, or comparisons made relative to his product, as opposed to a competitive product.

Occasions for the sales talk are many. We might say that any time a speaker appears before one or more persons with the purpose of selling, he makes a sales talk. The groups, however, which compose the audience may be any one of these: a school board, a high school or college class, a gathering of church officials, a purchasing committee for a business house, a city council, a ladies' aid society, or a group of farmers who have met at a country school house to observe the demonstration of a new tractor hitch. The main idea is that prospective customers can be any kind of people and be met anywhere and at any time.

SUGGESTED TOPICS FOR A SALES TALK

Build your speech around one of the following suggestions which you attempt to sell:

1. Sporting equipment - golf clubs, tennis rackets, etc.
2. Hunting equipment - guns, ammunition, clothing, etc.
3. Fishing equipment.
4. Tractors.
5. Plows or drills, etc.
6. Horses.
7. A vacuum sweeper.
8. An electric razor.
9. A pen or pencil.
10. Stationery.
11. A watch.
12. A book or magazine.
13. An insurance policy.
14. A correspondence course.
15. Real estate.
16. A box of chocolates.
17. Clothing (any article).
18. Old coins or stamps.
19. Ticket to a movie.
20. Speaker's choice.

HOW TO CHOOSE A TOPIC FOR A SALES TALK

Choose a product for sale that you believe in; then build your talk around it. Be sure to select something your audience needs and can use. If none of the above suggestions is suitable, select something else. Do not put off a choice because you cannot make up your mind. You can choose a topic if you want to.

HOW TO PREPARE A SALES TALK

First of all, follow the regular steps of preparation used for any speech. You know these. Pay particular attention to diagnosing your audience. It would be fatal to misjudge your prospective buyers. You should know as much as possible about these items concerning their personal situations: probable incomes, credit ratings, occupations, religions, education, local beliefs, and anything else that concerns them. A wise salesman will find out what other salesmen have sold or tried to sell the group in the way of competitive products. He will also be familiar enough with these products that he can make comparisons favorable to his own.

It will be advisable in all cases to demonstrate whatever you are selling. This means that you must know how to show it to the best advantage. Be sure, very sure, that it is in good appearance and working order. Let your customers try it out. If it is candy, pass samples of it around. If it is a car, have them drive it - but demonstrate.

It is essential that you be ready to sign order contracts. This will necessitate your having pen and ink, order forms, credit information, check books, and receipts for use. Do not make a buyer wait if he is ready to buy.

Another point is to be prepared to greet the audience promptly. Go to the designated meeting place early. Have everything in proper and neat arrangement before your audience arrives. After you think you have every display most advantageously placed, all sales forms in order, and everything in tip-top shape, go back for a final check. If you have omitted nothing, then you are ready, not before.

As for your speech, have it well in mind. Do not use notes. It would be foolish to attempt to sell something while referring to notes in order to discover the good points of your product.

The organization of your speech should be well thought out. One plan which can be recommended is the one that follows.

1. Give a friendly introduction, stating your pleasure in meeting the audience. Be sincere.

2. Present information about yourself and your product. Who are you? What position do you hold? How long have you been with this company? Why did you choose to work for your particular company? What is the name of the company? How old is it? Is it a nation-wide organization? Is it financially sound? Is it reliable? Does it stand behind its products? Does it guarantee its products? Does it quibble over an adjustment if a customer asks for one? Does it have a large dealer organization? Can you get parts and repairs quickly if these are needed? Does the company plan to stay in business? Is it constantly improving its products? Does it test all of its products before placing them on the market? How large is its business? What special recommendations does the company have? Of course, it may not be necessary to answer all of these questions; however, many of them will have to be answered by giving information which establishes you as a reputable salesman and your company as a reputable firm.

Now that you have laid the groundwork, you are ready to show and explain the goods you have for sale. The nature of the article you are selling will demonstrate how you do this. Probably, the first thing you will do will be to explain the purpose of your product; that is, you will tell what it is for. Next you will explain and demonstrate how it operates. In doing this, be sure to play up its advantages, its special features, new improvements, economy of operation, dependability, beauty, ease of handling, and the like. Give enough detail to be clear but not so much that you confuse your listeners.

At this point you have established yourself, your company, and you have explained and demonstrated your product. Your next step will require careful analysis of your audience. This is done to show how your product will benefit them: You must know their wants and needs and let them see vividly how your product satisfies these wants and needs. If the sales article is a tractor, the farmer will do his work more easily and economically by its use. If it is a box of chocolates, the housewife will delight her family and her friends by serving them. If the salesman is offering a correspondence school course, the buyer will make more money, gain prestige, secure advancements by buying the course. Whatever the sales item, you must show the advantages and benefits of the ownership of it. Sometimes it is helpful to mention the names of other persons who have bought the product from you and are now benefiting from ownership of it.

And now comes the last step. How may they buy it? Where? When? Who sells it, if you carry only samples? How much does it cost? Do you sell on the installment plan? What are the carrying charges? How much do you require as a down payment? How many months are allowed in paying for it? What is the amount of the monthly payments? Or is it cash? Is any discount allowed for cash? What special inducement is offered to those who buy now? How much can they save? Will future prices be higher? Do you take trade-ins? How much allowance is made on a trade-in? . . . Make it as easy and simple as possible to buy the goods you are selling. Be sure that your explanations are clear and exact. Do not use misleading terms or give wrong impressions. If your salesmanship will not withstand a full, complete, and candid examination, you will be wise to change your policies or change your vocation.

To be able to present the above information effectively, to demonstrate the product, to show the prospective customers how they will benefit from owning your goods, and how they may buy it, you will rehearse the demonstration and accompanying speech aloud many times. Do this until you have attained complete mastery of the entire speech. Avoid being trite, cocky, or insincere. Do your best, and all will be well.

HOW TO PRESENT A SALES TALK

Look good; be good. In other words have a neat and pleasing appearance, plus a friendly and polite attitude. These points are extremely important. Your own good judgment will tell you what is appropriate dress. Your common sense will provide the background for the right attitude. Generally, you should begin your speech directly, if this procedure is appropriate to the mood of your listeners. Avoid being smart or using questionable stories to impress your listeners. Put the group at ease and get on with your speech. Your manner should be conversational; your voice should be easily heard by all but not strained. Your bodily action should be suitable for holding attention, making transitions, and demonstrating what you are selling. Your language, of course, should be simple, descriptive, vivid, and devoid of technical terms. In using charts, pictures, diagrams, or the sales article itself, your familiarity with these should be so great that you can point out any information or refer to any part of the product while retaining a posture that permits focusing your attention on the audience. In answering questions you should be as clear as possible and sure that your questioner is satisfied with the information you give. Avoid embarrassing anyone. An alert and enthusiastic yet friendly attitude is most desirable.

SPECIAL HINTS

Do not knock your competitor or his product; it is better to praise him.

If you have any special inducements to encourage the buying of your products, be sure to present them at the appropriate time.

After concluding your talk allow your audience time to ask questions. It may be that some of them will wish to ask questions during your speech. If this is the case, be sure to answer them clearly; however, do not turn the meeting into a question and answer occasion before explaining your wares.

IMPROVE YOUR VOCABULARY

Trĕnchănt - (tren'chant) a. A trenchant remark is one that is cutting, sharp, keen, or biting. Example: The speaker had a trenchant wit which worried his hecklers. Use this word in this speech and five times a day for the next week. Make it yours. You can.

Awful and terrible - Omit these words. Do not use them for a week at least. They are fatigued to the point of exhaustion. Give your vocabulary new life by using synonyms. Examples: frightful, monstrous, monotonous, ill-bred, plain, homely, unlovely, ugly, odious, serious, overpowering, disgusting, etc., Be careful that you do not use synonyms inappropriately. Save your more powerful words for situations that they accurately describe.

BIBLIOGRAPHY FOR THE SALES TALK

Reager, Richard C., Crawford, N. P., and Stevens, E. L., You Can Talk Well, Rutgers University Press, Rev. ed., 1960, Chapter 14.
Simmons, Harry, How to Talk Your Way to Success, Prentice-Hall, Inc., 1954, Chapter 22.

SALES SPEECH

By Donald Rogers

What are your plans for next weekend? Are you planning to boat, hike, ski, fish, paint a room in your house, or participate in some other enjoyable form of relaxation? What was that? Painting -- an enjoyable form of relaxation? I think it can be, and in a few moments I'll show you how you can make painting a pleasurable experience.

My name is Don Rogers, representing Montgomery Ward's hardwares division, and I'm here to demonstrate a remarkable product that has revolutionized home decorating, along with eliminating many of the headaches that are traditionally involved.

Here I have two samples of wallboard painted identically with dark green glossy enamel. Beneath each is a gallon of paint. (Speaker kneels beside first can.) This one is a very fine latex interior paint. (Speaker moves to second can.) This is LIFE, Montgomery Ward's new interior latex enamel. For years all paint, particularly rubber latex paints, were pretty much the same in that they all came in lovely colors, were washable, and offered easy clean-up. Now LIFE interior latex enamel offers all these advantages plus several important differences.

Let me show you exactly why I think LIFE is like no other paint you have ever used. (Speaker goes to first open can of paint.) First I will paint a sample with this paint. (Speaker starts to paint with roller.) Notice how this paint applies smoothly and quickly. It is a very fine paint. (Speaker finishes the sample and moves to the second.) Now I will paint this sample with Ward's LIFE. (Speaker begins to paint second sample.) Notice that it too rolls on smoothly, quickly and with absolutely no spattering and, as you can see, (Speaker holds up roller full of paint) LIFE is totally dripless. (Speaker picks up both sections of wallboard and brings them forward to his audience.) If you will, please look at this sample I just painted (pointing to first sample) and you will see that it will surely need another coat in order to cover. Up to now this has not been uncommon, but look at the sample painted with LIFE. It is completely covered. There is absolutely no green showing through the new white coating. This, ladies and gentlemen, is one of the most remarkable qualities of LIFE paint. Here is the Montgomery Ward's one-coat guarantee printed on each can of LIFE:

"THIS PAINT IS GUARANTEED TO COVER ANY PAINTED SURFACE WITH ONE COAT WHEN APPLIED ACCORDING TO LABEL DIRECTIONS AT A RATE NOT TO EXCEED 450 SQUARE FEET PER GALLON. IF THIS PAINT FAILS TO COVER AS STATED HERE, BRING THE LABEL OF THIS PAINT TO YOUR NEAREST WARD'S BRANCH AND WE WILL FURNISH ENOUGH PAINT TO INSURE COVERAGE, OR, TO YOUR OPTION, WILL REFUND THE COMPLETE PURCHASE PRICE."

In addition to being a one-coat paint, LIFE interior latex is extremely durable and washable and can be expected to last six years or more, retaining its velvet finish through frequent clean-ups with harsh solvents and powders. LIFE is as tough as enamel, and with the soft quality of latex.

Not only is LIFE a durable, long-lasting, beautiful coating to any wall surface, but it is safe to use. The aroma, lightly evident while painting, is non-toxic as well as pleasant; and of extreme importance when small children are in the house, LIFE is totally lead-free. This paint is also sanitized to help retard the growth of bacteria on the surface of the paint.

LIFE is truly a superb interior paint. It comes in over eight hundred beautiful colors allowing you to decorate your home in any combination of hues and tints. There is no need to pamper this improved paint. It satisfies the decorator's demands for a soft-look, flat-finish that can be washed repeatedly without losing its luxurious appearance. LIFE is dripless and spatterless, easy to clean up (with just soap and water) and is easy to apply (drying in thirty minutes). Again, LIFE paint is unconditionally guaranteed to cover any painted surface in one coat, which brings us to the best point of all. LIFE is inexpensive to use. You can paint a ten by twelve foot room with one gallon, at a cost of ten dollars and forty-nine cents, and do it in half the time.

Because Montgomery Ward is a nation-wide department store, LIFE interior latex is readily available almost anywhere. Since the one-coat guarantee is good at all Ward stores you can buy the paint in Chattanooga, Tennessee and Ward's will replace it, if desired, in beautiful downtown Burbank.

I urge you to try LIFE interior latex the next time you paint, and I'm sure you will find that for quality and convenience it cannot be duplicated. LIFE is as near as your Montgomery Ward store. Purchase a gallon. Get that job done . . . you know . . . the one you have been putting off, and you'll be enjoying your favorite sport sooner than you think.

SPEECH OUTLINE

Construct a neat, complete sentence outline on this sheet, tear it out, and hand it to your instructor when you rise to speak. He may wish to write criticisms of the outline and speech in the margins.

Type of speech:_____   Name:_____

Number of words in outline:_____   Date: _____

Purpose of this speech: (What do you want your audience to learn, to think, to believe, to feel, or do because of this speech?)_____

_____

TITLE:

INTRODUCTION:

BODY:

CONCLUSION:

Instructor's comments may concern choice of topic, development of ideas, organization, language use, personal appearance, posture, physical activity, sources, and improvement.

(Write sources of information on back of sheet)

SOURCES FROM LITERATURE

(Fill out source requirements completely. Write "none listed" if an author's name or copyright date is not listed.)

1. Author's name _____

   Title of book or magazine used _____

   Title of article in above book or magazine _____

   Chapter and/or pages read _____

   Date of above publication _____

2. Author's name _____

   Title of book or magazine used _____

   Title of article in above book or magazine _____

   Chapter and/or pages read _____

   Date of above publication _____

3. Author's name _____

   Title of book or magazine used _____

   Title of article in above book or magazine _____

   Chapter and/or pages read _____

   Date of above publication _____

INTERVIEW SOURCES

1. Person interviewed _____ Date of interview_____

   His position, occupation, and location _____

   Why is he a reliable source? Be specific _____

   _____

2. Person interviewed _____ Date of interview_____

   His position, occupation, and location _____

   Why is he a reliable source? Be specific _____

   _____

PERSONAL EXPERIENCE OF SPEAKER

1. Tell (1) when, (2) where, and (3) conditions under which you became an authority on subject matter in

   your speech _____

   _____

   _____

   _____

Chapter 29

MAKING AN ANNOUNCEMENT

This speech is due:

Time limits: 2-4 minutes. (This means the total time to be used for all of your announcements combined.)

Speaking notes: Yes. Be sure you have exact information.

Special note to student: Prepare at least two or three announcements for this assignment.

Sources of information: If the announcements are real, state your sources of information on the outline form at the end of this chapter.

Outline your speech: Prepare a 20-40 word complete sentence outline for each announcement. Use the form at the end of this chapter.

PURPOSE OF MAKING AN ANNOUNCEMENT

Each year many millions of announcements are made. Each year many people who hear these announcements are left in a confused state of mind because the information presented was poorly organized, obscure, incomplete, or could not be heard. Often, as a result, attendance at clubs, schools, churches, and other organizations has been disappointing. It is true that you cannot force people to attend a gathering, but it is just as true that you can increase attendance by making absolutely certain that everyone within hearing distance of your voice is completely informed of and aware of the event that you are announcing. Because announcements are so very important, this speech experience is assigned to you.

EXPLANATION OF AN ANNOUNCEMENT

An announcement is a presentation of information. It is brief, concise, to the point, and pertinent. It tells specifically about something in the past (who won a prize), about immediate events to occur (the governor will appear in one minute, or, there will be an important business meeting following adjournment); it may concern a dance to be sponsored next month. An announcement should be crystal-clear in meaning, contain all necessary and helpful data, be stated in easily understandable terms, and be heard by everyone present. Occasions for its use arise at practically every kind of meeting where people convene.

SUGGESTED ANNOUNCEMENTS

Choose two or three of the following suggestions as bases for announcements:

1. A school dance.
2. A labor meeting.
3. A council meeting.
4. A skating party tomorrow night.
5. A picnic next week.
6. An all-school play next week.
7. Tickets for a barbeque supper.
8. A football game.
9. A basketball game.
10. A church meeting.
11. A convention.
12. A candy sale.
13. A contest with $1000 in prizes.
14. A class meeting.
15. A special Christmas sale.
16. A new train schedule.
17. A lecture.
18. A new schedule for classes.
19. A hunting expedition.
20. A ski meet.
21. A young people's convention.
22. The showing of a new car.
23. The demonstration of a new machine.
24. A typing contest.
25. New closing hours for library.
26. Sale of a new book.
27. A wrestling match.
28. A golf tournament.
29. Arrival of celebrities soon.
30. Speaker's choice.

HOW TO CHOOSE AN ANNOUNCEMENT

Study the above suggestions closely. Check the ones that attract you. From these select two or three that you think you would enjoy, as well as profit from, announcing. Remember that nothing will be gained by procrastination, insofar as choosing topics for practice announcements is concerned. If you make up your mind now, you will have much more time to prepare to present the information of the announcements you will make.

HOW TO PREPARE AN ANNOUNCEMENT

The chief purpose of an announcement is to inform. Keep this in mind as you prepare your material. Organize your information in the manner that you would organize any good speech. Have an interesting introduction and a strong conclusion, as well as good organization of the other necessary parts of a speech.

Your first job will be to gather information. Be sure you secure this from authentic and authoritative sources. Do not rely on hearsay. Be absolutely certain that your data are accurate and correct to the last detail. If there is any doubt at all, recheck the material before presenting your announcement. It is your responsibility to have in your possession any and all last minute information available. Ascertain whether any changes have occurred since you first received your information.

The organization of your announcement is important. You must determine the order in which you will present your information so that it will be in logical sequence. It is considered advisable according to some research to place your most important point first to achieve greatest effectiveness.

Generally, your announcement should follow an order of items for presentation similar to the following. Show that the event is timely and opportune. If there are known or probable objections, refute them impersonally; however, avoid going into defensive debate or offering a long list of excuses for the action your announcement proposes. (Show its value and happiness as related to the audience.) Second, name the exact place of the meeting and its location. Tell how to get there, if this is advisable. If it is necessary, indicate the advantage of the place. State the time. Give the date, the day, and the exact hour. If there is an admission charge, give the price or prices. If desirable, tell about the reasonableness of the charges, and where the money will go, especially when the project is a worthy one. If there are tickets, tell where, when, and how they may be secured. If reserved seats are available, explain any special conditions concerning them. Finally, summarize by restating the occasion, the place, the time, and the admission. Omit "I thank you" when you finish.

Not all of the above points will have to be included in every announcement. Your own judgment will tell you what should be omitted or added, as the case may be.

Prepare notes to be used in making your announcements so that nothing essential is omitted. Use cards at least three inches by five inches in size. Make your notes brief, orderly, and legible. Rehearse them until you have everything well in mind.

HOW TO PRESENT AN ANNOUNCEMENT

Your attitude will be one of alertness and politeness. There will be no great need for bodily action other than that which naturally accompanies what you have to say. You must speak clearly and distinctly. All places, dates, days, and times must be articulated so that no misunderstanding prevails when the announcement is given.

Your place should be before the audience where all can see and hear you, not back in an obscure corner or elsewhere among the crowd. Go to the front and stand near the center of the platform. Observe good posture. Pause until you have gained the attention of the audience. Your first words should be heard by everyone. In some cases you may need to raise your hand or rap on a table to get attention. However, do not attempt to talk above crowd noises if the audience is slow to respond. When referring to your notes, hold them up so that you can keep your eyes on the assembly and avoid talking to the floor. When you finish, simply resume your former position in the house by going unostentatiously to your place. There should be no display in your entire performance. Pleasantness and a desire to be understood are enough.

IMPROVE YOUR VOCABULARY

Debacle - (dē-bä'k'l) n. A sudden or unexpected break-up, a rout, a complete collapse, a stampede. Example: The failure of the giant corporation was the greatest debacle in the decade.

Lot - Here is a word that ordinarily receives too much attention. Try using synonyms in place of it. You will find it both enjoyable and enlightening. Examples: volume, multitude, mass, abundance, galaxy, horde, scores, numbers, profusion, host, wealth, etc.

BIBLIOGRAPHY FOR MAKING AN ANNOUNCEMENT

Hance, Kenneth G., and Others, Principles of Speaking, Wadsworth Publishing Company, Inc., 2d ed., 1969, pp. 323-324.
Oliver, Robert T., and Cortright, R. L., Effective Speech, Holt, Rinehart and Winston, Inc., 5th ed., 1970, Chapter 23.
Williams, Barbara, Purposeful Communication, Kendall/Hunt Publishing Company, 1970, pp. 194-196.

ANNOUNCEMENT

By Nancy Bunn

Members of the Student Body, as you know, it is that time of year again for our annual Homecoming game. This year the big game has been scheduled for Friday, October 15. The following announcements are to inform you of the activities planned.

Last year a special day was given to each class, to do anything they wished, within reason, to promote spirit. The activities will be conducted on the same line this year. The Freshman class will begin spirit week on Monday, October 11. The Sophomore class will pick it up, and it will be their day, Tuesday, October 12. The Juniors will be scheduled for Wednesday, October 13, and the Seniors, Thursday, October 14. Also each class is eligible to participate in the float-making contest. Winners will be announced at the game. The individual classes may have one class meeting on their own time before their scheduled day to decide on what they will do during spirit week. Now I know you're all very creative and will come up with some very original ideas to make this week a success.

On Friday, October 15, the day of the game, everyone will rally together in the gym after lunch for an hour long pep assembly. Which means getting out of class. The assembly will be lead by the cheerleaders at which time we will announce our Homecoming Queen from one of the three candidates our team has already chosen.

At 6:30 that night everyone will meet at the lot behind the bank for lighting of the bonfire and snake dance. Then it's off to the game, which is at 8:00 in our football field. Grab your friends or a date and come to support our team. Immediately following the game is our Homecoming dance which will last until 1:00. The dance will be held in the gym, and the band is "The Wandering Kind." Get your date and come, the admission is only two dollars per couple and one dollar and fifty cents for singles. The dress is casual.

Now remember, spirit week begins Monday, October 11, with the Freshmen; Tuesday, October 12, the Sophomores; Wednesday, October 13, the Juniors; and last, Thursday, October 15, the Seniors. Each class may participate in the float-making contest. Then Friday, October 15, a pep assembly will be held in the gym right after lunch. The bonfire is at 6:30 in the lot behind the bank. Don't forget the big game starts at 8:00 Friday, October 15, and will be held in the football field. Last will be the dance, immediately following the game, in the gym, and it will last until 1:00. The dress is casual.

There is a busy week ahead so everyone start making plans for it now because I can assure you it will be a great deal of fun.

Schedules of activities will be posted on the bulletin board in the main hall.

SPEECH OUTLINE

Construct a neat, complete sentence outline on this sheet, tear it out, and hand it to your instructor when you rise to speak. He may wish to write criticisms of the outline and speech in the margins.

Type of speech:_____   Name:_____

Number of words in outline:_____   Date:_____

Purpose of this speech: (What do you want your audience to learn, to think, to believe, to feel, or do because of this speech?)_____

_____

TITLE:

INTRODUCTION:

BODY:

CONCLUSION:

Instructor's comments may concern choice of topic, development of ideas, organization, language use, personal appearance, posture, physical activity, sources, and improvement.

(Write sources of information on back of sheet)

SOURCES FROM LITERATURE

(Fill out source requirements completely. Write "none listed" if an author's name or copyright date is not listed.)

1. Author's name _____

   Title of book or magazine used _____

   Title of article in above book or magazine _____

   Chapter and/or pages read _____

   Date of above publication _____

2. Author's name _____

   Title of book or magazine used _____

   Title of article in above book or magazine _____

   Chapter and/or pages read _____

   Date of above publication _____

3. Author's name _____

   Title of book or magazine used _____

   Title of article in above book or magazine _____

   Chapter and/or pages read _____

   Date of above publication _____

INTERVIEW SOURCES

1. Person interviewed _____ Date of interview_____

   His position, occupation, and location _____

   Why is he a reliable source? Be specific _____

   _____

2. Person interviewed _____ Date of interview_____

   His position, occupation, and location _____

   Why is he a reliable source? Be specific _____

   _____

PERSONAL EXPERIENCE OF SPEAKER

1. Tell (1) when, (2) where, and (3) conditions under which you became an authority on subject matter in

   your speech _____

   _____

   _____

   _____

Chapter 30

THE BOOK REVIEW

This speech is due:
Time limits: 15-16 minutes.
Speaking notes: Fifty word limit.
Outline your speech: Prepare a 75-150 word complete sentence outline. Designate the exact number of
    words in your outline. Use the form at the end of this chapter.

PURPOSE OF THE BOOK REVIEW

There are two reasons for this assignment of the book review. The first reason is that you should
have the experience of preparing and presenting a book review so you will know first hand how it is done.
While you are doing this, you will gain much valuable information and enjoyment from the book you are
reviewing. The second reason is that as a class project you will, as one member of the group, add much
to the knowledge of all of the members of the class. Because each member will review a separate book,
many different authors' ideas will be presented. This in turn will provide a general fund of information
that would otherwise be unattainable.

EXPLANATION OF THE BOOK REVIEW

An oral book review is orderly talk about a book and its author. This requires that you provide
pertinent information about the author as well as what he wrote. Generally speaking, you should include
an evaluation of his work relative to composition and ideas. The ends of your talk will be to inform, to
stimulate, to entertain, and, possibly, to convince.

The book reviewer is expected to know his material well, to be informed regarding the methods of
giving a review, and to be able to present his information in an organized and interesting manner. These
requirements demand an unusually thorough preparation.

Occasions for the book review can occur almost anywhere. They arise in scholastic, civic, religious, and other organizations. In practically any kind of club or society, school or church, a book review
often forms the basis of a program.

SUGGESTED TYPES OF BOOKS FOR A REVIEW

For this particular experience it is suggested that each student select a different speech book to
review. The book should not be a brief copy, a military edition, or other short text unless the instructor
specifically designates such a source. Whatever the book, it should be approved by the instructor before
preparation of the speech is begun.

If the instructor prefers to do so, he may assign any type of book for review; however, reviews
concerning speech will provide a wide coverage of speech and a wealth of information in a short time. Examine the bibliography near the end of this book.

HOW TO CHOOSE A BOOK FOR REVIEW

First of all, follow your instructor's assignment. If you are asked to review a speech text, go to
the library, check out a number of books, examine their tables of contents carefully, and then make your
selection upon the basis of their suitability, appeal, and interest to you and your audience. Be sure you do
not choose a highly technical or scientific treatise on phonetics, rhetorical analysis, speech pathology, or
similar subject unless you possess sufficient background to render a comprehensive and intelligible review. Now, should a book be approved that does not deal with speech, be sure that it is satisfactory for
the occasion, audience, yourself, and the physical environment in which you will review it.

HOW TO PREPARE A BOOK REVIEW

Every speech must have a purpose. The book review is no exception; for this reason, you should
determine your purpose whether it is to inform, to entertain, to convince, to stimulate.

Now you ask, "What should go into a book review and how should you go about organizing your material?" Succinctly, your procedure may follow this order if you consider it suitable.

Tell about the author. Who is he? What about his life? What anecdotes can you discover about him? Does he do more than write? What other books has he written? Where does he live? What is his environment? Has he written similar books? How old is he? Include other data of a similar kind.

Now, about the book. Why did you choose it? When was it written? Under what circumstances? Why was it written? Is it biographical, historical, fiction, what? What do the reviewers say about it? (Ask your librarian to show you lists of book reviews such as those in The New York Times, Christian Century, Saturday Review of Literature, New Republic, The Nation, and others.) What is your opinion? Formulate your own. Do not plagiarize someone else's evaluation of the book. Give examples and comments in answering the following questions: Are the plot and organization well constructed? Is the writer's style interesting? How are situations and characters portrayed? Do the characters seem real and alive? Does the story move forward to a climax? Is the information interesting and useful? Do you recommend the book? Why?

One of the best ways to master the above information is to read the book that you are preparing to review several times. First, read it through for enjoyment. The second and third times read for information you plan to use in your review. As for getting your material in mind, use your own method. It is advisable that you should either write the speech out in full or make a careful and detailed outline, after which you rehearse aloud until your sequence of thoughts has been firmly fixed in mind. If you use quotations, limit them to one hundred and fifty words each.

HOW TO PRESENT A BOOK REVIEW
First of all, have the review "in your head." Do not stand before your audience with the book in your hands so that you can use it as a crutch while you give your review by following previously marked pages, or occupy time by reading. This is not reviewing. Use the book only for your quotations and then for not more than one hundred and fifty words each. If you use notes, limit yourself to three words or less for each minute you speak.

Utilize all of the aspects of good speech - friendliness, animation, vigor, communicative attitude, bodily action, and gestures that are appropriate, a voice that is easily heard and well modulated, correct pronunciation, clear articulation, vivid and descriptive language, a neat appearance, poise and confidence. Utilize these and you cannot fail.

SPECIAL HINTS
1. Be sure you have an excellent introduction and conclusion.
2. Be sure your speech is logically organized all the way.
3. Do not fail to evaluate the book.

IMPROVE YOUR VOCABULARY
Enervate - (ĕn'ĕr-vāt') v. Weaken, make less vigorous, debilitate, unnerve, emasculate, unman, exhaust, jade, fatigue, tire, weary, enfeeble. Example: Hot weather enervates many persons but cold weather stimulates them. Use enervate in this speech and five times a day for a week. Next time you arise early and feel enervated, say so rather than using a commonplace term.

Wonderful - Omit this word. Give it a rest. Try a synonym for adding new life to your vocabulary. Examples: splendid, sublime, dazzling, superb, versatile, gifted, magnificent, amazing, astonishing, surprising, strange, admirable, rapturous, ecstatic, etc.

BIBLIOGRAPHY FOR THE BOOK REVIEW

Monroe, Alan H., and Ehninger, Douglas, Principles of Speech Communication, Scott, Foresman and Company, 6th brief ed., 1969, pp. 9-10.

Oliver, Robert T., and Cortright, R. L., Effective Speech, Holt, Rinehart and Winston, Inc., 5th ed., 1970, pp. 385-388.

SPEECH OUTLINE

Construct a neat, complete sentence outline on this sheet, tear it out, and hand it to your instructor when you rise to speak. He may wish to write criticisms of the outline and speech in the margins.

Type of speech:_____ Name:_____

Number of words in outline:_____ Date:_____

Purpose of this speech: (What do you want your audience to learn, to think, to believe, to feel, or do because of this speech?)_____

_____

TITLE:

INTRODUCTION:

BODY:

CONCLUSION:

Instructor's comments may concern choice of topic, development of ideas, organization, language use, personal appearance, posture, physical activity, sources, and improvement.

(Write sources of information on back of sheet)

SOURCES FROM LITERATURE

(Fill out source requirements completely. Write "none listed" if an author's name or copyright date is not listed.)

1. Author's name _____

    Title of book or magazine used _____

    Title of article in above book or magazine _____

    Chapter and/or pages read _____

    Date of above publication _____

2. Author's name _____

    Title of book or magazine used _____

    Title of article in above book or magazine _____

    Chapter and/or pages read _____

    Date of above publication _____

3. Author's name _____

    Title of book or magazine used _____

    Title of article in above book or magazine _____

    Chapter and/or pages read _____

    Date of above publication _____

INTERVIEW SOURCES

1. Person interviewed _____ Date of interview_____

    His position, occupation, and location _____

    Why is he a reliable source? Be specific _____

    _____

2. Person interviewed _____ Date of interview_____

    His position, occupation, and location _____

    Why is he a reliable source? Be specific _____

    _____

PERSONAL EXPERIENCE OF SPEAKER

1. Tell (1) when, (2) where, and (3) conditions under which you became an authority on subject matter in

    your speech _____

    _____

    _____

    _____

Chapter 31

READING ALOUD

This assignment is due:
Time limits: 4-5 minutes.
Sources for reading aloud: Study bibliography at end of this chapter. Consult school librarian.

PURPOSE OF READING ALOUD

Many persons find themselves in a quandary when confronted with a situation that demands oral reading. Too often they seemingly have no idea about the way oral reading should be done. As a result, excellent literary productions go unread or are so poorly read that much of their beauty and thought are lost. No one expects you to master the field of oral reading after concluding one appearance before your classmates, but certainly you should have a much clearer understanding of what is involved in reading aloud. This reading experience will help you improve your oral reading from the standpoint of personal enjoyment and ability to read for others.

EXPLANATION AND REQUIREMENTS OF ORAL READING

Oral reading, as we use the term here, is reading aloud from the printed page with the purpose of interpreting what is read so that its meaning is conveyed to those who are listening and watching. The purpose may be to inform, to entertain, to arouse, to convince, or to get action. Successful oral reading demands that the speaker must know his material well enough that he can interpret fully and accurately the ideas, meanings, and beauties placed in the composition by the author. To do this capably, a burden of careful, almost meticulous preparation is placed on the reader. Much attention must be given to understanding what the author is saying; the reader assumes the responsibility of discovering the author's meaning. When the reader starts to voice the author's ideas, he still faces the difficult problem of imparting accurate meanings and moods by properly using his voice and actions.

Occasions for oral reading are practically limitless. Any gathering at which it is appropriate to read aloud is suitable. School, church, and civic gatherings are common scenes of oral reading. Clubs, societies, private groups, private parties, and even commercial organizations, such as the radio, utilize oral reading largely for entertainment. We are not considering the hundreds of news casts and other types of radio and television programs which are read daily in the category of oral reading.

HOW TO CHOOSE A SELECTION FOR ORAL READING

Choosing a selection is not easy; it is hard work. First of all, be sure to make your choice of a selection for reading early enough that you will have adequate time to prepare it. Your selection should be made on several important bases. Among these are the following: The selection should be suitable to you as its reader. In other words, choose something that you are capable of preparing and later interpreting. For this particular reading experience, it will probably be advisable that you do an interpretation that does not require characterization other than your own. If you select wisely, this matter need not concern you farther. Of course, if you have had sufficient experience so that you are qualified to portray different characters and make the necessary transitions involved in more difficult interpretations, then go ahead with such a choice of subject. Give close attention to your prospective audience and the occasion. Your choice of a selection must be applicable to both. This means that you need to analyze both your audience and the occasion carefully; otherwise you may read something entirely unappropriate. You must ascertain the kind of environment in which you will be required to read. The size of the building, the seating arrangement in relation to you, the reader, outside noises, building distractions, and other factors will definitely influence your selection. If you observe closely all these bases of choosing a topic, you have a good chance of presenting a creditable oral reading. On the other hand, if you are indifferent and lackadaisical and do not make a careful choice of a selection for reading, then you should expect nothing better than an apathetic response from your audience.

Sources of material are available in your school library. Check the Card Catalogue for poetry, prose readings, and interpretations. Your instructor and the librarian will gladly help you.

HOW TO PREPARE ORAL READING

Some important steps in preparation are these: Know the meaning of every word, as well as the use of all punctuation. The author wrote as he did for a reason. Learn all you can about the author so that you may understand why he used certain words, punctuations, and phrases. Try to understand his philosophy and point of view. Acquire a knowledge of the circumstances surrounding the writing of your particular selection. Do the same for the setting of the article so that you may enjoy its perspective more adequately. Try hard to capture its mood.

Adequate preparation may necessitate your paraphrasing and pantomiming the selection to better understand its meaning. This will assist you in obtaining a more complete comprehension of what the author meant and what he might have done had he read his own poetry or prose.

Practice reading aloud until you have the entire selection well enough in mind that you can give most of your attention (eighty to ninety per cent) to your audience by maintaining eye contact. This will necessitate a form of memorization that will permit you to use the printed copy as a guide only.

HOW TO PRESENT ORAL READING

Do not forget that the audience is watching you at any time you are visible to it. This may be before and after you read. All this time, they are observing you and forming opinions. Thus it is imperative that you constantly maintain an alert, poised, and friendly appearance. When you rise to read, your confidence and poise should be evident. Do not hurry to your position, but rather take your place easily and politely without hesitation. Pause a few seconds to glance over your audience before beginning to read. Avoid being stiff and cold and unfriendly. Begin your presentation by telling why you made your particular selection; tell something about the author so that the listeners may better understand him; provide information concerning the setting of the prose or poetry; and include anything else that will contribute to appreciation and enjoyment of your reading.

Your body should be appropriate to your selection both in posture and action. Any activity and gesture that will add to the interpretation of your reading should be included. Whatever will assist in imparting the mood, emotion, and meaning should be a part of your interpretation. Be careful that you do not make the reading an impersonation.

Naturally, your voice must tell and imply much. Its variety as to pause, rate, pitch, melody, and intensity should be in keeping with what you are interpreting. All of these qualities should have been determined during the periods of rehearsal. If you can feel the emotions and meanings, so much the better.

Your book, or your reading material, should be held in such a way that it does not hide your face nor block the flow of your voice. Your head should not move up and down, as you glance from book to audience. One hand placed palm down inside the book will permit you to mark your place with a forefinger. The other hand held conveniently under the book palm up will act as a support. You need not hold your book in exactly one position, especially while you are looking at your audience. The point to remember is to raise your book in preference to dropping your head in order to read. The audience wants to see your face to catch emotions and meanings portrayed by its changing expressions.

When concluding a reading, pause a second or two before politely returning to your chair. Avoid quickly closing your book and leaving the stage when you are three words from the end of the last line.

If you are reading several selections, treat each one separately. Allow sufficient time between numbers that the audience may applaud and relax slightly and otherwise express enjoyment of what you have done.

By keeping in mind your audience, the occasion, your material and its meanings, the environment in which you are reading, and your place in the entire picture, you can do an excellent interpretation.

IMPROVE YOUR VOCABULARY

Enigmatic - (ē'nĭg-măt'ĭk) a. Puzzling, hard to understand because of obscurity, like a riddle.
    Example: He possessed an enigmatic personality. Use this word in this speech and five times a day for the next week. Make it yours.

Fix - Omit this word. Do not use it for a week, then not more than once a day thereafter. People use it so often it has lost its potency. Use a synonym. Examples of fix in the sense of bribe are: bribe, influence, corrupt, induce, persuade, cajole - other synonyms in the sense of mend are: repair, adjust, arrange, renew, restore, replace, redeem - still other synonyms for fix as a noun are: predicament, condition, plight, dilemma, quandary, crisis, trial, imbroglio, muddle, etc.

BIBLIOGRAPHY FOR READING ALOUD

Buehler, E. Christian, and Linkugel, W. A., Speech Communication, Harper & Row, Publishers, 1969, pp. 235-237.

Ecroyd, Donald H., Speech in the Classroom, Prentice-Hall, Inc., 2d ed., 1969, Chapter 7.

Gilman, Wilbur E., and Others, An Introduction to Speaking, The Macmillan Company, 2d ed., 1968, Chapter 8.

Hance, Kenneth G., and Others, Principles of Speaking, Wadsworth Publishing Company, Inc., 2d ed., 1969, pp. 270-271.

Jensen, J. Vernon, Perspectives on Oral Communication, Holbrook Press, Inc., 1970, Chapter 2.

Monroe, Alan H., and Ehninger, Douglas, Principles of Speech Communication, Scott, Foresman and Company, 6th brief ed., 1969, pp. 12, 114-126, 297-299.

Nadeau, Ray E., A Basic Rhetoric of Speech Communication, Addison Wesley Publishing Company, 1969, pp. 88-91.

Oliver, Robert T., and Others, Communicative Speaking and Listening, Holt, Rinehart and Winston, Inc., 4th ed., 1968, pp. 310-315.

Ross, Raymond S., Speech Communication, Prentice-Hall, Inc., 2d ed., 1970, pp. 68-70.

Samovar, Larry, and Mills, Jack, Oral Communication, Message and Response, Wm. C. Brown Company, Publishers, 1968, pg. 24.

Tacey, William S., Business and Professional Speaking, Wm. C. Brown Company, Publishers, 1970, Chapter 7.

Tanner, Fran Averett, Basic Drama Projects, Clark Publishing Company, 2d ed., 1972, Chapter 13.

ORAL READING SELECTIONS

* The following poems are suggested for oral reading. You will find most of these poems in the Pocket Library book #PL 505 Modern Verse, edited by Oscar Williams. These poems are suggested mainly because of the accessibility of this paperback in local and school book stores. (Or you may obtain it from the publishers: Pocket Library, 630 Fifth Ave., New York, N. Y., 10020.) You may find equally good selections in other anthologies and in your own literature books.

W. H. Auden, "The Unknown Citizen," "Musee des Beaux Arts"
Rupert Brooke, "The Great Lover," "The Soldier"
E. E. Cummings, "Chanson Innocente," "Sweet Spring"
Walter de la Mare, "The Listeners"
Emily Dickinson, "Success is Counted Sweetest," "Because I Could Not Stop For Death"
Robert Frost, "The Mending Wall," "Birches"
A. E. Housman, "When I Was One and Twenty," "Reveille"
Langston Hughes, "The Negro Speaks of Rivers," "Mother to Son"
Vachel Lindsay, "The Congo," "Abraham Lincoln Walks at Midnight"
Edgar Lee Masters, "Silence," "Lucinda Matlock"
Edna St. Vincent Millay, "Dirge Without Music," "To Jesus On His Birthday"
Ogden Nash, "Kindly Unhitch That Star, Buddy," "Bankers are Like Everybody Else, Except Richer"
Edward Arlington Robinson, "Richard Cory," "Mr. Flood's Party"
Christina Rosetti, "When I am Dead," "Remember"
Carl Sandburg, "Jazz Fantasia," "Cool Tombs"
Lew Sarett, "Four Little Foxes," "The World Has a Way With Eyes"
Karl Shapiro, "Auto Wreck," "Buick"
Dylan Thomas, "Poem in October," "Do Not Go Gentle Into That Goodnight"
William Butler Yeats, "Lake Isle of Innisfree," "The Second Coming"

---

* Reprinted from "Basic Drama Projects," by Fran Averett Tanner, Clark Publishing Company, P. O. Box 205, Pocatello, Idaho, 1966.

Chapter 32

PARLIAMENTARY LAW AND THE STUDENT CONGRESS

This assignment will begin:

Time limits of speakers: Unless otherwise stated, in the organization's constitution, ten minutes is generally recognized as the maximum amount of time any person may occupy the floor to speak upon a proposal in one speech.

Student motions: Each student will be required to place at least three motions before the assembly and seek their adoption. He will report the motions which are adopted to his instructor.

PURPOSE OF THIS PARLIAMENTARY LAW EXPERIENCE

A great many persons attempt to lead an assembly in which group discussion is paramount, or they endeavor to participate in a group discussion when they are totally uninformed regarding orderly and proper parliamentary procedure. The results of haphazard procedures are notorious. Ill-will, ruffled feelings, rife confusion, impeded progress, and circuitous thinking are but a few of the by-products of such incidents.

By mastering the rules of parliamentary procedure, you will be enabled to take your place in any gathering whether you are chairman or audience participant. Furthermore, you will be qualified to assist in carrying on all matters of business pertaining to the group's needs.

These experiences are offered in order that you may learn through usage of parliamentary law, the proper procedure for conducting or participating in a deliberative assembly.

EXPLANATION OF PARLIAMENTARY LAW

Parliamentary law is a recognized procedure for conducting the business of a group of persons. Its purpose is to expedite the transaction of business in an orderly manner by observing definite procedures. These procedures may and do vary according to the constitutions and by-laws adopted by various groups. In the many state legislatures and the national congress, parliamentary procedures are basically the same, but differ in numerous interpretations. The rules of each assembly determine the procedures which prevail for that assembly. There is no one set of rules which applies to all assemblies, despite the fact they may all adopt the same text on parliamentary procedure. The laws followed by a group are their own laws, adopted by themselves, interpreted and enforced by themselves. Kansas and Indiana legislatures might adopt Roberts Rules of Order as their rule book for conducting business, yet in actual practice differ widely. In fact, the House and Senate in the same state legislature normally operate under different regulations. This is true of the two houses in the national Congress. One of the obvious divergences here is the Unlimited Debate Ruling in the Senate (this is the reason for the Senate filibusters) and the Limited Debate allowed in the House. There are other dissimilarities which need not be discussed here. The fundamental point is that assemblies do operate under definite laws and regulations.

Occasions for using parliamentary law arise any time a group meets to transact business. Whether the occasion is a meeting in a church, a school house, a pool hall, a corporation office, or any one of ten thousand other places, the opportunity for practicing parliamentary procedure arises. The formality which will govern the extent of the use of parliamentary procedure is dependent upon the group and their knowledge of its rules. Generally, the larger organized groups are more formal and observe their regulations more closely than do small informal gatherings.

HOW TO USE THE CHART OF PRECEDENCE OF MOTIONS AND THEIR RULES

The best, if not the only, way to prepare for participation in parliamentary law is to be familiar with the precedence of motions and their applications. This can be done with a reasonable amount of study through the use of any standard parliamentary law book. Without this knowledge, you will flounder in any assembly and slow down the entire proceedings. You will find the fundamentals discussed in the following paragraphs; however, it is necessary that you study a parliamentary text in considerable detail if you wish to master many of the technicalities.

Here are fundamentals you should know:

Precedence of motions - This term means that motions are debated in a certain order. To ascertain the meaning of this, study the chart entitled Chart of Precedence of Motions and Their Rules. You will notice that number 13 is a main motion. An example of a main motion would be a motion "that the Parliamentary Law Club have a party." This main motion is what the assembly must discuss. It is the only

CHART OF PRECEDENCE OF MOTIONS AND THEIR RULES

Key to Abbreviations of Their Rules:

No - S. -- No second required
Und. -- Undebatable
Int. -- May interrupt a speaker
2/3 -- Requires a 2/3 vote for adoption
Lim. -- Limited debate

PRIVILEGED MOTIONS:

1. To fix the time to which to adjourn. . . . . Lim.
2. To adjourn (unqualified). . . . . Und.
3. To take a recess . . . . Lim.
4. To rise to a question of privilege . . . . Int., Und., No-S
5. To call for orders of the day . . . . Int., Und., No-S

SUBSIDIARY MOTIONS:

6. To lay on the table . . . . Und.
7. To move the previous question (this stops debate) . . . . Und., 2/3
8. To limit or extend the limits of debate. . . . . Lim., 2/3
9. To postpone definitely. . . . . Lim.
10. To refer to committee. . . . . Lim.
11. To amend . . . .
12. To postpone indefinitely. . . . .
13. A Main Motion
   a. "To reconsider" is a specific main motion. . . . . Int.

INCIDENTAL MOTIONS:
(These have no precedence of order)

To suspend the rules. . . . . Und., 2/3
To withdraw a motion . . . . No-S, Und.
To object to a consideration. . . . . Int., No-S, Und., 2/3
To rise to a point of order . . . . Int., No-S, Und.
To rise to a point of information (parliamentary inquiry). . . . . Int., No-S, Und.
To appeal <u>from</u> the decision of the chair. . . . . Int., Lim.
To call for a division of the house. . . . . Int., No-S, Und.
To call for a division of a question . . . . Und.

main motion that can be under discussion. It must be disposed of before any other main motion can legally be entertained by the assembly. If the group, after discussion, votes to have a party, the main motion is disposed of. If it votes not to have a party, the motion is disposed of. But supposing the Club does not want to adopt the motion as it stands. This raises another question.

Amendments - You see, as the motion stands, it simply states that the "Parliamentary Law Club have a party." It does not say when. It is obvious that a change will have to be made. Now look at number 11 on the Chart of Precedence of Motions. It is "To amend." It is in a position above the main motion on the chart. Hence, someone moves "to amend the main motion by adding the words 'Saturday night, June 16'." This is in order. It is discussed and voted on. If it carries, the group has decided to add the words "Saturday night, June 16" to the motion. If it fails, the main motion stands as it was originally made and is open to discussion or ready to be voted on. Assuming for a moment that the amendment carried, the business before the house becomes that of disposing of the main motion as amended. It is debated and voted on.

If an assembly wishes to, it may amend an amendment in the same manner it amends the main motion. It then discusses and votes on the amendment to the amendment. If this does not carry, the amendment remains untouched. If it does carry, the amendment as amended is next discussed and voted on. If it, in turn, does not carry, then the main motion remains unchanged and the amendment plus the amendment to it is lost. If it does carry, the main motion as amended is debated and voted on.

It is illegal to change an amendment beyond adding one amendment to it.

Other motions - Supposing the group decided to amend the main motion by adding the words "Saturday night, June 16," but still is not ready to decide definitely about having a party. You will note that number 10, the motion directly above number 11, is "to refer to a committee." If someone wishes, he may move "to refer the motion to a committee;" all amendments automatically go with it. The motion "to refer" will be debated and voted on. If it carries, the main motion is disposed of and the house is ready for another main motion. If the motion "to refer to a committee" fails, then the main motion remains before the house as though the motion "to refer to a committee" had never been offered.

Now look at your Chart of Precedence of Motions again. You will note many more motions are listed above number 10. The higher you move up this list, the smaller the number of the motion is, but the more important it becomes, until you arrive at the very top of the list, at number 1. This is the most powerful motion of all. The motions on the chart may be placed before the assembly any time during debate on a main motion, provided you always put a motion on the floor that has precedence. In other words, John moves a main motion; Jim immediately moves number 9, to postpone the main motion definitely; George moves number 6, to lay the main motion on the table; Mary follows by moving number 3, to take a recess. This is all in order. However, when George moved number 6, Mary could not move number 8, since George's motion, number 6, had precedence.

Actually, the precedence of motions in its simplest form means that a person may place any of the motions on the floor at any time they are in order if he follows the rule of precedence. You have to understand that the numbers appearing before each motion are not put there to count them. Those numbers tell you exactly what motion has precedence over other motions. The most important motion, as far as having power over other motions is concerned, is number 1; to fix the time to which to adjourn. The second most important motion in order of precedence is number 2, to adjourn - unqualified; next is number 3; then number 4; and so on, clear down to number 13, the main motion itself.

Now let us look at the Chart of Precedence of Motions once more. You see the thirteen motions divided into three specific groups; namely, Privileged Motions from number 1 through number 5, Subsidiary Motions from number 6 through number 12, and last you see Main Motion, number 13, which can be a motion about anything from hanging Hitler to having a party. Here is the point you should get from studying these thirteen motions. After you have a main motion on the floor, there are seven actions you can take on it. These are the motions numbered 6, 7, 8, 9, 10, 11, 12. They are called subsidiary because they pertain to things you can do to a main motion. At a glance you can see that an assembly can do anything from postponing a motion indefinitely to laying it on the table and taking it off again. These motions do not conflict with the ruling that you can have only one main motion before the house at a time. They are not main motions. They are the ways you change (amend) or dispose of a motion (postpone indefinitely, refer to a committee, lay on the table . . . .). Of course, you can dispose of a motion by adopting or rejecting it. It is obvious that once you have a main motion before the assembly, you have to do something with it and rules concerning precedence of motions tell you how to do it.

If you will now examine the privileged motions, 1 to 5 inclusive, you will see that they do not do anything to a main motion. They are the actions a group can take <u>while</u> it is disposing of a main motion. For example, if the club were discussing a main motion to have a party, someone could move number 3, to take a recess. If the group wanted to take a recess, they would vote to do so and then recess for five minutes, or whatever time the motion to recess called for. When the recess was over, they would convene again and once more start discussing the main motion where they left off when they voted to recess.

The section entitled <u>Incidental Motions</u> is largely self-explanatory. You will note that it concerns those things a person would normally do <u>during debate</u> on a motion. For example, if the assembly were debating the motion "to have a party," you might want to find out whether it was in order to offer an amendment to the main motion at that time, because you were not quite sure of the status of such a move. In this case you would "rise to a point of information," sometimes called "point of parliamentary inquiry." If you observed an infraction of the rules which the chair overlooked, you would immediately "rise to a point of order." You will notice that most incidental motions require "no second" and also permit you to interrupt a speaker. This is true because certain matters must be clarified while debate is in progress. Otherwise too many corrections would have to be made after a motion was adopted or defeated.

IMPORTANT INFORMATION YOU SHOULD KNOW

1. <u>The chairman's duties:</u> To call the meeting to order, to conduct the business of the assembly, to enforce rules, to appoint committees and their chairmen, to appoint a secretary for each meeting if one is not elected. He refrains from discussing any motion before the house.

2. <u>The secretary's duties:</u> To keep an accurate record of all business transacted by the house. This includes all motions, whether carried or defeated, who seconded the motions and the votes upon them. Also a record of all committees appointed and any other actions of the assembly.

3. <u>If the chairman wants to speak on a proposal,</u> he appoints a member to take his place; then he assumes the position of a participant in the assembly. He gains recognition from the chairman he appointed, makes his remarks on an equal basis with other members of the group, and then resumes the chair at any time he desires.

4. <u>To gain recognition from the chairman:</u> Rise and address the chairman by saying "Mr. Chairman" or "Madame Chairman," depending on the sex of the chairman. The chair will then address you by name, Mr. _____, or he may nod to you, point towards you, or give some other sign of recognition. You are not allowed to speak until you get the chair's permission to do so, in other words, his recognition.

5. <u>How to place a motion on the floor:</u> Gain recognition from the chair; then state your motion by saying, "I move that _____."

6. <u>How to dispose of a motion:</u> Either adopt or reject it or apply subsidiary motions to it.

7. <u>How to second a motion:</u> Simply call out the word "second." You need not rise or have recognition from the chairman.

8. <u>How to change (amend) a motion:</u> Gain recognition; then say, "I move to amend the motion or amendment by adding the words _____" or "by striking out the words _____" or "by striking out the words _____ and inserting the words _____."

9. <u>How to stop rambling or extended debate:</u> Move the previous question, number 7, on all motions before the house. This will include the main motion and any subsidiary motions.

10. <u>How to ask for information:</u> Rise without gaining recognition, interrupt a speaker if necessary, and say, "Mr. Chairman, point of information" - or you may say, "Mr. Chairman, I rise to a point of parliamentary inquiry." When the chair says, "State your point," you will ask your question.

11. <u>How to ask a member of the assembly a question:</u> Gain recognition; then say, "Will Mr. _____ yield to a question?" The chairman then asks the person if he will yield. If the member says "yes," you may ask one question. If he says "no," you cannot ask your question.

12. How to exercise personal privilege: Rise without recognition, interrupt a speaker if necessary, and say, "Mr. Chairman, personal privilege!" The chair will say, "State your privilege." You may then ask to have a window closed because a draft is blowing on you, or you may ask whatever happens to be your privilege.

13. How to call for "division of the house:" Without rising to gain recognition, simply call out, "Division of the house." This means that you want the voting on a measure to be taken by a show of hands or by asking members to stand to indicate their vote. "Division of the house" is called for when a voice vote has been taken which was so close it was hard to determine what the vote actually was.

14. What does "question" mean when called out? This means the person who calls out "question" is ready to vote. It is not compulsory that the chairman put the motion to a vote. However, he generally does so if enough persons call out "question." This has nothing to do with the motion for the previous question.

15. How do you reverse a ruling made by the chairman? Just as soon as the chairman makes the ruling, the person who disagrees with it calls out without recognition, "Mr. Chairman, I appeal from the decision of the chair." A second is necessary to make the appeal valid. If it is forthcoming, the chair asks the person who made the appeal to state his reasons for doing it. This done, discussion follows after which the chair asks for a vote from the assembly by saying, "All those in favor of sustaining the chair raise their hands," then after counting the votes he says, "those opposed, the same sign." He then announces the vote by saying "The chair is sustained by a vote of seven to three" or "The chair stands corrected by a vote of six to four."

16. How is a meeting adjourned? Adjournment may be made by the chairman who declares the meeting adjourned, or it may be made after the motion to adjourn is placed on the floor, voted on and carried.

17. How do you know what order of business to follow? The assembly agrees upon an order of business. It is the chair's duty to see that it is followed unless rules are suspended by the group, which will permit a change temporarily.

18. How do you suspend the rules? A motion is put before the house "that the rules be suspended to consider" certain urgent business. If the motion carries by a two-thirds vote, the rules are suspended.

19. How do you vote on a motion? The chair asks for a vote. It may be by voice ("yes" and "no"), roll call, show of hands, by standing, or by ballot.

20. How does a person object to the consideration of a motion? Rise without recognition, interrupt a speaker if necessary, and say, "Mr. Chairman, I object to the consideration of the motion (or question)." No second is required. The chair immediately asks the assembly to vote "yes" or "no" as to whether they want to consider the question. If two-thirds vote against consideration of the question, it cannot be considered. The objection must be made immediately after the motion to which the member objects is placed before the assembly.

21. How do you conduct nominations for office? The chair opens the floor to nominations for a certain office. A member rises and says, "Mr. Chairman, I nominate_____." The secretary records nominations. After a reasonable time, the chairman rules that all nominations are closed, or someone moves that all nominations be closed. This is a main motion. It is seconded, debated, and voted on. If it carries, nominations are closed. If not, they remain open. The chair may rule a quick "motion to close nominations" out of order if it is obviously an attempt to railroad a certain party into office before other nominations can be made.

22. How does a chairman receive a motion and put it before the assembly? If it requires a second he waits a short time to hear the second. If it does not come, he rules the motion dead for want of a second. If a second is made, he repeats the motion as follows: "It has been moved and seconded that the Parliamentary Law Club have a party Friday night. Is there any discussion?" This officially places the motion in the hands of the assembly.

HOW TO CONDUCT PARLIAMENTARY LAW SESSIONS

Your instructor will advise you in this matter. However, every class member should take his turn acting as chairman at one time and secretary another. It is advisable that the chairman be appointed by the instructor until the class learns how to nominate and elect a chairman. The following steps may then be carried out:

1. The chairman should appoint a committee to draw up a proposed constitution and by-laws. (The committee may be elected if the group wishes to do it this way.) If time is limited, the instructor may dispense with drawing up a constitution and by-laws.

2. An order of business should be set up. Normally, it will be something similar to the following:

    A. Call the meeting to order.

    B. Read the minutes from the preceding meeting. Make any necessary changes, then adopt them.

    C. Ask for old business. This may be unfinished business.

    D. Ask for committee reports.

    E. Ask for new business.

    F. Adjourn.

3. In carrying out practice parliamentary law sessions, it is necessary that motions be placed before the assembly. Each student is required to put at least three motions on the floor and seek their adoption. At the end of this chapter he should write out five prospective motions which he will submit to the assembly. These should be written on the chart labeled Motions To Be Placed Before the Assembly. Examples are: (a) A motion to petition teachers that all written examinations be limited to one hour. (b) A motion that tardy students should pay a twenty-five cent fine for each time tardy, the money to be contributed to a school social building fund.

- -

MOTIONS TO BE PLACED BEFORE THE ASSEMBLY

(Be prepared to hand this list to your instructor on request)

1. _____

2. _____

3. _____

4. _____

5. _____

Motions adopted were:

_____

(Signature)

A STUDENT CONGRESS

A student congress may be composed of a house and senate with different speech classes acting in each capacity or one group may form a unicameral legislature. In either instance the group purpose is to formulate bills, discuss them, and adopt or reject them by vote. To accomplish these activities the group must know parliamentary law and conduct its business in an orderly manner. This involves (1) determining the scope of legislation to come before the assembly, (2) organizing the legislature by electing officers, forming committees, and assigning seats, (3) holding committee meetings to consider and/or draft bills, and (4) debating and disposing of bills brought before the assembly.

The First Meeting of the General Assembly

At the first meeting of the general assembly a temporary chairman and a temporary secretary will be appointed or elected. Both will take office immediately. The instructor will act as parliamentarian unless one is elected or appointed. The temporary chairman will then open the meeting to nominations for a permanent chairman (speaker of the house or president of the senate) who will take office as soon as he is elected after which he will call for nominations for a permanent secretary who will be elected and take office at once. As next business the presiding officer will appoint standing committees and a chairman for each. The assembly may then discuss matters relative to its general objectives and procedures. Adjournment of the first meeting follows.

Committee Meetings

Committee meetings are next in order and, though informal, parliamentary procedure is advisable with an elected or appointed secretary to keep minutes for the group. A committee may originate its own bills and consider bills submitted by members of the assembly which the speaker of the house has referred to them. It will report bills out or "kill them" in committee, according to votes taken after discussion in the committee.

Sample Bill

Keep bills short, not over 175 words. They must have a title, an enacting clause, and a body. A preamble is optional. The body is composed of sections and each line is numbered. Note the following example:

A BILL PROVIDING FOR LIMITING STUDENT DRIVERS AT BLANK HIGH SCHOOL

WHEREAS, Space is limited around Blank High School, and
WHEREAS, Parking on the street is limited to one hour, and
WHEREAS, Student enrollment is increasing each year, and
WHEREAS, Many students are within walking distance of Blank High School, therefore,

BE IT RESOLVED BY THE BLANK HIGH SCHOOL SPEECH CLASS, THAT:

1   SECTION I. The governing officials of Blank High School should prohibit all students
2 living within one mile of this school from operating a car to and from school as a means
3 of transportation.

This bill introduced by _____

If a bill originates in a committee a member of the committee should be selected to present it to the general assembly. Another member should agree to second the bill. Other members might well prepare to speak for the bill. In case there is a minority report against the bill, their presentation should be similarly organized, even to offering a substitute bill.

The General Assembly In Deliberation

Some student congresses follow the procedures and rules of their state legislatures. Others follow established rules of parliamentary procedure by designating a certain text as their guide. In either case, an agreed procedure must be used. To have a successful general assembly members should know parliamentary procedure and how to use it. Especially important to know are precedence of motions, how to apply the privileged and subsidiary motions. Incidental motions, which have no order of precedence, are of vital importance in the general conduct of the assembly's deliberations and should be thoroughly familiar to all participants.

Under a bicameral student congress the requirement is that each bill must pass the house in which it originates. It is then filed with the secretary of the other house after which the presiding officer of the house refers it to the proper committee. If reported out of this committee and passed by the second house it may be considered as "passed" unless there is a governor in which case he must act on it before it can be considered as "passed." When a governor is used, a lieutenant governor is ordinarily elected and serves as presiding officer in the senate. It thus becomes doubly important that all plans be laid before a student assembly convenes for the first time in order to know what officials to elect, what their duties are, what committees to set up, and what all procedures will be relative to activities of the congress.

A Suggested Order of Business

The following order of business meets most student congress needs:

1. The meeting is called to order.

2. Minutes of the last meeting are read and adopted as read or corrected.

3. The presiding officer announces the order in which committees will report and the group decides on (a) time limits for individual speakers and (b) the total time allowable on each bill.

4. The spokesman for the first committee reads the bill, moves its adoption, gives a copy to the secretary. Another member seconds. If the bill belongs to an individual, he presents it in a similar manner when granted permission by the chairman. A friend seconds. Whoever presents a bill then speaks for it. The bill is debated and disposed of according to the rules of the assembly.

5. Each succeeding committee reports and the process of discussing and disposing of each bill is continued until all bills have been acted upon.

6. The secretary announces the bills that were passed and those that were defeated.

7. The assembly conducts any business that is appropriate.

8. Adjournment is in order.

IMPROVE YOUR VOCABULARY

Obstreperous - (ŏb-strĕp'-ĕr-ŭs) a. Noisy, clamorous, vociferous, unruly, difficult to control, etc., Example: An obstreperous person in an assembly shouts loudly, but thinks little. Use this word three or four times daily until it becomes a natural part of your vocabulary.

Mix - Omit this word. Use synonyms for variety and new shades of meaning. Examples are: amalgamate, associate, blend, commingle, compound, fuse, merge, unite, confuse, intermingle, etc.

BIBLIOGRAPHY FOR PARLIAMENTARY LAW AND THE STUDENT CONGRESS

Gilman, Wilbur E., and Others, An Introduction to Speaking, The Macmillan Company, 2d ed., 1968, Chapter 7.

Hance, Kenneth G., and Others, Principles of Speaking, Wadsworth Publishing Company, Inc., 2d ed., 1969, pp. 336-343.

Kruger, Arthur N., Effective Speaking, a Complete Course, Van Nostrand Reinhold Company, 1970, Chapter 16.

Monroe, Alan H., and Ehninger, Douglas, Principles of Speech Communication, Scott, Foresman and Company, 1969, pp. 404-405.

Nadeau, Ray E., A Basic Rhetoric of Speech Communication, Addison Wesley Publishing Company, 1969, Chapter 13.

Oliver, Robert T., and Cortright, R. L., Effective Speech, Holt, Rinehart and Winston, Inc., 5th ed., 1970, Chapter 7.

Oliver, Robert T., and Others, Communicative Speaking and Listening, Holt, Rinehart and Winston, Inc., 4th ed., 1968, pp. 291-300.

Strother, Edward S., and Huckleberry, A. W., The Effective Speaker, Houghton Mifflin Company, 1968, Chapter 15.

Chapter 33

DISCUSSION - THE PANEL

This discussion is due:

Participants: Three to six and a chairman.

Time limits: 30 minutes for most classroom performances. Others vary according to the amount of time available.

Speaking notes: Participants usually find it necessary and convenient to have notes which provide data such as figures, facts, sources, etc. concerning the points of view and information they present.

Sources of information: Three or more should be studied.

Outline of discussion: See "How To Prepare For a Panel Discussion" next page.

PURPOSE OF DISCUSSION - THE PANEL

There is no better method for resolving the world's problems than by "talking them over." The panel discussion, when operating successfully, utilizes this method. It is democracy at work. Every citizen and, certainly, every student should have the experience of deliberately sitting down in the company of other persons to find the answers to problems of mutual concern. This assignment will give you this vital experience; hence you should study it carefully.

EXPLANATION OF THE PANEL DISCUSSION

A panel discussion occurs when a group of persons sit down together to try to solve a problem or problems by pooling their knowledge and thus arriving at decisions satisfactory to the majority. If they reach these decisions, their purpose is fulfilled. This requires that the discussants enter the panel <u>with open minds and a willingness and desire to hear other viewpoints, opinions, and evidence.</u> Thus by gathering all possible information (facts) and by pooling it, the group can examine a problem bit by bit, point by point, and arrive at a logical solution. No one should consent to join a panel if he does so while harboring preconceived ideas, prejudices, and opinions, which he is unwilling to change in the light of evidence which he does not possess. An attitude of <u>open mindedness</u> is the most valuable asset a panel speaker or anyone else can possess. This does not mean he is vacillating but rather that he will easily and gladly change his mind when confronted by information which perhaps he did not know was in existence.

A panel may vary greatly in the number of members; however, if there are too many participants, progress tends to be slow and laborious. It is, therefore, advisable to limit membership to a maximum of five or six persons besides the chairman.

Occasions for a panel discussion are as numerous as the problems that face any group of people. Every club, every society or organization has recourse to the panel as a method of problem solving. Naturally, if an organization has a large membership, its problems will be submitted to committees which will in turn attack them through the discussion method, that is to say, the panel. Today the radio often features the panel as a public service. The student should not be led to believe that every panel must have an audience or that certain TV programs dominated by sarcasm, acrimony, and quibbling represent true discussion. Such discussions are not in any sense of the word good panel discussions because they often lack the quality of open mindedness and a sincere desire to solve a problem.

SUGGESTED PROBLEMS FOR PANEL DISCUSSION

(Note that topics are phrased in the form of questions. This is considered desirable since the questions imply that their answers are to be found in the form of solutions.)

1. What is the most desirable minimum age for voters?
2. How may more people be encouraged to vote?
3. How may more efficient and capable persons be placed in public office?
4. How may white collar workers' salaries be raised?
5. How may political bosses be controlled?
6. How may more educational facilities be offered?
7. What should be done to decrease illiteracy in the U. S. ?
8. What should be done to improve high school and college curriculums?
9. What should be done about cheating at school?
10. What should be the policy relative to paying athletes or granting them special privileges?
11. What should be the policy in regard to charging admission fees at school dances?
12. How should sororities and fraternities be improved?
13. What should be done to improve school spirit?

14. What should students practice in regard to dating "steady"?
15. Should required courses in marriage be taught in high schools?
16. Should teachers be retired automatically at a certain age?
17. Should all physically and mentally capable students be required to attend school until eighteen years of age, or until graduated from high school?
18. What should a young person's attitude be toward taking out life insurance?
19. Should the government assist young married couples by subsidizing their marriages?
20. Panel's choice of subject for discussion.

HOW TO CHOOSE A PROBLEM FOR PANEL DISCUSSION

If the problem is not assigned, the panel should meet under the leadership of the chairman. At the meeting, various problems should be considered and a selection of a topic for discussion be made by majority vote. The selection should be based on interest to the discussants and the availability of material for research and study. If the discussion will be conducted before a group, then the audience should be considered when the choice is made. In either case the group should select a question they are capable of adequately discussing. In other words, a technical problem should be avoided, such as: How should the Federal Reserve System be organized?

HOW TO PREPARE FOR A PANEL DISCUSSION

Participants should give careful thought to the purpose of a panel discussion, which is to solve a problem. They should prepare their material with this thought uppermost. Their attitude should be that of a farmer who sees a strange plant growing in his field. What should he do about it? Is it harmful? Is it valuable? Should he dig it out by the roots or cut it off? Who can tell him what kind of a plant it is? In other words, the student should not jump at conclusions immediately after selecting a problem, but, like the farmer, he should find out all he can about the question (plant) under discussion and then make up his mind regarding what opinions he should hold and what he should do about them.

Let us assume for a moment that the problem has been selected and that the discussants are ready to begin searching for possible solutions. Here are the steps each participant should follow in arriving at possible answers:

The Problem: What should be done to decrease the number of divorces?

Procedure to follow in arriving at possible solutions: (Keep detailed notes on the following data.)

1. Find out all the effects of divorce, both good and bad. Ask your teacher and librarian to help you locate sources of information.
2. Find out what caused these good and bad effects.
3. Now that you know the results of divorces and what causes them, you should decide that anything you suggest as solutions to the problem must meet certain standards. For example,
   (a) Any solution must be fair to both the man and woman.
   (b) Any solution must be fair to the children of divorced parents.
   (c) Any solution must be legal and constitutional.
   (d) Any solution must be acceptable to the church.
   (e) Etc.
4. State several tentative (possible) solutions to your problem of divorces. Be sure these answers meet the standards you set up. Under each suggested solution list both the advantages and the disadvantages of it. (Remember that you are not to be prejudiced for your solutions. You will soon say to the other discussants, "Here are my ideas with their good and bad points. This is what I believe on the basis of the information I could find. However, I'm willing to change my views if your information indicates I should.")
5. Now select the one solution which you think is the best from all those you have constructed.
6. Suggest ways and means to put your best solution into action. For example, newspaper publicity, beginning with your school paper.

Note: Outline all of your points, one through six, using complete sentences. State all your sources of information, giving dates, authors, names of books or magazines, pages, volumes, . . Be sure to identify your authorities. Hand outline to your instructor as evidence of preparation.

Now that you have gathered all of the information on your problem, outlined it, and learned its contents sufficiently well, you are ready to meet with other members of the panel to see what they have discovered. Each one of them has done the same thing you did in trying to find out what should be done to decrease the divorce rate. You will all get together and pool your knowledge. Obviously you will not all have the same information, because you did not all read the same magazines and books and talk to the same people. This means you will not all agree with each other because your information is different. Your possible solutions will be different too. Nevertheless, you will pool your knowledge and after thoroughly talking it over and examining all the data carefully, you will decide on possible solutions that are agreed on by a majority of the panel. These solutions will represent the cooperative effort of all of you, rather than only one person.

HOW TO PRESENT A PANEL DISCUSSION

In presenting a panel you merely meet as a group and discuss the information and ideas each one has brought with him. To do this effectively, each discussant should approach the panel with an open mind. He must have a desire to find the answers to the mutual problem of the members, not a desire to propound and seek adoption of his personal ideas and solutions. This attitude of open mindedness is probably the most important aspect of discussion.

Now let us assume that the members of the panel have assembled. The chairman should have arrived first and previously placed the chairs in a semi-circle so that each person can easily see everyone else during the discussion. The chairman will sit near the middle of the group. If an audience attends to hear the panel, the chairman should be sure the discussants are all seated in such a manner that they are visible to the listeners. The speakers, in turn, should be just as sure that their remarks are easily heard by everyone present, and they should direct their voices toward the audience as well as the panel.

Before the actual participation begins, each speaker should remind himself that he is not to dominate the occasion, neither is he to withdraw and say little or nothing. Each one should remember further that he will not become angry, impolite, sarcastic, or acrimonious. He will be very earnest and sincere, however, and even persistent if necessary.

The chairman, in turn, will insist - gently, but firmly - on a policy of fairness. He will encourage the more timid to speak their minds. He will promote harmony and good will among the group. He will permit some digression from the main question but direct the discussion in such a way that the main problem is explored. He will note the passing of time and make certain that the discussion progresses rapidly enough to be completed within the allotted time.

Now we are ready to begin the discussion. The chairman will make brief introductory remarks in which he will mention the occasion and reasons for discussing the topic at hand. He will introduce members of the panel (if there is an audience) and tell where each is from, his occupation, and anything else appropriate. If there is no audience, the chairman should be certain that all members of the panel are acquainted with each other.

The procedure for the actual discussion should be entirely informal throughout. It should be a spontaneous give-and-take affair with free and easy questions, answers, and contributions from everyone without promptings from the chairman. This does not mean the chairman may not call on a member if he thinks that it is necessary to do so.

The points to discuss should develop in the following order through informal talk.

1. Define the terms. Be sure you all agree on what you are talking about.
2. Limit your subject if it is too broad. Perhaps you should talk about decreasing divorces in the United States only, or in one state, one city, or in one church. (Note: The statement of your question does not limit the discussion in this respect.)
3. Talk about the effects of the high divorce rate.
4. Discuss the causes of the effects of the high divorce rate.
5. Set up standards on which you will base any solutions to your problem.
6. Arrive at several tentative solutions or conclusions to your question. Be sure you discuss advantages and disadvantages of each one.
7. Select one tentative solution as the best one to put into action.
8. Decide on ways and means to go about putting your solution into action.
9. The chairman should summarize briefly what the panel has accomplished.

10. If it is desirable, the chairman will permit the audience (if there is one) to direct questions to the panel members. He will have to rule on questions that obviously have no bearing on the discussion or other questions that are out of order.
11. The chairman will conclude the meeting with a brief summary at the end of the allotted or appropriate time.

Note: To follow through all of these steps will necessitate a constant alertness on the part of all discussants and the chairman. Of course, if a number of meetings are scheduled, you may move gradually through the various stages of arriving at a solution. It is not wise, however, to prolong the sessions until the members become tired.

IMPROVE YOUR VOCABULARY

Versatile - (vŭr'sȧ-tĭl) a. Being able to do many things easily - easy to adjust to new situations. Example: A versatile secretary is a valuable person. Use this word in your conversation several times a day throughout the next week so that you can really call it your own.

Swell - Here is that word! Everybody owns it and works it to death. Why not omit it and use synonyms? Examples are: matchless, unequalled, priceless, gorgeous, costly, choice, rare, peerless, superlative, rich, capital, inimitable, ornate, etc.

BIBLIOGRAPHY FOR DISCUSSION - THE PANEL

Gilman, Wilbur E., and Others, An Introduction to Speaking, The Macmillan Company, 2d ed., 1968, Chapter 6.

Hance, Kenneth G., and Others, Principles of Speaking, Wadsworth Publishing Company, Inc., 2d ed., 1969, Chapter 20.

Monroe, Alan H., and Ehninger, Douglas, Principles of Speech Communication, Scott, Foresman and Company, 1969, Chapter 14.

Oliver, Robert T., and Cortright, R. L., Effective Speech, Holt, Rinehart and Winston, Inc., 5th ed., 1970, Chapter 6.

Oliver, Robert T., and Others, Communicative Speaking and Listening, Holt, Rinehart and Winston, Inc., 4th ed., 1968, Chapter 13.

Ross, Raymond S., Speech Communication, Prentice-Hall, Inc., 2d ed., 1970, Chapter 12.

Samovar, Larry A., and Mills, Jack, Oral Communication, Message and Response, Wm. C. Brown Company, Publishers, 1968, pp. 205-216.

Strother, Edward S., and Huckleberry, A. W., The Effective Speaker, Houghton Mifflin Company, 1968, Chapter 14.

Verderber, Rudolph F., The Challenge of Effective Speaking, Wadsworth Publishing Company, Inc., 1970, Chapter 19.

Chapter 34

DISCUSSION - THE SYMPOSIUM

This assignment is due:
Participants - Three to four speakers and a chairman.
Time limits for each speech: 5-6 minutes.
Speaking notes: None for the speakers. The chairman may use notes in order to be sure that the order of
    speakers, topics for discussion, and other information do not become confused.
Sources of information: Three or more should be studied.
Outline of speech: None is required for instructor. Prepare your own to insure proper organization.

PURPOSE OF DISCUSSION - THE SYMPOSIUM
    The symposium, one type of discussion, is being used more and more as a means of informing and
enlightening the public. Many persons are unaware of the different types of discussions and the advantages or disadvantages inherent in each of them. Because it will be to your advantage to understand the
workings and the technique of the symposium, it is offered here as a new speech experience for you.

EXPLANATION OF THE SYMPOSIUM
    The symposium is a method of presenting representative aspects of a problem. Usually three or
four speakers talk about one general question, with each speaker presenting his views on a particular aspect. A chairman acts as moderator and leader. He synchronizes the different speeches so that unifica-
tion of ideas rather than a series of unrelated lectures is present. Each speaker is charged with the responsibility of fitting his remarks into the main question by making sure that he contributes to the proposition being explored. The time allotted each speaker is the same, except that the length of the speeches
may vary from a few minutes to fifteen or twenty each if time allows. Following the conclusion of the
speeches, the participants may form a panel, after which the audience is invited to ask questions of the
speakers. Either one of the latter procedures may be omitted - the panel or questioning by the audience.
The whole program may continue as long as an hour and a half or more if the audience is quite active and
the discussants capable, and if time permits.

    The purpose of a symposium is to inform and stimulate the listeners. This purpose is accom-
plished by virtue of the fact that each speaker may support a given point of view.

    Occasions for the symposium may present themselves any time a group of persons meets. It may
be the meeting of a club, a society, a religious, fraternal or business organization, an educational group,
any civic gathering or other assemblage. Today radio and television utilize the symposium frequently on
certain types of programs.

SUGGESTED TOPICS FOR A SYMPOSIUM
    1. How may world organizations for peace be improved?
    2. What should be done to insure permanent peace in Europe?
    3. What should be done to promote progress in China?
    4. What should be done with atomic power?
    5. How should debts to the United States be settled?
    6. What should be done to improve American-Russian relations?
    7. What are the aspects of a federal world government?
    8. Should the United States have compulsory military training?
    9. Should the federal government subsidize high schools and colleges?
  10. Should colleges be tuition free?
  11. What should be done to stabilize marriage?
  12. Should a national minimum age for marriage be established?
  13. Should scholarships be given to all high school graduates with outstanding records?
  14. Should parents exercise more control over their children?
  15. What should be done to improve school dances?
  16. What should be done to decrease juvenile delinquency?
  17. How may moving pictures be improved?
  18. What is a student's responsibility to his home?
  19. What is a student's responsibility to his school?
  20. Symposium's choice.

HOW TO CHOOSE A TOPIC

The members of the symposium should meet with their chairman and then by general agreement decide on a proposition. They should choose one that is interesting to everyone, if possible. However, if all of the members of the group do not agree, the one most suitable to the majority should be the choice. It is not to be expected that you can choose a topic on which everyone is well informed. Be sure that your selection is one about which you can secure information by interviews and reading. Make your decision soon.

HOW TO PREPARE A SYMPOSIUM

First of all, it should be kept in mind that the individual speakers should prepare their speeches according to the suggestions laid down for any speech to inform or stimulate. All the steps of preparation should be included from audience analysis to rehearsal.

The mechanics of overall preparation may be as follows:

I. The members should meet with the chairman.
   A. The topic to be discussed should then be divided by mutual agreement among the speakers so that each one presents a different aspect of it. For example, if the topic is "What should be done to improve the streets of our city?" the three speakers (if that is the number) could set up these questions: (1) What should the city administration do to improve the streets? (2) What should the citizens do to improve the streets? (3) What should be done to improve the efficiency and use of present equipment?

II. Having agreed on the above divisions of the question, each speaker is next obligated to prepare his discussion making sure, of course, that he observes his time limits closely.

The chairman should be well prepared on the entire subject, because he will direct discussion on it. A routine responsibility of the chair is to set up the order of speakers. Having completed this, the chairman must prepare brief introductory remarks. These remarks will include these facts: (1) a history and statement of the proposition, (2) reasons for its discussion, (3) relationship and importance of the topic to the audience, (4) definitions of terms of the proposition, (5) names, topics, and order of the speakers, and (6) the manner in which the symposium will be conducted. The chairman should familiarize himself generally with the point of view each speaker will take. He should also be aware of the necessity for a brief summary at the conclusion of the performance by the speakers and after the questions are asked by the audience.

Let us assume now that everyone is ready for the symposium. A final check should provide answers to these questions: Does each speaker have sufficient authorities and accurate data to back up his information, ideas, and conclusions? Are these proofs in a form which he can use while he is being questioned by a member of the symposium or the audience? Does each member know how to answer questions from his own group or the audience, to meet objections, to restate arguments, to summarize his point of view? Will the speakers keep their heads, their sense of humor, and remain polite when under fire? Does the chairman know how to lead the symposium when they form a panel? Does the chairman know how to lead the audience and direct questions to the speakers? Does he know what types of questions to permit as legitimate and which to rule out of order? If the answers to these questions are not known to the participants, they are obligated to discover them by studying suggested references.

HOW TO PRESENT A SYMPOSIUM

Throughout the entire symposium, good speech practices should be followed. Aside from keeping these in mind, the procedure may be as follows:

1. The members of the symposium may be seated side by side with the chairman at one end.
2. The chairman will make his introductory remarks, will introduce members of the symposium, and then will present the first speaker and his topic.
3. The first speaker will deliver his speech after which the chairman will present the other speakers in a similar manner.
4. At the conclusion of the speeches the chairman will briefly summarize the ideas of the speakers.

5. Following the chairman's summary, the symposium will be continued according to one of the alternatives listed below:
   (a) The speakers will form a panel for a limited time and discuss the ideas that were presented after which the chairman will summarize briefly, then adjourn the meeting.
   (b) The speakers will form a panel as indicated in a preceding, after which the audience will be permitted to question the speakers for a limited or unlimited time by directing questions through the chairman. The chairman will conclude the symposium with a brief summary followed by adjournment.
   (c) Following the speeches and the chairman's brief summary, the audience will be permitted to question the speakers a definite or indefinite time by directing questions through the chairman. At the conclusion of audience participation, the chairman will summarize the matter of the individual speakers, and then adjourn the meeting. In this case there is no panel by the speakers.

IMPROVE YOUR VOCABULARY

Redolent - (rĕd'ô-lĕnt) a. Fragrant, odorous, aromatic, spicy, balmy, etc. Example: The odors of the redolent flowers filled the air. Use redolent in your vocabulary several times each day during the next week.

Sure - Sure is another slave. When used to mean certainly it is an error because it should be surely. Let us give it emancipation and enliven our vocabularies at the same time. Examples of synonyms are: certainly, unquestionably, gladly, undoubtedly, assuredly, unmistakably, decisively, decidedly, definitely, clearly, inevitably, undeniably, unavoidably, incontestably, conclusively, etc.

BIBLIOGRAPHY FOR DISCUSSION - THE SYMPOSIUM

Gilman, Wilbur E., and Others, An Introduction to Speaking, The Macmillan Company, 2d ed., 1968, Chapter 6.

Hance, Kenneth G., and Others, Principles of Speaking, Wadsworth Publishing Company, Inc., 2d ed., 1969, Chapter 20.

Monroe, Alan H., and Ehninger, Douglas, Principles of Speech Communication, Scott, Foresman and Company, 1969, Chapter 14.

Oliver, Robert T. and Cortright, R. L., Effective Speech, Holt, Rinehart and Winston, Inc., 5th ed., 1970, Chapter 6.

Oliver, Robert T., and Others, Communicative Speaking and Listening, Holt, Rinehart and Winston, Inc., 4th ed., 1968, Chapter 13.

Ross, Raymond S., Speech Communication, Prentice-Hall, Inc., 2d ed., 1970, Chapter 12.

Samovar, Larry A., and Mills, Jack, Oral Communication, Message and Response, Wm. C. Brown Company, Publishers, 1968, pp. 205-216.

Strother, Edward S., and Huckleberry, A. W., The Effective Speaker, Houghton Mifflin Company, 1968, Chapter 14.

Verderber, Rudolph F., The Challenge of Effective Speaking, Wadsworth Publishing Company, Inc., 1970, Chapter 19.

Chapter 35

THE LECTURE FORUM

This speech is due:
Time limits: 7-8 minute speech. Questioning period 5 minutes.
Speaking notes: 15 word maximum limit.
Sources of information: Three are required, preferably four. For each source give the specific magazine
    or book it was taken from, title of the article, author's full name, date of publication, and the chap-
    ter or pages telling where the material was found. If a source is a person, identify him completely
    by title, position, occupation, etc. List these on the outline form.
Outline your speech: Prepare a 75-150 word complete sentence outline. Designate the exact number of
    words in your outline. Use the form at the end of this chapter.

PURPOSE OF THE LECTURE FORUM

Persons who give speeches often do so without knowing how many unanswered questions they leave in the minds of their listeners. These questions are unanswered because the hearers have no chance to voice their questions. It is becoming evident daily that speakers can be more helpful to their listeners if the speakers remain on stage following their lectures to answer questions which have arisen in the minds of their audience.

Most students do not receive training in answering questions about the material they present in speeches; thus, when they are confronted with a forum (question period) following a speech they are in danger of awkwardly handling themselves and their audience. This lecture forum type of speech is de-signed to provide experience in speaking as well as answering questions. It should be both enlightening and challenging to student speakers. See what you can do with it.

EXPLANATION OF THE LECTURE FORUM

The lecture forum is a speech followed by a period in which members of the audience are permitted to direct questions to the speaker. The purpose of the lecturer generally is to inform his hearers on a worthwhile subject. He could present a speech intended to stimulate or one to convince; however, the speech to convince would probably not suit the lecture forum atmosphere so well as the speech to inform. We cannot preclude the speeches to stimulate and to convince, because they can well be followed by periods of questioning and often should be; but we <u>can</u> and <u>do</u> suggest that for most lecture forums the speaker should <u>utilize his time by discussing an informative subject</u>. The reason for this is that usually an expert or someone else equally informed is asked to speak for a group to analyze a subject. If, during his lecture the expert does arrive at a decision regarding a policy that he believes should be carried out, he does so scientifically, in the presence of his audience. Having reached a solution does not change his purpose to inform to that of attempting to convince the audience that they should adopt his solution. He <u>stops</u> when he reaches the solution, although he may <u>suggest</u> means for carrying it out. If the audience <u>wants</u> to follow his advice, that is their privilege. The speaker should not urge it on them.

The lecture forum demands that the speaker be well informed, better informed than any member of his audience. It demands further that he be capable of receiving and answering questions from an audience. In short, he should be something of an expert and an excellent speaker.

Occasions for the lecture forum occur whenever an informative speech is in order. These speeches may be given before committees, business groups, church organizations, civic audiences, educational meetings, fraternal orders, and the like. There is scarcely a limit to the occasions for lecture forums.

SUGGESTED TOPICS FOR A LECTURE FORUM

1. How may our government be improved?
2. The problem of juvenile delinquency.
3. The influence of motion pictures.
4. Comic books and good reading.
5. Making the highways safe.
6. Radio or television programs.
7. Honesty in advertising.
8. Women in industry.
9. School assemblies.
10. The status of high school or college athletics.

11. The question of how much insurance to carry.
12. The problem of the feeble-minded.
13. How to live cheaply but well.
14. Proper clothes for the student.
15. Today's music.
16. The future of airplanes.
17. Beneath the ocean.
18. The difficulties of landing on the moon.
19. The problem of keeping peace.
20. Better service stations.
21. New methods in selling.
22. Graduation requirements.
23. New information about space.
24. New sources of water.
25. Oil supplies of the world.
26. The best vacation spots in the United States.
27. Choosing companions.
28. Etiquette while with a date.
29. Industrial schools.
30. Speaker's choice.

HOW TO CHOOSE A TOPIC FOR A LECTURE FORUM

You will be expected to know your subject unusually well, since you will appear before your audience to inform them and be present to open the meeting to questions centered around your remarks. Thus, it is advisable to choose a topic of interest to you and your listeners, as well as a subject about which you can secure plenty of information. Do not select a subject for which there are only limited sources. An apology to an audience for ignorance on your subject is not conducive to confidence in you as a speaker. Base your choice then, on interest, appropriateness, and the availability of source materials.

HOW TO PREPARE FOR A LECTURE FORUM

Since this is an informative speech, you should read the chapter in this text entitled The Speech To Inform. Here you will find complete information relative to preparing this type of speech. Follow it closely.

HOW TO PRESENT A LECTURE FORUM

You should read the chapter in this text entitled The Speech To Inform. It will tell you how to present your speech but not how to conduct the period of questioning from your audience. A discussion of this point follows.

Immediately after the conclusion of your lecture the audience will be advised by the chairman or yourself that they may question you. In making this announcement several points should be explained politely but thoroughly, such as:
1. Tell the audience to please confine their questions to the material presented in the lecture, because you are not prepared to answer questions outside this scope.
2. Request your audience to ask questions only, unless you wish to permit short speeches on the subject. Whatever policy you intend to follow - that is, strictly a questioning period or a question and short speech period - must be specifically announced and understood, or you will run into trouble with those persons who want to make short speeches. If you allow short speeches, announce a definite time limit on them. For the classroom one minute is enough. In large public gatherings, three minutes is adequate.
3. If the audience is small and informal, permit the speakers to remain seated during the forum period; that is, do not ask them to stand while participating. If the gathering is large, require them to stand. Conduct yourself in a like manner, that is, by standing, or seating yourself.
4. Announce the exact amount of time which will be given to the period of questioning. Do not make this questioning period too long. You can always extend the time if the questions are coming briskly at the moment you are scheduled to close. On the other hand, do not continue to hold an audience for the announced time if it becomes obvious that they no longer care to ask questions. It is better to have them go away wanting more than having had too much.
5. Once your announcements are made, open the question and answer period by telling the audience to direct their questions to you. Also explain that you will answer the questions in the order in which they are asked. Thus, if two persons speak at once you will designate which one may ask his question first. The speaker should be urged to speak out rather than to raise his hand, and then wait to be called on.

Having made the above explanations to your audience, tell them you will be glad to answer their questions as best you can. Do not promise to answer all questions, since it is likely that no one could do that. (After all, you are human.) If a question is raised that you do not feel qualified to answer, tell your interrogator you do not have the information necessary to give him a reliable answer. However, if you do not know the answer because you are poorly prepared, you will quickly lose the confidence and respect of your audience - and you should.

If questions are asked which do not pertain to the subject under discussion, politely tell the interrogator that the question is beyond the scope of your talk and you are not prepared to answer it. Should you by chance possess information which will enable you to answer it, state briefly that the question is somewhat afield but you know that _____; then make a very brief reply. Do not let this take you off your subject more than a moment.

Should a heckler trouble you, handle him politely but firmly. Do nothing drastic. Read the chapter in this text dealing with heckling speeches if you want more information.

If some questions are obscure and long drawn out, it may be necessary for you to rephrase them. If you do this, inquire of the person who gave the question as to whether or not your rephrasing asks what he wants to know. At other times it may be necessary for you to ask for a restatement of an inquiry. Do this anytime that you do not hear or understand the question clearly.

Observe acceptable speaking practices throughout your lecture and the period following. Retain an alert and friendly attitude. Do not become ruffled when you meet obvious disagreement or criticism. Simply explain your position firmly but politely. Do not engage in a debate or an exchange of unfriendly remarks and accusations. Dismiss the matter and move on to the next question. If some of the questions are "hot" and they will be, keep your head, add a touch of humor to cool them off if it seems advisable; then reply as capably as you can.

When you are ready to turn the meeting back to the chairman, conclude with appropriate remarks in which you sincerely express your pleasure for having been with the audience. Also compliment them for their interest in the subject.

IMPROVE YOUR VOCABULARY

Criterion - (krĭ-tē'rĭ-ŭn) n. Standard - such as a standard for judging; a gage, a measure, proof, rule, test, yardstick, etc. Example: There was no criterion for the action he took. Use this word three times daily until it becomes a part of your speaking vocabulary.

Complain - Try using synonyms for this word. They will express many new shades of meaning. Here are examples: find fault, grunt, repine, murmur, remonstrate, croak, growl, grumble, grieve, etc.

BIBLIOGRAPHY FOR THE LECTURE FORUM

Gilman, Wilbur E., and Others, An Introduction to Speaking, The Macmillan Company, 2d ed., 1968, Chapter 6.

Monroe, Alan H., and Ehninger, Douglas, Principles of Speech Communication, Scott, Foresman and Company, 1969, Chapter 14.

Oliver, Robert T., and Cortright, R. L., Effective Speech, Holt, Rinehart and Winston, Inc., 5th ed., 1970, Chapter 6.

Ross, Raymond S., Speech Communication, Prentice-Hall, Inc., 2d ed., 1970, Chapter 12.

Samovar, Larry A., and Mills, Jack, Oral Communication, Message and Response, Wm. C. Brown Company, Publishers, 1968, pp. 205-216.

Strother, Edward S., and Huckleberry, A. W., The Effective Speaker, Houghton Mifflin Company, 1968, Chapter 14.

SPEECH OUTLINE

Construct a neat, complete sentence outline on this sheet, tear it out, and hand it to your instructor when you rise to speak. He may wish to write criticisms of the outline and speech in the margins.

Type of speech:_____ Name:_____

Number of words in outline:_____ Date:_____

Purpose of this speech: (What do you want your audience to learn, to think, to believe, to feel, or do because of this speech?)_____

_____

TITLE:

INTRODUCTION:

BODY:

CONCLUSION:

<u>Instructor's comments</u> may concern choice of topic, development of ideas, organization, language use, personal appearance, posture, physical activity, sources, and improvement.

(Write sources of information on back of sheet)

SOURCES FROM LITERATURE

(Fill out source requirements completely. Write "none listed" if an author's name or copyright date is not listed.)

1. Author's name _____

   Title of book or magazine used _____

   Title of article in above book or magazine _____

   Chapter and/or pages read _____

   Date of above publication _____

2. Author's name _____

   Title of book or magazine used _____

   Title of article in above book or magazine _____

   Chapter and/or pages read _____

   Date of above publication _____

3. Author's name _____

   Title of book or magazine used _____

   Title of article in above book or magazine _____

   Chapter and/or pages read _____

   Date of above publication _____

INTERVIEW SOURCES

1. Person interviewed _____ Date of interview _____

   His position, occupation, and location _____

   Why is he a reliable source? Be specific _____

   _____

2. Person interviewed _____ Date of interview _____

   His position, occupation, and location _____

   Why is he a reliable source? Be specific _____

   _____

PERSONAL EXPERIENCE OF SPEAKER

1. Tell (1) when, (2) where, and (3) conditions under which you became an authority on subject matter in

   your speech _____

   _____

   _____

   _____

Chapter 36

DEBATE

This debate is due:

Time limits: 10 minutes on main speeches, 5 minutes for rebuttals. These time limits may be shortened proportionately for class debates if the instructor finds it necessary. Conventional debates require them, however.

Speaking notes: Use notes sparingly, but efficiently. They are necessary in good debating.

Sources of information: You will need many. In your debate you will be required to state your sources of information to prove the validity of your statements.

Outline of speech: Prepare a 75-150 word complete sentence outline to be handed to your instructor before the debate starts. Write the number of words in the upper left hand corner of the paper.

Number of speakers on a team: Two speakers on a team is the conventional number. A one-speaker team is not uncommon.

PURPOSE OF THE DEBATE

This assignment is proposed because many persons want the experience of debating. It is proposed also because debating can be done in speech classes without the long periods of training undergone by contest debaters. This does not mean that long periods of practice are not desirable. They are. Such training produces truly superior speakers. But debating can be done effectively and with good results in speech classes. It provides excellent experience in communicating, since it pits two or more speakers with opposing ideas against each other. It tests their ability to express these ideas and to defend them under direct challenge. This teaches tact, resourcefulness, ability to think on one's feet, and it teaches that ideas must be backed by evidence, not by mere conjecture and opinion. Experience of this kind is beneficial and should be a part of every speech student's life.

EXPLANATION OF A DEBATE

A debate is a speaking situation in which two opposing ideas are presented and argued. The ideas represent solutions to a problem. The proponent of each solution attempts to convince his audience that his idea should be adopted in preference to all others. Actually, a debate, in the sense used here, consists of two opposing speeches to convince.

A debate team may be composed of one, two, or more persons. Today most teams have two speakers. One-speaker teams are not uncommon. Three speakers on a team may permit more exhaustive arguments, but they will take more time and unless they are skilled, much repetition and haggling may be encountered, which will dull the debate.

Debates are divided into main speeches and rebuttals. In carrying out a debate, the usual order of speakers for main speeches is: (1) first affirmative, (2) first negative, (3) second affirmative, (4) second negative. For rebuttals the order is: (1) first negative, (2) first affirmative, (3) second negative, and (4) second affirmative. It is at once apparent, when matching two-speaker teams, that the affirmative team leads off and closes the debate. Now should you have a one-speaker team, the affirmative will lead off with (for example) a ten-minute speech. The negative will reply for fifteen minutes, after which the affirmative will conclude with a five-minute rebuttal. This arrangement gives each debater an equal amount of time. Other arrangements are easy and add variety. For example, an arrangement for two-speaker teams can be worked out by permitting each of the speakers to present a ten-minute main speech in the usual order of speaking, but immediately following each speech an opponent rises to cross examine the speaker for five minutes before the speaker leaves the floor. To bring the debate to an end, after the speeches and cross examinations, one member of the negative team presents a final five minute summary of the negative's position, after which one member of the affirmative concludes the debate with a like summary of his team's position.

It will be advisable to practice the conventional type of debating rather than the cross examination system. The cross examination method involves too many technicalities to be settled by a chairman or judge during the cross examining periods. Unless the rules are well known to the participants and the judge, confusion instead of cross examination reigns.

Occasions for debates occur in practically all academic classes, although regularly organized debate groups and speech classes enjoy them most frequently. Inter-school debates among high schools are nation-wide, as are inter-college contests. Debates provide excellent program material in schools, over

TV, radio, before civic organizations, churches, business groups, clubs, . . . Any group of persons willing to listen to a sound discussion of opposing ideas always welcomes good debate. For sheer enjoyment with, perhaps, some thought thrown in, humorous debates are a fine type of entertainment. Even though they are light in treatment of subject matter and their purpose is to entertain, they require the same skillful preparation that the regular debate does.

SUGGESTED TOPICS FOR DEBATE

1. Resolved that federal population controls should be established.
2. Resolved that the closed shop should be abolished by law.
3. Resolved that inter-racial marriages should be prohibited by law.
4. Resolved that national speed laws should be established.
5. Resolved that national uniform traffic signals should be established.
6. Resolved that all car owners should be compelled to carry liability insurance.
7. Resolved that hitch hiking should be made illegal.
8. Resolved that the national government should establish and maintain roadside parks at established intervals on all national highways.
9. Resolved that the federal government should establish permanent rent controls.
10. Resolved that the national government should be prohibited from spending more than it receives in taxes.
11. Resolved that all high school graduates should attend college at least one year.
12. Resolved that minimum wages should be established for all teachers.
13. Resolved that students working their way through school should be required to carry lighter credit loads than unemployed students.
14. Resolved that fraternities and sororities should be established in all high schools.
15. Resolved that smoking should be permitted in designated lounge rooms in high schools.
16. Resolved that students should be permitted to choose all subjects they wish to take for academic credit.
17. Resolved that beer should be served in designated lounge rooms in colleges.
18. Resolved that all high schools should teach courses in sex education.
19. Resolved that students who have unexcused absences totaling ten per cent or more of any class periods should automatically "flunk" those courses.
20. Resolved that persons convicted of killing wild game illegally should be prohibited from purchasing hunting licenses for at least one year from date of conviction.
21. Resolved that the federal government should own and operate all munitions industries.
22. Resolved that college athletes should be subsidized.
23. Resolved that wealth as well as men should be drafted in time of war.
24. Resolved that women as well as men should be drafted in time of war.
25. Resolved that a special tax should be levied to raise funds for the support of state hospitals.
26. Resolved that it is more desirable to own a _____ car than a _____ car.
27. Resolved that women with children under the age of fourteen should be prohibited from working away from home.
28. Resolved that tipping should be abolished.
29. Resolved that students caught cheating should be expelled from school.
30. Resolved that liquor should be rationed, distributed and sold by the federal government.
31. Resolved that colleges should restrict enrollments to the higher intellectual students.
32. Resolved that inter-collegiate football should be abolished.
33. Resolved that every high school should require a course in speech for graduation.
34. Resolved that no price of admission for movies should exceed fifty cents.
35. Resolved that mercy killing should be legalized.
36. Resolved that capital punishment should be abolished.
37. Resolved that corporal punishment in schools should be abolished.
38. Speaker's choice.

HOW TO CHOOSE A TOPIC FOR DEBATE

Since two teams will be concerned with the choice of topic, it will be well to consult your opponents, at which time all of you will agree on a subject for debate. Remember that one team will uphold the proposition under debate, while the other will argue against it. So, in choosing a topic, it should also be decided which team will debate affirmative (for the topic) and which will debate negative (against it).

In arriving at an agreement on the subject, be sure that all of you have an interest in the subject and that you can find information about it. If you are in doubt about the availability of source materials, check with your school and city librarians before making a final decision.

If you decide to argue a proposition which is not listed in Suggested Topics For Debate, remember it must be phrased so that it proposes a specific proposition to be adopted or rejected. In other words, be sure that you have a debatable subject.

There should be no procrastination in deciding on a question for debate. An honest effort to select a subject should be made by the persons concerned. This does not imply that a hurried decision should be reached. It simply means that a logical approach to topic selection is necessary and that the inability of debaters to agree on a question for debate is no excuse for not having a subject.

One answer to the problem of what to debate is to ask your instructor to assign the subject and the side you will argue.

HOW TO PREPARE A DEBATE

As stated earlier in this chapter, a debate is really two or more opposing speeches to convince. Your purpose, then, is to convince your audience that you are correct in your point of view. To refresh your memory about the speech to convince, reread the chapter bearing this heading.

Because a debate is an activity in which two colleagues team against two other colleagues, it is necessary that preparation for the contest be made jointly by each pair of debaters. This can best be done if the following suggestions are carried out:

1. Decide who will be first speaker.
2. Make a mutual agreement that both colleagues will search for materials to prove your side of the question. Later these materials can be exchanged to help each of you to strengthen your cases.
3. Begin your hunt for information on your subject. Whenever you find something pertinent, take notes on it. Be sure to be able to give the exact reference for the information. Record the following items: The author's name and who he is, the name of the article, the name of the magazine, newspaper, or book in which you found the item, and the exact date of publication. Take your notes on four inch by six inch cards; then at the top of each card write briefly what the notes on that card concern.

How to Organize a Debate Speech

After you have gathered your material, you will begin organizing your case. This part of your preparation will require some stiff head work; however, it is not particularly difficult. The following suggestions will tell you how to organize a debate case.

I. Divide your entire case into three parts. These parts are called stock issues. An affirmative must prove all three issues; a negative can win by disproving any one of the issues.
   A. Show a need for the specific proposal you are offering.
   B. Show that your proposal is practical. In other words, show that it will do what you say it will do.
   C. Show that your proposal is desirable. This means to show that the way in which it will work will be beneficial. If you are arguing that capital punishment should be abolished, the question arises as to whether or not it will be desirable for the nation to pay taxes to keep convicted murderers alive for thirty years.

II. Your finished case should be set up as follows:
   A. State your proposition.
   B. Define your terms. If you are arguing that compulsory military training should be established in the United States, you must tell what you mean by "compulsory." Will anyone be excepted? What does "military training" mean? Does it refer to the infantry, the air force, or a technical school for atomic specialists? In other words, state exactly what you are talking about.
   C. Show that your proposal is needed (stock issue).
      1. To prove the need give examples, illustrations, opinions of authorities, facts, and analogies which all point to the need for your proposition. Give enough of these proofs to establish your point.
   D. Show that your proposition is practical (it will work). This your second stock issue.
      1. Give proofs as you did to establish your need in point C, above.
   E. Show that your proposal is desirable (its results will be beneficial). This is your third stock issue.
      1. Give proofs as you did in point C, above.
   F. Summarize your speech, then close it by stating your belief in your proposal.

III. Colleagues should divide their case.
  A. The first speaker often defines the terms and sets up the need. If time permits, he may establish the practicality and desirability of the proposal; however, the second speaker usually takes one or both of these points. This matter must be settled and agreed on by colleagues before cases are organized. A speaker should not spread himself so thin that he proves nothing. A second speaker should re-establish the need set up by his colleague if an opponent attacks it. After doing this, he goes into his points.

IV. Rebuttal is easy if you follow a plan.
  A. Colleagues should agree ahead of time regarding which points each one will defend. This agreement should be adhered to, otherwise confusion results.
  B. In refuting points, try to run the debate. Take the offensive. This is easy but you must follow a plan. The plan is to take your main speech point by point. Reiterate the first point you made, tell what the opposition did to disprove it; then give more evidence to re-establish it. Now take your second point, do exactly the same thing over again. Continue this strategy throughout your rebuttal and close with a summary, followed by a statement of your belief in the soundness of your proposal.
  Do not talk about points brought up by your opponents, except as you refer to them while you re-emphasize your own points. You must carry out this plan of advancing your own case or you will be likely to confuse yourself and your audience. Refuse to be budged from the consideration of your plan for advancing your own case.

V. The points (stock issues) listed above apply to both affirmative and negative speakers. When each team tries to run the debate, that is, take the offensive, there is a real argument. Because each plays upon his own case, the two proposals and their arguments are easily followed.
  It should be noted, too, that negative cases oppose affirmative cases by showing that any one of the stock issues does not hold, that is, the proposal is not needed, not practical, or not desirable. By disproving any one of these points, a negative causes an affirmative to fall, since the affirmative must prove all of them.

VI. Colleagues should plan their cases together and rehearse them together. They should have their material so well in mind that they need make little reference to their notes, except when bringing up objections raised by the opposition. Practice should be continued until a student feels complete mastery of his material. He should not memorize a debate speech word for word. He should know his sequence of points and his evidence to prove his point. Besides this, he needs a well-planned introduction and conclusion.

HOW TO PRESENT A DEBATE

A debater's attitude should be one of confidence but not "cockiness." He should be friendly, firm, polite and very eager to be understood. A sense of humor is helpful if well applied.

Bodily actions, gestures, and use of notes should be without awkwardness. Posture should be one of ease and alertness.

The voice should be conversational in quality, earnest, and sincere. Everyone should hear it easily. Shouting, "preaching," grandiloquence, "stage acting," and similar displays have no place in debate - or any good speaking. If a speaker is aroused and means what he says, generally, his voice will tell his story. He must, however, not permit his voice to slip from his control.

When a debater rises to speak, he should address the chairman, and then greet his audience and opponents by saying "Friends." No more is needed. Many debaters utter trite, stereotyped phrases which would be better left unsaid. The debater should make a few introductory remarks about the occasion, the audience, and pleasure of debating a timely question. He should move into the debate by defining his terms. This should all be done informally and sincerely in a truly communicative manner. There is no reason why a debate should be a formal, cold, stilted, unfriendly affair. The reason that some debates are conducted in this formal manner is probably a carry-over of last century's ideas concerning the formality of debating. Such practice, however, does not have a place in modern debating.

After a debate is concluded and the decision announced by the chairman, it is customary and advisable for the teams to rise, meet in mid-stage, and shake hands all around.

HOW A DEBATE IS CONDUCTED

1. The two teams sit at tables on opposite sides of the platform. They face the audience. A chairman sits between the tables or in some other convenient place on stage.
2. A time-keeper sits on the front row in the audience. He signals the debaters by raising his fingers. If two fingers are up, he means that the speaker has two minutes left. When time is "up," he raises his hand palm out, or he stands. The speaker should stop speaking within ten seconds after the final signal.
3. One, three, or five judges may be used. They are provided with ballots which carry spaces in which to write their decisions. After a debate is concluded, the judges, without consultation, immediately write their decision, sign the ballots, and hand these to the chairman who acts as collector. The chairman may appoint someone to collect the ballots if he wishes. He then reads the decisions from the stage.
4. To start a debate, the chairman reads the debate question to the audience, introduces the speakers, the judges, and the time-keeper. He then announces the first speaker, who opens the debate. He announces each speaker thereafter in turn. If desirable, after once introducing the speakers, the chairman may refrain from further introductions of speakers. The debaters simply rise in their proper order and present their cases.
5. Debaters may refer to their team mates by name, such as "Mr. Jones," or "my colleague." Opponents may be referred to by name or as "my opponent" or "the first speaker for the opposition" or "the second speaker for the opposition" or "the negative" if that is their side of the debate. Debaters may refer to themselves as "we," "my colleague and I," "our position is _____," . . .

IMPROVE YOUR VOCABULARY

Propitious - (prō-pĭsh'ŭs) a. Favorable, fortunate, favorably disposed, opportune, promising, conducive to success, etc. Example: The senator's speech was so propitious for the occasion that he received the nomination. Use this word three or four times daily in your conversation until you completely master it. Use it propitiously at every opportunity.

Trip - Here is a word that can stand a few synonyms. Try omitting it for a while. Examples of synonyms are: journey, cruise, excursion, passage, voyage, tour, expedition, pilgrimage, mission, etc.

BIBLIOGRAPHY FOR THE DEBATE

Culp, Ralph Borden, Basic Types of Speech, Wm. C. Brown, Publishers, 1968, Chapter 3.

Gilman, Wilbur E., and Others, An Introduction to Speaking, The Macmillan Company, 2d ed., 1968, Chapter 5.

Jensen, J. Vernon, Perspectives on Oral Communication, Holbrook Press, 1970, Chapter 4.

Oliver, Robert T., and Cortright, R. L., Effective Speech, Holt, Rinehart and Winston, Inc., 5th ed., 1970, Chapter 7.

Oliver, Robert T., and Others, Communicative Speaking and Listening, Holt, Rinehart and Winston, Inc., 4th ed., 1968, Chapter 13.

Ross, Raymond S., Speech Communication, Prentice-Hall, Inc., 2d ed., 1970, Chapter 12.

Strother, Edward S., and Huckleberry, A. W., The Effective Speaker, Houghton Mifflin Company, 1968, Chapter 14.

Verderber, Rudolph F., The Challenge of Effective Speaking, Wadsworth Publishing Company, Inc., 1970, Chapter 17.

SPEECH OUTLINE

Construct a neat, complete sentence outline on this sheet, tear it out, and hand it to your instructor when you rise to speak. He may wish to write criticisms of the outline and speech in the margins.

Type of speech:_____   Name:_____

Number of words in outline:_____   Date:_____

Purpose of this speech: (What do you want your audience to learn, to think, to believe, to feel, or do
because of this speech?)_____

_____

TITLE:

INTRODUCTION:

BODY:

CONCLUSION:

Instructor's comments may concern choice of topic, development of ideas, organization, language use, personal appearance, posture, physical activity, sources, and improvement.

(Write sources of information on back of sheet)

SOURCES FROM LITERATURE

(Fill out source requirements completely. Write "none listed" if an author's name or copyright date is not listed.)

1. Author's name _____

    Title of book or magazine used _____

    Title of article in above book or magazine _____

    Chapter and/or pages read _____

    Date of above publication _____

2. Author's name _____

    Title of book or magazine used _____

    Title of article in above book or magazine _____

    Chapter and/or pages read _____

    Date of above publication _____

3. Author's name _____

    Title of book or magazine used _____

    Title of article in above book or magazine _____

    Chapter and/or pages read _____

    Date of above publication _____

INTERVIEW SOURCES

1. Person interviewed _____ Date of interview_____

    His position, occupation, and location _____

    Why is he a reliable source? Be specific _____

    _____

2. Person interviewed _____ Date of interview_____

    His position, occupation, and location _____

    Why is he a reliable source? Be specific _____

    _____

PERSONAL EXPERIENCE OF SPEAKER

1. Tell (1) when, (2) where, and (3) conditions under which you became an authority on subject matter in your speech _____

    _____

    _____

    _____

Chapter 37

RADIO AND TELEVISION SPEAKING

This speech is due:
Time limits: See your instructor for the exact time.
Speaking notes: Unless your instructor directs otherwise, you will write out your speech word for word.
    A copy of your speech should be in your instructor's hands at least one day before you are sched-
    uled to speak.
Sources of information: Two or more. List them at end of your written speech.
Outline of speech: None is required for instructor.

PURPOSE OF RADIO AND TELEVISION SPEAKING

If one understands preparation and presentation of radio and television speech through first-hand knowledge and experience, he is much freer to evaluate and appreciate it as well as actually to participate in it. Real experience in studios provides at least an acquaintance. Such experience should enlighten and interest all speech students. It will pose real problems while answering many questions for all who take part.

Special note to the instructor: The instructor may arrange with a local broadcasting company for time at their studios. He will reserve two rooms, one with a microphone from which to broadcast, the other in which to seat the class to receive the broadcasts and write criticisms on them at the conclusion of each speech. Even though the talks will not go on the air, this experience will be practical. Television studios may be arranged similarly. If real studios are not available, the school auditorium or other suitable rooms and loud speaker systems may be substituted. By speaking behind a curtain or off-stage and using a microphone while seating the class in the auditorium or an adjoining room excellent results may be obtained.

EXPLANATION OF RADIO AND TELEVISION SPEAKING

Radio and television speech is that which is broadcast by means of radio or television. It may be dramatization, debate, discussion, or any of the many different types of speech. Its chief characteristics are its strict adherence to definite time limits and language usage suitable to an audience of average people. Generally such speeches are read, which permits a person to meet these requisites of time and diction. The requirements of these mediums of public speaking are: a pleasing voice, proper speech construction, good English, correct pronunciation, clear enunciation, desirable appearance, stage presence, and cooperation of all who make the broadcast. Willingness to rehearse and promptness at the studio are of major importance. The person who is tardy or who arrives only five minutes before time to go on the air has no business near a studio.

SUGGESTED TOPICS FOR RADIO AND TELEVISION SPEAKING

1. Politics
2. Education
3. Schools
4. Hunting
5. Wild Life
6. Travel
7. Sports
8. Curricula
9. Aeronautics
10. Personality
11. Recreation
12. Marriage
13. Ships
14. Government
15. Courtship
16. Automobiles
17. Atomic Power
18. Crime
19. Religion
20. Speaker's Choice

HOW TO CHOOSE A TOPIC FOR RADIO OR TELEVISION SPEAKING

Follow all of the principles set up for selecting any subject but keep in mind that a radio or television audience is the most diverse and varied in the world. Hence, unless you deliberately intend your speech for a limited group of persons, you will select a topic that can be presented to cross sections of listeners.

HOW TO PREPARE A RADIO OR TELEVISION SPEECH

All principles involving the preparation of the type of speech you intend to present apply here. It will be wise to do review work regarding your speech, whether it be informative, a eulogy, a goodwill speech, or any other kind of speech. After deciding what kind of speech you will present, prepare it by giving special attention to details and correctness. No excuses can be offered for errors when you have a written copy lying before you. It should be typed double-space for easy reading.

The final preparation should be the submission of your speech to the instructor for approval. After the preparation is completed, numerous rehearsals will be required before you are ready to step before the microphone. If possible you should practice with a microphone while a friend listens critically and offers suggestions for improvement. The use of a recording machine for practice will add greatly to the quality of your speech. If desirable, after several rehearsals, you may write time signals in the margins of your paper to tell you where you should be at the end of two, three, or four minutes, etc. These may be checked with the studio clock while you present your speech.

HOW TO PRESENT A RADIO OR TELEVISION SPEECH

Ordinarily, these speeches are presented with the thought that the audience will be scattered far and wide throughout the nation, possibly the world. They may be congregated in groups of two, three, four, or there may be only one person in a home. Your presentation should be so tempered that it meets all situations. If you ask yourself how you would speak were you to step before these small groups of people in person, your type of presentation becomes quite clear. It should be remembered that only your voice will be heard. This means that enough animation, clarity, force, and emphasis are needed to give interest. If you utilize television, then of course you are in full view for all to see and hear. This calls attention to posture, gestures, bodily action, and appearance.

In presenting your speech avoid rustling your paper in any way. Do not cough, sneeze, clear your throat, or shout into the mike. In radio speaking keep a uniform distance from the mike all the time. This will prevent fading or sudden increase in volume. If you feel like gesturing, go ahead. It will add life to your speech. Just be sure to talk into the microphone, with or without gestures. If you stand about ten inches from it you will be close enough provided the mechanism is sensitive. The best plan is to rehearse with a live microphone and thus be fully prepared. (If it is desirable each speaker may be assigned to another person who will introduce him. This will add realism to the project.)

In television speech various kinds of mechanical devices are used to give the impression the speaker is looking directly at the viewer although in reality he may be reading his speech. Microphones are kept out of camera range or may be in full view depending on the program. Should you be scheduled to speak on television, inquire ahead of time at the studio regarding the clothes that will look best, facial make-up, use of jewelry, what signals the manager will give, how to identify and respond to the "live" camera, and numerous other details, especially those concerning the stage crew. A visit to a television station will reveal many methods utilized to make speeches more effective when telecast. Become acquainted with them.

BIBLIOGRAPHY FOR RADIO AND TELEVISION SPEAKING

Fang, Irving E., Television News; Writing, Filming, Editing, Broadcasting, Hastings House, Publishers, Inc., 1968.

Gordon, George N., and Irving, A. F., TV Covers the Action, Julian Messner, Publishers, 1968.

Hance, Kenneth G., and Others, Principles of Speaking, Wadsworth Publishing Company, Inc., 1969, pp. 327-332.

Hilliard, Robert L., ed., Writing For Television and Radio, Hastings House, Publishers, Inc., 2d ed., 1967.

Julien, Daniel J., Jr., and Others, Radio and Television in the Secondary School, National Textbook Corporation, 1968.

Monroe, Alan H., and Ehninger, Douglas, Principles of Speech Communication, Scott, Foresman and Company, 6th brief ed., 1969, Chapter 13.

Oliver, Robert T., and Cortright, R. L., Effective Speech, Holt, Rinehart and Winston, Inc., 5th ed., 1970, Chapter 17.

Ross, Raymond S., Speech Communication, Prentice-Hall, Inc., 2d ed., 1970, pp. 245-249.

Willis, Edgar E., Writing Television and Radio Programs, Holt, Rinehart and Winston, Inc., 1967.

(For additional materials write to The Northwestern Press, 315 Fifth Avenue South, Minneapolis, Minnesota, 55415. They list numerous radio and television books and plays.)

Chapter 38

THE RADIO PLAY

This production is due:
Place of production is:
Time limits: See your instructor for exact time limits. Fifteen minutes should be adequate. Whatever it
    is, the variance should not be more than thirty seconds.

PURPOSE OF THE RADIO PLAY

A radio play will provide great enjoyment and add much to a person's background and experience.
It will acquaint students with numerous problems relative to this type of production. It will build confidence in those who participate and give them improved stage poise. It offers an opportunity for self-expression not presented before. Sometimes students show a marked personality improvement after participation in dramatic productions. It is for these reasons that this experience is suggested.

EXPLANATION OF A RADIO PLAY

A radio play is a dramatic production for radio broadcast. It is characterized by musical backgrounds, involved sound effects, time limits, and lack of stage action by the players. The various parts
are read, rather than memorized. An announcer is used to narrate or describe, according to the requirements of the drama. The purpose of radio drama is largely that of entertainment, although the purpose
may be altered to suit any type of occasion and audience.

Requirements for a radio play are these: a cast, a director, a play, and an announcer, music and
sound effects. The coordination of all these constitutes the play.

Occasions for radio plays are innumerable. Practically every station produces them in one form
or another.

SUGGESTIONS FOR SELECTING RADIO PLAYS

Under your instructor's supervision, visit your school library and/or your dramatics department.
Secure copies of different plays, read a number of them, and assist in selecting one or more for radio
production.

It is probable that the selected play will have to be edited, cut considerably, or rewritten for radio
adaptation. It might be helpful to ask your English or dramatics teachers for assistance. Further help
can be secured by visiting a local radio station. The chances are that the staff at the radio station will
supply you with some excellent scripts. If not, you should write to any of the large broadcasting companies for help. They are usually very willing to give free materials of good quality.

HOW TO PREPARE A RADIO PLAY

It should be kept in mind that you are not expected to be professional in this production. However,
you are expected to do your best.

The following things must be done:

1. Be sure that radio studios or a loud speaking unit is available.
2. The instructor will appoint (or use some other method) a student director or chairman for each
   play.
3. Casts must be chosen. They should not be too large (four or five persons as a maximum) or
   difficulty in broadcasting may be encountered. In casting the players, it is desirable to select
   persons who have definite contrasts in voice so that listeners may identify them easily.
4. Narrators or announcers must be designated. They should prepare their own scripts in conjunction with those of the players.
5. Sound effects technicians must be designated and their equipment assembled. Considerable experimentation should be conducted until the desired effects are attained. Practice in timing
   sounds is extremely important. A door may slam too soon, or other sounds happen too late, if
   care is not exercised.

6. Scripts for the players may be secured by copying the various parts from the play books. This should be done only if a play is being produced for the class audience; otherwise, copyrights may be violated. If desirable, each group may write and produce its own play.

7. All players must follow the director's instructions willingly, regardless of any personal differences in interpretations.

8. Many rehearsals must be scheduled and held. For all practical purposes they should be conducted with a live microphone when possible.

HOW TO PRESENT A RADIO PLAY

The entire presentation must be a coordination of all the characters, sound effects, music, announcing, and timing so that they become a unit. Every detail should be so well-planned and worked out that there are no weak spots, breaks, or embarrassing silences.

Successful presentation demands close attention to scripts and cues, and absolute quiet from all players not engaged in speaking or producing sound effects. Special attention should be given to the mechanics of production, such as distance from the microphone and turning from it to create an illusion of distance. Rustling papers, careless whispers, clearing the throat, coughing, and incorrect reading must be avoided.

Players must read their parts in such a way that they impart the naturalness and ease of everyday, normal speaking individuals. Characters must be made to live each time a player reads, and the reading must seem to be a particular character caught on life's stage for a few moments.

The timing should be executed to the point of perfection. This can be done successfully by using scripts which are marked to show just how far the play should have progressed at the end of three, five, ten minutes, . . .

The director should use prearranged signals to indicate to the actors how the performance is progressing. These signals are well established among radio personnel and should be used. The more basic ones are listed in the following order:

1. <u>Get ready or stand by</u> - This is a warning signal which may be used to precede other cues. Its most general use is to warn the performers of the first cue which will place the program on the air. This stand-by cue consists of raising the arm vertically above the head.

2. <u>Cue</u> - The cue is the green light or go ahead signal which tells any member of the cast to execute whatever should be done at a particular moment. The actor will know what to do because the script will tell him. The cue consists of pointing to the actor who is to execute it. It should be made from the stand-by position by lowering the arm to horizontal and pointing to the person who is to execute the cue.

3. <u>Speed up</u> - If the director wishes the cast or any person in it to pick up the tempo, he indicates this by rotating an index finger clockwise. The speed of the rotating finger will indicate whether to speed up just a little or a great deal.

4. <u>Slow down</u> - The signal to stretch the time or slow the tempo is indicated by a movement which appears as though the director were stretching a rubber band between his two hands. The amount and manner of stretching will show how much slowing down is needed.

5. <u>On the nose</u> - When the director touches the tip of his nose with his index finger he means that the program is running on time.

6. <u>To move closer to the microphone</u> - To indicate this action the hand is placed in front of the face, <u>palm inward</u>.

7. <u>To move away from the microphone</u> - To indicate this action the hand is placed before the face, <u>palm outward</u>.

8. <u>To give more volume</u> - The signal for more volume is made by extending the arm, palm upward, then raising the hand slowly or quickly to indicate how much volume is wanted.

9. <u>To give less volume</u> - The signal for less volume is made by extending the arm, palm down, and lowering the hand quickly or gently, depending on how much the volume should be decreased.

10. <u>Everything is okay</u> - This signal is a circle made with the index finger and thumb while extending the hand toward the performers. Whenever given it means that as of that moment all is going well.

11. <u>Cut</u> - The cut signal is given by drawing the index finger across the throat. It means that the director wants somebody or something to stop. It may pertain to sound effects, crowd noises, or something else.

IMPROVE YOUR VOCABULARY

<u>Assuage</u> - (ă-swāj') v. To ease the feelings, to lessen or to allay, to soothe. Example: It is difficult to <u>assuage</u> the grief of a bereaved parent.

<u>Do</u> - This verb is called on for much, too much, work. Try using a synonym for greater effectiveness. Examples are: perform, perpetuate, affect, fulfill, finish, create, commit, consummate, achieve, actualize, accomplish, etc.

BIBLIOGRAPHY FOR THE RADIO PLAY

Burack, Abraham S., ed., <u>Four-Star Radio Plays for Teenagers</u>, Plays, Inc., Publishers, 1959.

Hackett, Walter, <u>Radio Plays For Young People</u>, Plays, Inc., Publishers, 1964.

Kozlenko, William, Comp., <u>100 Non-Royalty One-Act Plays</u>, Grosset and Dunlap, Inc., Publishers.

Olfson, Lewy, <u>Dramatized Classics For Radio Style Reading</u>, Plays, Inc., Publishers, Rev. ed., 1969.

Olfson, Lewy, <u>Radio Plays From Shakespeare</u>, Plays, Inc., Publishers.

Taylor, Loren E., <u>Radio Drama</u>, Burgess Publishing Company, 1965.

STUDENT SPEECH APPRAISALS

One part of a speech course is that which provides a student the opportunity to listen to a speech and to evaluate it. To appraise a speech is especially helpful because a student becomes a more careful listener, which enables him to better judge the worth of a speech.

The form shown below is a sample speech appraisal form which the instructor may duplicate for class use and which the student is to fill out at the instructor's direction. One-half to one-third of the class, depending on its size, may be assigned to write criticisms for an individual speaker. At the conclusion of each speech, those persons who write criticisms will pass them to the instructor. (By doing this, the criticisms of each speaker will not have to be sorted later in order to place them in one group.) As soon as the appraisals have been examined by the instructor, he will give them to the speaker so that he may study them and thus learn just what his audience thought of him as a speaker.

From time to time throughout the course the instructor will assign certain speeches which will be appraised by the students.

SPEECH APPRAISAL

The student listener should conscientiously complete this form and hand it to the instructor to study before he gives it to the speaker.

SPEAKER _____   SUBJECT _____

Date _____

	Poor	Very weak	Weak	Fair	Adequate	Good	Very good	Excellent	Superior	Write comments
	1	2	3	4	5	6	7	8	9	
1. Introduction										
2. Clarity of purpose										
3. Choice of words										
4. Bodily act.-gest.-posture										
5. Eye contact & facial express.										
6. Vocal expression										
7. Desire to be understood										
8. Poise & self-control										
9. Adapting material to aud.										
10. Organization of material										
11. Conclusion